PACKING THE COURTS

EDITED BY HERMAN SCHWARTZ

The Burger Years: Rights and Wrongs in the Supreme Court, 1969–1986

PACKING THE COURTS

The Conservative Campaign to
Rewrite the Constitution

HERMAN SCHWARTZ

CHARLES SCRIBNER'S SONS   New York

Charles Scribner's Sons
Macmillan Publishing Company
866 Third Avenue, New York, N Y 10022
Collier Macmillan Canada, Inc.

Library of Congress Cataloging-in-Publication Data
Schwartz, Herman, 1931–
    Packing the courts.
    Bibliography: p.
    Includes index.
    1. Courts—United States.   2. Political questions
and judicial power—United States.   3. Judges—
United States—Selection and appointment.   4. Civil
rights—United States   I. Title.
KF8700.S35   1988   347.73′1   88-3257
ISBN 0-684-18953-4   347.3071

Macmillan books are available at special discounts for bulk purchases for sales promotions, premiums, fund-raising, or educational use. For details, contact:

> Special Sales Director
> Macmillan Publishing Company
> 866 Third Avenue
> New York, N.Y. 10022

10 9 8 7 6 5 4 3 2 1

Printed in the United States of America

$19.95

FOR MY CHILDREN

Susan, whose sweetness and sparkle brighten the day,
and

Danny, who would have approved

Contents

Preface

This is not a book written in tranquil recollection of things past. I wrote it while engaged in many of the controversies it discusses, with more in the offing. It was written in the belief that it would be useful for Americans to know in some detail from someone involved in these battles what was at stake and why a topic that, in Senator Patrick Leahy's words, usually generates less spirited debate than National Pickle Week was suddenly thrust into the headlines and onto the nation's television screens.

Despite my involvement, I have tried to be as objective and accurate as I can, particularly about positions with which I disagree. Any failures on that score are failures of execution, not of will.

I hope *Packing the Courts* will make some contribution to the history of our times. I enjoyed writing it very much and I want to acknowledge the enormous help of several friends and associates.

First and foremost, I thank my beloved wife, Mary, who went over every line of the manuscript with fear and trembling that I might have gone off the deep end. Her careful analysis of the substance and her insistence on clear expression were invaluable. And her tolerance of my more difficult moments should earn her many credits at Judgment Day.

I also want to thank those who read the manuscript, all of whom made helpful suggestions: Nan Aron, Victor Navasky, Norman Redlich, David Rothman, Sheila Rothman, Norman Rosenberg, and Peter Schrag. Had I adopted more of their ideas this would probably be a better book, but authorial pigheadedness is nothing new.

I am also grateful to my editor, Robert Stewart, for his many perceptive suggestions and comments.

Finally, I want to acknowledge my debt to Sophie Cooper, my indefatigable and resourceful research assistant, who overcame her libertarian scruples to dig up most of the sources I rely on; to Cindy Jones, my other research assistant, who helped at the windup; and to my secretary, Sharyl Van Bogart, whose skill and never-failing good humor overcame an indecipherable script, innumerable changes, and unreasonable deadlines.

Washington, D.C.
March 1988

Introduction

This book was written in 1987, the year of the Bicentennial of the Constitution. It was also the year of the most bitterly disputed Supreme Court nomination in our history, the unsuccessful nomination of Judge Robert H. Bork to the United States Supreme Court.

The coincidence was remarkable. It lifted celebration of the Bicentennial from a ritual self-congratulation about what a marvelous document we live under to an intensive national examination of what the Constitution means, how it should be interpreted, and in particular the role of the federal judiciary in the way we govern ourselves.

Controversy over the proper role of national courts in a democratic society is not new. It began soon after the founding of the Republic and has never been permanently resolved. In the last half century, as the federal courts have begun to breathe life and vigor into the constitutional guarantees of justice and liberty—to make them more than what the great Judge Learned Hand once called "merely admonitory or hortatory"—the debate has intensified.[1]

This book is about that debate and about the conservative efforts to overturn what the courts have done in the past half century on behalf of the constitutional imperative to "establish justice . . . and ensure the blessings of liberty." It focuses on the Reagan Administration's systematic campaign to reduce the judicial role in civil rights and civil liberties enforcement to what it used to be.

For the fact is that only since the 1930s have the federal courts made serious efforts to enforce the Bill of Rights and the right to equal protection of the law. During much of our history, the Supreme Court and the lower federal courts were either indifferent to these concerns or actively hostile to them. In 1857 the infamous *Dred Scott* decision read blacks out of the Constitution and probably helped bring on the Civil War. When the freed slaves were constitutionally mandated equality by the post–Civil War amendments, *Plessy* v. *Ferguson,* at the threshold of the twentieth century, legitimized Jim Crow.[2]

The rights and liberties of others treated unfairly by society fared little better in the courts, except occasionally. Discrimination against women was tolerated until the 1970s; free speech and religion received almost no judicial protection until 1930. The only rights and liberties to which the courts gave significant protection were those of property and business.

The Supreme Court's public school desegregation decision in 1954 changed all that. In *Brown* v. *Board of Education* and the other school cases, the Court showed how federal courts, equipped with judicial power and with the majesty of the Constitution and the law behind them, could protect constitutional rights. And not only for blacks. *Brown* and its progeny provided a model for similar efforts on behalf of women, protesters, prisoners, mental patients, and others long mistreated or neglected by society.[3]

The courts' role as guardian against official abuse extended beyond the Constitution's mandates. Judges also insisted that public officials and those in positions of private power honor the rights created by the many statutes passed by Congress to protect minorities and women, health, the environment, the workplace, and a free and honest market.

The consequence was, as Harvard professor Abram Chayes has noted, that federal courts now "deal with grievances over the administration of some public or quasi-public program and to vindicate the public policies embodied in the governing statutes or constitutional provisions. As a result, courts are inevitably cast in an affirmative, political—activist, if you must—role. Whether they realized it or not," observed Chayes, "the Justices in *Brown* had committed the federal courts to an enterprise of profound social reconstruction," an enterprise that soon reached far beyond school desegregation.[4]

This is not to say that the courts have always been responsive.

Even when cases are won, the victories often gain far less than had been sought or expected. Many courts have ordered improvements in prison conditions, for example, but most prisons remain unfit for humans to live in. Also, courts have limited powers—they do not have the power of the purse, for example—and may often be unable to do much. And important cases were lost. Many judges are unwilling to involve themselves in these issues or to push too far, and even a sympathetic judge may have his hands tied, for the law does not always permit a just, merciful, or liberty-favoring result.

Nevertheless, real changes were made, often when none of the other institutions in the society seemed able to respond to a pressing need or a gross injustice.

Those who were troubled by these and other cultural changes that were generated by the postwar era turned on the federal courts, attacking the legitimacy of both judicial activity and specific decisions. A new conservatism developed, sometimes called the "new right" or the "radical right." Some of its adherents were former Democrats attracted to Alabama governor George Wallace, who felt threatened by civil rights gains and the increased protections for the criminally accused. Others were fundamentalist Christians upset by the Supreme Court's abortion and school prayer decisions and by what they considered an overall decline in public morality as reflected in high divorce rates, illegitimacy, premarital sex, homosexuality, pornography, and a disrespect for religion.[5]

A more traditional element in this conservatism consisted of business interests and others hostile to government intervention in the economy and to increased taxes. These people were now able to draw on the intellectual framework developed by economists Frederick A. von Hayek and Milton Friedman, for whom government intervention in the market is not only grossly and inevitably inefficient but also a threat to basic freedoms.

There are differences among these elements of the conservative coalition. Libertarians and businessmen who look to von Hayek and Friedman do not necessarily share the Religious Right's hostility to abortion. By contrast, "cultural conservative" Paul Weyrich of the Free Congress Research and Education Foundation has criticized the free-market conservatives for thinking that "if the free economy leaves some people destitute—so be it." Nevertheless, the groups share enough to overcome their differences most of the time, especially in criticizing the courts.[6]

At first they had little success, but in 1980, when Ronald Reagan won the presidency and many right-wing conservative senators ousted liberal and moderate Democrats, their goals seemed within reach.

These conservatives took varying approaches to attain those goals, and we shall see in the pages that follow why they finally settled on ideological judge-picking.

PACKING THE COURTS

1
The Conservative Court-Packing Campaign

*The Reagan legacy is probably going to be found in his court appointments
. . . far beyond any legislative initiatives.*
                              *Patrick McGuigan, Director, Judicial Reform Project
                                   of the Institute for Government and Politics*

"Conservatives have waited over thirty years for this day," exulted *Conservative Digest* founder Richard Viguerie, when President Ronald Reagan nominated Judge Robert H. Bork on July 1, 1987, to succeed retiring Supreme Court justice Lewis F. Powell, Jr.[1]

And so they had. Ever since the Supreme Court prohibited racial segregation in public schools in 1954, barred official school prayers, and began to insist on constitutional rights for the accused, meaningful remedies for discrimination, fairer electoral district apportionment, freer expression, and recognition for women's rights, a growing new conservative movement has tried to cripple the Court and the rest of the federal judiciary.

It made no difference that by 1981, Presidents Richard Nixon and Gerald Ford, both conservative Republicans, had appointed a majority of the Supreme Court. The Court led by Nixon appointee Chief Justice Warren E. Burger was attacked even more harshly by

Reagan's attorney general, Edwin Meese III, and his allies than its predecessor, the Court led by Chief Justice Earl Warren. As late as 1987, James McClellan, founder of the ultraconservative legal think tank the Center for Judicial Studies, and a former aide to Senators Jesse Helms and Orrin Hatch, the senatorial leaders of the new conservatives, lamented that "most Supreme Court Justices appointed by Republican Presidents since Franklin Roosevelt have turned out to be votaries of Rooseveltian constitutional principles and precedents."[2]

The election of Ronald Reagan in 1980 raised hopes on the right that this time the courts could be brought under control. Reagan had identified himself with almost all the cultural and economic aspirations of the new conservatives, and his Administration drew heavily on conservative scholars like McClellan, political scientist Gary McDowell, University of Chicago Law School professor Richard Epstein, and Bruce Fein of the Heritage Foundation, and on lawyers like Paul Kamenar and Daniel Popeo of the Washington Legal Foundation and Patrick McGuigan of the Institute for Government and Politics.[3]

And the Reaganites did try. From their first days in office, in Congress, in court, in public speeches and interviews, in every forum they could find, President Reagan and his lieutenants campaigned to turn the clock back.

By and large, they failed. Anti-abortion proposals got nowhere; the courts repeatedly rebuffed the Justice Department; Congress strengthened the Voting Rights Act in 1982 despite intense Administration opposition; most environmental, health, and safety measures remained in force.

Polls, election results, and the resounding defeat of the Bork nomination showed why: The American people just didn't buy this part of the president's agenda. In disgust, James McClellan complained in 1984—and he could have repeated this in 1987—"It is a melancholy fact that, in spite of the campaign rhetoric and the Republican Party Platform of 1980, which held out hope of judicial reform, nearly all of the Supreme Court doctrines and decisions which brought us to our present state of affairs remain securely intact."[4]

4

In 1984–85 the Administration began to try another approach, slower and less certain but more effective and longer-lasting: packing the federal courts with "right-thinking" judges. Through a combination of normal attrition and eighty-five newly created judgeships, by the end of his eight years, President Reagan will be able to appoint over four hundred judges, including a chief justice of the Supreme Court and three associate justices. Reagan will therefore be able to name more judges than any other president in history and a majority of the judges on active duty; in this century, only Franklin D. Roosevelt and Dwight D. Eisenhower were able to name a majority. The culmination of this effort was to be the appointment of the ultraconservative Robert Bork to succeed the more moderate Lewis Powell, Jr.

Although it was not pursued intensively until 1985, Reagan's plans to bend the federal judiciary to the right were made very early. In September 1980, "signals from Mr. Reagan's camp suggested that the former governor, determined to fill the federal bench with persons who share his conservative philosophies, may be ready to challenge a centuries-old system that has given U.S. Senators virtual appointment power over judges." As governor of California, he had closely screened judicial candidates for their conservative ideology, after making a mistake with one appointment to the California Supreme Court. Said one veteran Californian court-watcher, "Anybody Reagan as president will nominate is going to have one helluva survey done on him."[5]

The conservatives' model judges were described in the 1980 Republican platform as:

> women and men who respect and reflect the values of the American people, and whose judicial philosophy is characterized by the highest regard for protecting the rights of law-abiding citizens . . . is consistent with the belief in the decentralization of the federal government and efforts to return decision-making power to state and local elected officials . . . who respect traditional family values and the sanctity of innocent human life . . . [and] who share our commitment to judicial restraint.[6]

5

What this means in practice was explained by one of Meese's advisers and speechwriters, Bruce Fein, a former associate deputy attorney general in the Reagan Justice Department, and a frequent spokesman for conservatives on legal matters. According to Fein, Supreme Court justices appointed by Reagan would overrule the decisions

- creating a broad constitutional right to abortion,
- prohibiting voluntary prayer in public schools,
- endorsing racial preferences in employment,
- mandating busing to achieve racial balance in classrooms,
- ordaining strict one-person, one-vote standards for political apportionment, and
- sharply curbing police interrogation of suspects and the use of reliable but illegally seized evidence in criminal proceedings.

Fein added that a Reagan Court would also relax constitutional prohibitions of discrimination against women, reduce citizen access to the courts, permit more public assistance to church schools, and be "less sympathetic to individual rights . . . [to] free speech and press." The rulings and views of most of the justices who have sat on the Court during this century would be overturned.[7]

The conservative conception of "judicial restraint" on the lower courts, where the issues are often more specific, appeared in an early study by McClellan's Center for Judicial Studies. In concluding that "the Reagan judiciary, so far [through 1982], has lived up to expectations," the center noted with satisfaction that the Reagan judges had dismissed suits by Medicare patients whose funding was terminated without a hearing, prevented union members from suing their union, and had rejected claims by public assistance recipients, refugees, American Indians, handicapped children, the elderly, victims of Securities Act violations, public housing tenants, antitrust plaintiffs, and, of course, prisoners and others suing under any of the various civil rights acts.[8]

Nor has "activism" always been condemned by the devotees of "judicial restraint." The Wall Street Journal and several of Meese's advisers (one of whom, Bernard Siegan, has been nominated for an appellate court judgeship) have urged that judges vigorously protect and expand business and other property rights, what they call "economic civil rights," against legislative and other interference. Some of them, like Siegan and his mentor, Richard Epstein of the University of Chicago Law School, would overturn the entire New Deal and take us back to the generally condemned probusiness courts of a hundred years ago.[9]

To produce a constitutional revolution, a major transformation of the Supreme Court is required, and if Lewis Powell's successor is like Bork, Scalia, or Rehnquist, the president may achieve that. But even if Reagan fails, some significant reshaping of that Court is inevitable and soon, because three justices—William J. Brennan, Thurgood Marshall, and Harry Blackmun—are eighty or older.

Even without a profound turnaround in Supreme Court jurisprudence, the Reagan Administration's successful packing of the lower courts will produce many changes in the lives of the American people. These lower federal courts are the courts of last resort, both formally and practically, in hundreds of thousands of cases each year. Between July 1, 1986, and June 30, 1987, a typical year, the federal courts of appeals decided 18,199 cases. In most of these, the appeals courts will be the last stop, since the U.S. Supreme Court can review only about 100 to 150 federal appellate cases annually. Most cases involving criminal law, school desegregation, discrimination, prison conditions, and antitrust law never get beyond the court of appeals level.

The FBI's tactics in the Abscam cases, where government agents created a massive sting operation, often involving crooked middlemen, to catch easily tempted senators and congressmen, are good examples of the importance of the appeals courts. The cases raised many troubling legal and ethical issues about the ethics of tempting people to crime, the choice of targets, and the use of criminals as middlemen, but the Supreme Court did not review any of these cases.[10]

The courts of appeals are particularly significant in the regulatory area, which affects almost everything from the price of natural gas to the safety of children's toys. Regulatory law is a joint product of initial agency action and review by the courts of appeals. These courts usually examine about twenty-five hundred to three thousand agency actions per year, no more than ten to fifteen of which will be reviewed further by the Supreme Court. A good illustration of how important these appellate courts can be is telephone service, the cost and quality of which were transformed by some lower court decisions that were not reviewed by the Supreme Court. In one, a 1978 decision of the Court of Appeals in Washington, D.C., required the local Bell companies to give the Bell system's then-potential competitors in the long-distance business equal access to local networks, thereby introducing competition in long-distance service. The result transformed long-distance service, introducing vigorous competition and much lower rates. It also led, indirectly, to the breakup of the Bell system. This decision was never reviewed by the Supreme Court.[11]

Until recently, many of the appellate courts have also exercised some check on the Reagan Administration's campaign to dismantle fifty years of bipartisan regulatory effort to deal with the problems of an industrial society. As more Reagan judges have taken office, particularly on the Court of Appeals in Washington, D.C., that check has been weakening.

Who sits on the district courts to try federal cases is also crucial. In 1986–87 these courts issued hundreds of thousands of rulings, most of which are not reviewed by an appellate tribunal. Again, telephone service is a good example. Local phone service, for example, was transformed by a Washington, D.C., district court, which approved and has been supervising an agreement to separate the local companies from AT&T, thereby restructuring the entire American communications industry.[12]

These trial courts also determine the facts of what happened, and this often decides the outcome. An appellate court's review of the facts is quite limited, and its decision may be predetermined if the facts found by the trial court point unambiguously to a particular decision.

Every president wants judges who will see the world the way he does, and most have tried to pick Supreme Court and other judges who will vote on issues that are important to the president the way he wants them to; contrary to popular mythology, that effort has usually been successful. Thus most recent Republican appointees are considerably more hostile to civil rights, economic regulation,

8

and other liberal programs than their Democratic colleagues, though the opposite has sometimes been true—few Democratic appointees have done more for civil rights than Eisenhower nominees Earl Warren and Frank Johnson or Nixon nominee Harry Blackmun, while John Kennedy, Lyndon Johnson, and Jimmy Carter all nominated many reactionary judges.

But the current conservative campaign to achieve ideological purity throughout the federal judiciary goes beyond prior efforts. It is aimed at a much wider range of issues than any previous president has tried to affect, and it is being pressed with much greater determination and much more systematically.

This heightened zeal is not just because Ronald Reagan or Edwin Meese is unusually fervent about the conservative cause, although that is certainly a factor. Reagan, like every other Republican president, has had a very practical political problem that will continue long after his Administration is gone: There is probably no other feasible way to maintain the enthusiastic loyalty of the former Democrats and religious right newcomers who are now an indispensable element in the new Republican coalition.

Despite landslide elections and Reagan's great personal popularity, the Administration has been unable to deliver much of substance to these groups. It cannot invade Nicaragua, it must at least try to do business with the Russians, and it has been unable to deliver on the social agenda. It lost both the Bork and Douglas Ginsburg Supreme Court nominations and has had to settle for the apparently more moderate Anthony Kennedy.

Presidents can, however, usually deliver judgeships—only one Reagan nominee was voted down by the Senate and only three or so were forced to withdraw, out of some 350 nominations as of Decmber 31, 1987. A president dependent on right-wing support thus has good reason to concentrate on conservative court packing.

2
Abortion and School Prayer

Scarcely any question arises in the United States which does not become, sooner or later, a subject of judicial debate.
                                   Alexis de Tocqueville, Democracy in America

The conservative crusade is aimed at not just a few decisions or doctrines of the liberal Warren Court, or even of the more conservative Burger Court. The target is the transformation of American life and law that began in the 1920s: the increased openness and freedom; the refusal of those who had always been outside the favored circle of power and privilege like women, blacks, and homosexuals, to stay in their place; the ever more powerful role of government in social and economic matters, and concomitant with that, the implicit denigration of the rugged, Darwinian individualist. "This is our country," declared conservative congressman Trent Lott of Mississippi, "and it's time we conservative, God-fearing, hardworking Christian people take it back."[1]

The federal courts, under the leadership of the Supreme Court, had helped make this transformation possible. The Court's decrees against racial segregation and other forms of discrimination; its abortion, school prayer, and apportionment rulings; and its efforts to protect the rights of the criminally accused were often crucial to the changes, and in some cases initiated them. These courts were thus a natural target for the reaction.[2]

The anticourts attack is on many fronts. First, specific constitutional decisions are attacked: *Roe* v. *Wade,* the abortion decision; the rulings banning mandatory school prayer in the public schools; the decisions allowing school busing and racial and gender preferences; the *Mapp* v. *Ohio* decision excluding illegally obtained evidence from criminal trials; and *Miranda* v. *Arizona,* barring the use of statements from an accused who hadn't been told of his or her rights.[3]

Second, for both strategic and philosophic reasons, the critics assail not just the specific rulings themselves as either legally or logically flawed but the very legitimacy of the courts' involvement in these matters. The federal courts' role in American government has always been somewhat problematic and controversial. While Americans have usually been content with the principle of judicial review—the power of courts to tell other branches of the federal and state governments what they may or must do—specific exercises of that power have often drawn intense criticism. The Supreme Court's first major ruling in 1793, upholding a person's right to sue a state, promptly produced the Eleventh Amendment to the Constitution overturning that decision.[4]

That ambivalence is being exploited by today's conservative critics. They castigate the courts for being unconstitutionally activist and charge them with ignoring the original intent of the framers of the Constitution in order to impose their own subjective views of morality. Basic and long-standing doctrines and principles about the constitutional role of the states come under fire. The ultimate goal is to undermine the federal courts' authority and thereby prevent them from actively promoting all those individual rights and governmental powers resented by conservatives.

In most respects the conservatives have failed. Their philosophic attack has come under severe criticism, which frequently verges on the disdainful, and the social agenda still is not achieved. Despite the strenuous efforts of Ronald Reagan, Senator Jesse A. Helms of North Carolina, and Jerry Falwell, the abortion decision still stands and official school prayer still is prohibited.

The abortion and school prayer stories provide the best illustrations of the conservative efforts and their failures and why court-packing is so vital to them.

ABORTION

Roe v. *Wade,* the Supreme Court's 1973 decision recognizing a woman's constitutional right to an abortion, is the number one target of the social counterrevolution. The attack on *Roe* provides an invaluable political issue to Republican candidates, for it appeals to both the religious right and to Catholic blue-collar groups, crucial elements in any conservative political coalition continuing beyond the Reagan presidency. The case also offers a good constitutional stick with which to cudgel the Court, for some liberals have criticized its opinion on legal grounds, making hostility to the decision intellectually respectable.

First, some history.[5]

Strict state laws against abortion date only to the mid-nineteenth century. Before then, abortions were quite common, and often were done by unlicensed medical practitioners. Even where anti-abortion statutes were in force, they were not vigorously enforced.

During the last third of the century, attitudes changed, and by the 1950s most states banned almost all abortions except if a live birth endangered the woman's life. Abortions continued at a very high level, but at the doctor's discretion, for only a doctor could make the judgment that a live birth would endanger the mother's life.

The effect of this situation on poor women was devastating. Although abortions were readily available to those who could find and pay a reliable doctor, here or abroad, poor women had to resort to the coat hanger, quack medicines, or to inept back-alley abortionists. Botched abortions were a major cause of maternal deaths, accounting for approximately 20 percent of such deaths in the ten years before *Roe* v. *Wade* was decided. Juries, however, were still unwilling to convict illegal abortionists, and abortion laws remained rarely enforced.

During most of its history, the Supreme Court paid little attention to problems of marriage or childbearing. In 1927, for example, the Court had no trouble upholding sterilization of mentally defective criminals. The patrician justice Oliver Wendell Holmes, Jr., disposed of the case with a flip, "Three generations of imbeciles are enough."[6]

When sterilization again came before the Court in 1942, the New Deal judges displayed a very different attitude. Justice William O. Douglas's opinion for the majority opened with, "This case touches a sensitive and important area of human rights. Oklahoma deprives certain individuals of a right which is basic to the perpetuation of a race—the right to have offspring." A unanimous Court went on to deny Oklahoma the authority to sterilize certain criminals.[7]

In the 1950s and 1960s, laws making it a crime to use contraceptives or to provide birth control information were challenged. At first the Supreme Court ducked the issue, but in 1965, a 7–2 majority of the Supreme Court struck down a Connecticut statute that made it a crime for married couples to use contraceptives or for a doctor to advise married people about contraceptive devices or articles. Justice Douglas wrote that some six different amendments in the Bill of Rights and their "penumbras" created zones of privacy that included the marital relationship, "a right of privacy older than the Bill of Rights."[8]

The opinion was criticized by legal experts, but popular reaction was favorable; most people agreed with Justice Potter Stewart (in dissent) that such laws were "uncommonly silly." In 1972, the Court redefined this right of privacy as "the decision to bear or beget a child," and extended it to unmarried people.

A combination of technology and changes in sexual mores and women's life-styles soon brought abortion laws under scrutiny. Under the guise of saving the life of the mother, doctors had performed abortions for a wide variety of reasons, including rape, incest, and a potentially defective fetus. As technology progressed, however, it became obvious that a woman's life was rarely threatened by a live birth. The doctors' evasion of the law became more notorious, and they began to worry.

At the same time, women were changing their life-styles and becoming more concerned about family and career plans that could be upset by an accidental or otherwise unwanted child.

Abortion laws began to loosen up. In 1959 the American Law Institute, a prestigious association of distinguished judges, law professors, and lawyers, proposed to allow abortions when the pregnancy endangered the physical or mental health of the mother, when there probably would be a serious birth defect, or when the pregnancy resulted from rape or incest; in the next dozen years, fourteen states adopted statutes modeled on this proposal. In 1967 California governor Ronald Reagan signed the most liberal abortion law in the nation. In 1970 the New York law against abortion was repealed.

The major medical organizations were also becoming sympathetic. In 1970 the American Medical Association approved abortion as a procedure that could be performed if the law permitted it, and the American Public Health Association urged that "rapid and simple abortion referral . . . be readily available."[9]

The struggle for change also was carried on in court. By 1972 fourteen lower federal courts had considered challenges to state abortion laws and nine had struck down the law. Some half-dozen state courts also nullified their states' anti-abortion laws, including the California Supreme Court, one of the most respected in the nation. And seven times between 1968 and 1970 the U.S. Supreme Court was asked to review a strict abortion law, but for procedural and other reasons it declined.[10]

By 1971, the Court was ready to rule. A young unmarried woman from Texas, who identified herself only as "Jane Roe," became pregnant. She could not afford the $650 demanded by one doctor she found willing to perform the illegal abortion. She was, however, able to find a young lawyer willing to challenge the Texas law barring abortions, which dated back to 1854, as a public duty— Sarah Weddington, who later became an adviser on women's issues to President Jimmy Carter. "Roe" went to federal court and won. Texas appealed to the U.S. Supreme Court.

Going to the federal courts for a reform that was unavailable elsewhere had become very natural by the mid-1960s and 1970s. Starting with the *Brown* v. *Board of Education* school desegregation case in 1954 and picking up speed in 1961, the Supreme Court had made it clear that it was willing to strike at the grosser forms of injustice.

14

Chief Justice Earl Warren's favorite question from the bench was "Is it fair"?[11]

Many of the Court's landmark rulings were by narrow majorities, however, often over angry dissents. Some of these produced intense public hostility from those who preferred things as they had been. Charging that the Court was coddling criminals and making the streets unsafe, police organizations assailed the 1961 *Mapp* decision, which excluded unconstitutionally obtained evidence from state criminal trials, and the 1966 *Miranda* ruling, which required police warnings before a suspect in custody could be interrogated. Southerners angered by the desegregation rulings posted "Impeach Earl Warren" signs. Evangelical Christians complained that God had been forced out of the schools. Television evangelist Jimmy Swaggart, who was later suspended from his ministry for frequenting prostitutes, thundered, "The Supreme Court has banished God from the hearts of our children." Conservatives attacked the Court for acting "unjudicially" in even getting into these issues and called for "judicial restraint."[12]

These attacks, plus the domestic turmoils of the late 1960s, had their effect. By 1968, all reform passion seemed spent. The Court itself began to backtrack, and Richard M. Nixon, following the example of Barry Goldwater in 1964, campaigned on a law-and-order platform against the Court on behalf of the "peace forces," promising a Supreme Court that would adhere to principles of "judicial restraint."

In 1969 Earl Warren was succeeded by very conservative Court of Appeals judge Warren Burger, who had made a reputation attacking the Supreme Court. Burger was quickly joined by Judge Harry Blackmun, a boyhood friend of Burger's, who replaced the liberal Abe Fortas; Burger and Blackmun soon were dubbed the "Minnesota Twins" (though that was not to last very long). In an interview published on July 4, 1971, the new chief justice told Fred Graham of *The New York Times* that young lawyers should not look to the courts for social reform and promised them "some disappointments" if they tried. A few months later, Justices Hugo Black and John Harlan died within weeks of each other, to be replaced by the conservative Lewis F. Powell, Jr., and the ultraconservative William H. Rehnquist, both of whom, like Burger, had severely criticized the Warren Court.[13]

With this background, the 7–2 decision in *Roe* v. *Wade* recognizing a woman's right to an abortion was a shocker. With dissents from only Justices Byron White and Rehnquist, the Court, in an exhaustive opinion by Nixon appointee Justice Harry Blackmun, ruled that the right of privacy recognized in the 1965 contraception case and in other cases going back fifty years included a woman's right to an abortion, subject to but two limitations: During the fourth through the six month of pregnancy, the state could impose restrictions to protect the woman's health, and from the seventh month on, when the fetus was viable, abortions were available as a matter of constitutional right only if a live birth would endanger the mother's health.

Abortion opponents were outraged. Terence Cardinal Cooke of New York City exploded, "How many millions of children prior to their birth will never live to see the light of day because of the action of the majority of the Supreme Court today?" Justice Blackmun received numerous death threats from those who wanted to save the life of a fetus. The attorney general of Texas, where racial segregation had been deeply entrenched, compared the decision to the infamous 1857 *Dred Scott* case, which denied blacks citizenship. As late as 1986, an anti-abortionist minister urged prayers for Justice William Brennan's death so that President Ronald Reagan could appoint an anti-abortion justice in his place.[14]

There was criticism from expert liberal quarters as well. Although many commended the Court's decision, Yale Law School professor John Hart Ely, later dean at Stanford, said the decision was not only bad constitutional law but was "not constitutional law" at all, because the Court had not explained to his satisfaction how it derived the right to an abortion from the Constitution. Watergate special prosecutor Archibald Cox of Harvard Law School faulted the Court for "not articulating a precept of sufficient abstractness to lift the ruling above the level of a political judgment based upon the evidence currently available from the medical, physical, and social sciences." All this gave ammunition to those who were eager to challenge the legitimacy of not only the abortion decision but also all the Court's other liberal rulings.

Other legal experts acclaimed the decision, however. They pointed out that the Court had been developing privacy doctrine in cases involving the family, marriage, and sexual relations for almost half a century without much criticism and that the Ninth Amendment to the Constitution clearly indicated that there were "rights retained by the people" in addition to those explicitly stated in the Constitution. Much of the nation also supported liberalized abortion. Polls showed that in 1969, readily available abortions during the first trimester were favored by 40 percent and opposed by 50 percent. By 1974, however, 47 percent reported themselves favoring the Supreme Court's decision and 44 percent opposed. By August 1987 the score was 62 percent in favor of the decision and only 24 percent against; 81 percent thought abortion ought to be left to a woman and her doctor, without governmental interference. And Judge Bork's hostility to the right to privacy established by the Court was a major factor in his defeat, though how much of a role was played by his hostility to *Roe* v. *Wade* in particular is not clear.[15]

Most politicians expected—and hoped—the abortion issue would fade away, but it did not. The anti-abortion minority recovered from its shock and organized to overturn or undermine the decision, one way or another. Catholics who had been preoccupied with divisive controversies about contraception shifted their attention to abortion. Anti-abortionists made up hit lists of members of Congress and senators who did not vote for anti-abortion measures; state and local laws restricting abortions were passed; and abortion clinics were bombed.[16]

The abortion issue brought into American politics people who had never been politically active before and were interested only in that single issue. Many of them were religious fundamentalists who flocked to right-wing preachers like Jerry Falwell and his Moral Majority, Jimmy Swaggart, Jim Bakker, and Pat Robertson (who ran for the Republican nomination for president in 1988) and through them to the right wing of the Republican Party.

In the mid-1970s the religious right joined with the political new right and Catholic anti-abortionists to form a powerful anti-abortion coalition, which made substantial gains in the 1978 elections. Robertson boasted, "We have enough votes to run the country." Jim Bakker, a protégé of Robertson's and later the center of a financial and sexual scandal, proclaimed, "Our goal is to influence all viable candidates on issues important to the church. We want answers. We want appointments in government." The zeal, energy, and dedication of these newly active anti-abortionists made them into a force to be wooed assiduously by anyone seriously aspiring to the Republican presidential nomination.[17]

And woo them Ronald Reagan did. His signing one of the most liberal abortion laws in the nation was pushed into the past—he later said he hadn't realized how much it would allow—and he placed himself among the most ardent of all opponents of *Roe* v. *Wade,* commenting, "I don't that feel I'm trying to do something that is taking a privilege away from womanhood, because I don't think that womanhood should be considering murder a privilege." He pledged to appoint judges who believed in the "sanctity of human life" and "traditional family values." When Jimmy Carter could not rescue himself from the twin calamities of sixty-three American hostages in Iran and double-digit inflation, Reagan won the White House.[18]

The 1980 election was not just a victory for the Republican Party, which for the first time since 1954 controlled not only the White House but the Senate as well. The election also seemed to be a repudiation of liberal Democratic policies. Twelve Democratic senators were denied reelection, and many, like Birch Bayh, Gaylord Nelson, John Culver, and Frank Church, were leaders in the party's liberal wing. Their replacements were almost all from the Republicans' extreme right wing, like Charles Grassley of Iowa and Steve Symms of Idaho.

Additionally, the old segregationist Dixiecrat J. Strom Thurmond of South Carolina replaced Edward Kennedy as chairman of the Judiciary Committee, and the ultraconservative Orrin Hatch of Utah became chairman of the Constitution Subcommittee.

For its part, the Reagan Administration came prepared to undo much of the past fifty years. Aided by a small but vocal cadre of constitutional theorists like James McClellan of the Center for Judicial Studies, Texas law professor Lino Graglia, Chicago law professors Richard Posner, Antonin Scalia, and Frank Easterbrook, and Robert Bork of Yale, the Administration, under the leadership of Reagan's close associate Edwin Meese III, began to strike at the

Warren and Burger courts. The primary targets were the Court's decisions on abortion, school prayer, busing, and affirmative action. The tactics would include constitutional amendments, legislation, litigation, and executive orders and appointments.

The Senate was given the lead on the abortion issue. Since 1973, the anti-abortion forces had failed to get a constitutional amendment outlawing abortion even out of committee. Senator Jesse Helms of North Carolina, the far right's leader in the Senate, had tried an end run around the problem by introducing "court stripping" bills to take away the federal courts' authority over abortion issues, but these, too, failed.

To take advantage of the new Senate majority, Helms and House member Henry Hyde of Illinois decided to try to ban abortions by ordinary legislation declaring that human life begins at conception, without the need for a constitutional amendment. Senator Orrin Hatch took a more traditional approach and proposed a constitutional amendment allowing the states to restrict abortions.

The Helms and Hatch proposals got out of the Republican-controlled Senate Judiciary Committee but not much farther. The anti-abortion forces could not agree on a unified strategy, and the country was not behind them. After a six-month debate in 1982, they gave up. The *coup de grâce* was administered on June 28, 1983, when they could not get even close to the two thirds necessary for a constitutional amendment overturning *Roe* v. *Wade,* falling eighteen votes short.

The Administration not only supported Helms and Hatch but also tried to persuade the Supreme Court to reverse or limit *Roe.* Akron, Ohio, and Kansas City, Missouri, each passed local ordinances requiring abortions to be in a hospital, thus making them much more difficult and expensive to get; other restrictions also were created in the guise of health regulations. When the ordinances came before the Supreme Court in the 1982–83 term, the Administration filed a friend-of-the-court brief supporting them. Solicitor General Rex Lee chose not to make a frontal assault on the *Roe* case by asking the Court to overrule it, for as he later wrote, "no lawyer worth his salt would think of going before the Supreme Court or any appellate tribunal, and telling its members point blank that they were wrong on some case they decided just several years before. . . ." Lee suggested instead that the Court defer to local legislative judgments about how available an abortion should be.[19]

The Court resoundingly rejected the government's argument—even the dissenters refused to buy it—and a 6–3 majority strongly reaffirmed the *Roe* decision in an opinion by Justice Powell.[20]

The surprise was the new Justice Sandra Day O'Connor. In the Arizona state legislature in 1970 and 1974, she had supported legislation recognizing a woman's right to an abortion and had opposed restrictive laws against abortion. At her confirmation hearing, Senators John East of North Carolina, Helms's protégé, and Jeremiah Denton of Alabama grilled her relentlessly to learn where she stood on the issue, but she refused to respond.

In the *Akron* case, however, she vindicated the most ambitious hopes of her Administration sponsors. In her first judicial statement on abortion, a scathing dissent for herself and Justices White and Rehnquist, she attacked the *Roe* case and its basic underpinnings.[21]

Liberal critics of the decision accepted the inevitable. *Roe* v. *Wade,* John Hart Ely told an interviewer in 1986, "is now part of an elaborate system of legal doctrine. . . . I haven't changed my mind about the merits of the original judgment . . . [but] if I were on the Court I would feel bound to uphold the decision."[22]

The Administration was unmoved by such considerations, and it did not stop trying to overturn the 1973 decision. Unhappy with the cautious approach Solicitor General Lee had taken, James McClellan and other conservatives demanded a direct attack on *Roe.*

In 1985, another case involving restrictive local regulations came before the Court. Edwin Meese was now attorney general and there was also a new, more ideologically aggressive solicitor general, Harvard Law School professor Charles Fried. Ignoring Lee's advice about avoiding a frontal attack on a recent decision, Fried asked the Court to overrule *Roe.* The Court refused, but this time the vote was 5–4, as Chief Justice Burger voted to uphold the restrictions.[23]

While the Administration was trying to get *Roe* overturned in the courts, anti-abortion forces moved legislatively, and in 1986 put referenda on the ballot in Arkansas, Massachusetts, Oregon, and Rhode Island. Again they went down to defeat. All four referenda lost, and only in Arkansas was it even close; between 1978 and

1986, anti-abortionists lost twenty-one of twenty-two such referenda.

When the Senate returned to Democratic hands as a result of the 1986 elections, the anti-abortionists lost their best legislative opportunities. They had come very close in the Supreme Court, however. With the departure of Justice Powell, a woman's constitutional right to an abortion is now very much in jeopardy.

SCHOOL PRAYER

"We are a Christian people," said the Supreme Court in 1931. As late as 1952, Justice William O. Douglas could write, "We are a religious people whose institutions presuppose a Supreme Being" and get five other justices to join him. Regardless of whether these statements were accurate when they were made, they were true for much of our earlier history.[24]

Dominance by Protestant sects, often at odds with each other, began early in American colonial history. Most colonies had established churches. In the eighteenth century, however, the Enlightenment stress on rationalism and Deism, as well as the spirituality of the religious revival known as the Great Awakening, helped develop a tolerance for religious disagreement and a desire to separate church and state. Led by Southerners, the newly created states began the process of disestablishment, and by the end of the eighteenth century only three New England states still had established churches.

Virginia was the leader. Jefferson's Bill for Religious Liberty and James Madison's Memorial and Remonstrance against Religious Assessments in 1785 were the landmarks; it was Jefferson who used the influential metaphor of a wall of separation between church and state, earlier coined by a great apostle of religious tolerance, Roger Williams of Rhode Island. These ideas were incorporated in the First Amendment to the Constitution, which provided that Congress could make no law "respecting an establishment of religion, or prohibiting the free exercise thereof."

The First Amendment refers only to Congress, however, and not to the states. In 1844 the Supreme Court declared unequivocally that "the Constitution makes no provision for protecting the citizens of the respective states in their religious liberties." As a result, states were left completely free of constitutional restraints with respect to religious matters.[25]

Even the ban on Congress was ambiguous, and today historians disagree over whether the original intent of the First Amendment was to bar all aid to religion and mandate complete neutrality between religion and irreligion, or whether it was meant only to prohibit a preference for one religion over another and to allow the state to promote religion if all faiths are helped equally.

Despite disestablishment, the idea of a Christian community persisted. In the early years of the nineteenth century, many states had religious tests for office, and throughout the century mainline Protestants tried, with a good deal of success, to make America a Protestant nation. In 1892 the Supreme Court declared that the Christian religion was part of the law, adding that "American life as expressed by its laws, its business, its customs and its society . . . [show] everywhere a clear recognition of the same truth . . . that this is a Christian nation." And that meant Protestantism, for anti-Catholicism and anti-Semitism were rampant.[26]

Religious influence in the schools was especially strong. One geography book asserted that "Christian nations are more powerful and much more advanced in knowledge than any others. . . . There is little doubt that in the course of a few generations, the Christian religion will be spread over the greater part of the earth." The school day often began with prayers, and there were numerous programs of "released time" during school hours for religious instruction. There was little financial aid to parochial schools, however, for the Protestants didn't have parochial schools, and Catholic efforts in the nineteenth century to obtain such assistance had failed.[27]

Shortly after World War I, Protestantism began to lose its commanding position in America's life, as the many new immigrants, few of whom were Protestants, began to take their place in American society. The Court began to "incorporate" various provisions of the Bill of Rights into the Fourteenth Amendment, the Civil War amendment that prohibited the *states* from denying any person due process of law. State and local officials now had to honor these provisions.

The process was a gradual one. It was not until 1940 that the Court first applied the religion clauses of the First Amendment to the states, and not until 1947, in *Everson* v. *Board of Education* that it issued its first church-state separation decision. The issue was public aid to parochial schools—in this case, free public transportation.[28]

The Court's opinion in *Everson* spoke in two directions. On the one hand, Justice Hugo Black said that "the First Amendment means at least this: Neither a state nor the Federal Government can set up a church. Neither can pass laws which aid one religion, aid all religions, or prefer one religion over another." He nevertheless went on to rule for a 5–4 majority that a board of education could reimburse parents of parochial school pupils for bus transportation. In what was to become a recurrent pattern, both the dissent and the majority looked to history for support and found it.[29]

Anti-Semitism and anti-Catholicism were widespread, and the school transportation case aggravated the already strong religious antagonisms. And the Court drew more fire when it ruled the following year that religious instruction could not be given schoolchildren on school premises during the "released time" periods.

Other church-state controversies flared during the 1940s, but they were mild compared with what was to come in the 1960s. In 1962 the Court handed down the first of its two major school prayer decisions. In an almost unanimous decision, the Court barred New York from requiring children to recite a nondenominational prayer composed by the Board of Regents. A year later, in another 8–1 decision, the Court banned Bible reading and recitation of the Lord's Prayer as part of the school day's opening exercises.[30]

Protestantism was no longer America's quasi-official religion. As historian Robert Handy put it, "long-familiar patterns through which a Protestant tone had been given to public schools" had been "swept away."[31]

Religious fundamentalists assailed the decisions as "godless secularism." One Alabama congressman protested that "They put the Negroes in the schools. Now they have driven God out." South Carolina's powerful congressman L. Mendel Rivers announced that the Court "has now officially stated its disbelief in God Almighty."

The first of many proposed constitutional amendments to overturn the Court's decisions was introduced, but it got nowhere. Senator Jesse Helms's bills to strip the federal courts of authority to hear school prayer cases also failed.[32]

Many public schools nevertheless continued to require Bible reading, for despite the Court's rulings, separationist groups found it difficult to find people willing to face the inevitable local ostracism that would befall anyone who challenged the practice. Over twenty years later, a Justice Department official boasted to a judgeship candidate that his hometown in Texas had never stopped opening the school day with a prayer.[33]

In 1968, the year before Chief Justice Earl Warren retired, the Court ruled that Arkansas could not bar the teaching of evolution from its public schools. For a while this issue remained quiescent. In the 1980s it rose again as the growing fundamentalist movement, unable to exclude evolution from the schools, induced state legislatures to insist that evolution could be taught only if creationism was also taught. A solid 7–2 majority (Chief Justice Rehnquist and Justice Scalia dissenting) concluded that such a Louisiana statute was religiously motivated and therefore unconstitutional.[34]

Ronald Reagan campaigned for the vote of the antiseparationists, and even though Jimmy Carter was a bona fide born-again Christian, Reagan got it. To the Catholics, Reagan promised that as soon as elected, he would "ask the . . . [Congress] to pass tuition tax credit legislation to aid parents who send their children to nonpublic elementary, secondary, and postsecondary schools," most of which would be Catholic schools. He shared the podium at fundamentalist Christian rallies with Jerry Falwell and, telling his cheering audience that he considered himself a "born-again" Christian, Reagan declared that "it is an incontrovertible fact that all the complex and horrendous questions confronting us at home and worldwide have their answer in that single book"—the Bible. He also announced that he had "a great many questions" about evolution and thought that the biblical story of creation should be taught as well as Darwinian theory. The religious right loved it, worked zealously for his election, and is credited with having contributed significantly to it. Exit polls indicated that 12 to 15 percent of Reagan's vote in 1980 and 1984 came from the born-again Christians.[35]

As with the other social issues on the president's agenda, school prayer at first took a back seat as he concentrated on lowering taxes and increasing the defense budget. Not for Jesse Helms. On February 16, 1981, just a few weeks after the Ninety-seventh Congress convened, with its first Republican-controlled Senate since 1954, he introduced another court-stripping bill to deny the Supreme Court the power to review state court decisions on school prayer. With a new Republican Senate majority and a very popular conservative in the White House, few thought he would again fail.

When the economy started to slide in 1981–82, "the White House turned to prayer," as one religious right activist put it. It prepared a constitutional amendment in the summer of 1982, to which were later added proposals by Senators Orrin Hatch and Howard Baker, and began to push for it.

All in vain. For the second time in twelve years, a school prayer amendment failed. The Reagan proposal fell far short of the necessary two thirds, despite Republican control of the Senate. On September 10, 1985, the Helms court-stripping bill was also decisively defeated, the tenth time in seven years that a school prayer court-stripping bill was rejected by the Senate.

Failure dogged the Administration in the courts as well as in Congress. In its first major decisions after the 1980 election, the Court veered from separationism in a series of closely divided 5–4 decisions. In 1983 the Court allowed Minnesota to give tax deductions for parental school expenses, even though public school parents had virtually no expenses, and 96 percent of the children in private schools were in religious schools. The decision seemed inconsistent with an earlier decision and laid the constitutional groundwork for a tuition tax credit plan proposed by the Administration. That same year, the Court permitted Nebraska to pay chaplains to open the legislative sessions with prayer, and in 1984, it allowed Pawtucket, Rhode Island, to place a Nativity scene on public grounds at Christmas.[36]

The hopes raised by these decisions quickly vanished. In a 1985 case involving an Alabama law mandating a minute of silence for meditation and prayer, the Court found that the only purpose of the law, in the sponsor's words, was "to return voluntary prayer to our public schools," and invalidated it by a 6–3 majority. The Administration took a strong position in the case, and it lost badly. The Court left open the possibility that a moment-of-silence law that was not religiously motivated would pass muster. In two other church-state cases involving school aid, the Court also rejected Administration arguments and barred the aid, but the votes were very close.[37]

Justice Powell's was a crucial vote in these cases, as had been true in all the other close church-state decisions. The future of the school prayer and other state-religion issues thus depends on how his successor views these issues.

CIVIL RIGHTS, ECONOMIC REGULATION, AND CRIMINAL PROCEDURE*

Conservative critics did just as badly in other areas.

In civil rights matters they were unable to get Congress or the courts to ban school busing for desegregation or to invalidate racial or gender preferences in employment and other contexts. The Justice Department and conservative senators led by Orrin Hatch were unable to prevent extension and strengthening of the 1965 Voting Rights Act; Congress passed the extension by votes of 389–24 and 85–8.

The Administration suffered the additional indignity of having Congress block Attorney General Edwin Meese's effort to promote Assistant Attorney General William Bradford Reynolds to associate attorney general. Reynolds was in charge of the Administration's civil rights activities. His record was described by a group of distinguished establishment lawyers as "reflect[ing] an abdication of responsibility for the enforcement of civil rights and, even more disturbing, a disregard for the rule of law as it governs those rights." Reynolds's rejection by a majority of the Senate Judiciary Committee, including two Republicans, was because of this record.[38]

---

*A more detailed discussion of how these parts of the conservative agenda fared during the Reagan years is in Appendix I.

The Administration's only civil rights successes were in relaxing enforcement, where it obviously had almost complete control.

Enforcement was also the area where the conservatives achieved their most significant victories in economic matters, another major goal of the conservative revolt. Under Stanford Law School professor William F. Baxter, a devout believer in the efficacy of an unregulated market, the Antitrust Division virtually bowed out of antitrust enforcement. "I have a fairly deep-seated conviction," Baxter told a congressional committee at his confirmation hearing, "that companies will always—I should not say always but almost invariably act to maximize what they conceive as their profit opportunities . . . [which] generally results in favorable outcomes and should not be interfered with." The division gave its blessing to almost any corporate merger or restraint on distribution. In one of his few failures, Baxter tried to persuade the Supreme Court to allow a manufacturer to prevent a retailer from selling at a discount from the manufacturer's suggested resale price, but an irate Congress, led by Republican Senator Slade Gorton, forbade Baxter even to argue the point.[39]

The conservatives were much less successful in the regulatory area. Despite strong public support for deregulation, the Administration's campaign to deregulate for the sake of deregulation was stymied by both Congress and the courts. The Transportation Department's decision to rescind the requirement that carmakers install airbags as safety devices was overturned unanimously by the Supreme Court. By November 1986 a deregulation enthusiast grumbled that "the bureaucracy under Reagan spews out regulations only slightly more slowly than it did before."[40]

In matters affecting the rights of the accused and capital punishment, the conservatives did score real successes. Even there, however, those resulted from Nixon and Ford appointments, for the assault on the great landmarks of the Warren Court era—the rule excluding illegally obtained tangible evidence and the requirement that before questioning a suspect in custody, the police must apprise the suspect of his or her rights—was well under way as early as 1972, when the four Nixon justices were in place. Attorney General Meese continually attacked these decisions, at one point referring to them as "infamous." In a formal interview with *U.S. News & World*

Report, he declared, "If a person is innocent of a crime, he is not a suspect."[41]

Despite these attacks, the Court seemed quite content to keep the decisions themselves in force but to whittle them down with numerous exceptions.

3
The Attack from Principle

The tricky thing has been and remains that of devising a way or ways of protecting minorities from majority tyranny that is not a flagrant contradiction of the principle of majority rule.

John Hart Ely, Democracy and Distrust

I think there are certain movements that the Department of Justice [under Edwin Meese] is making which could be interpreted as trying to undermine the Supreme Court itself, which is of course impossible. They can't separate the political from the legal. They write political speeches and put the word "brief" on them.

Justice Thurgood Marshall in an interview with Carl Rowan,
December 13, 1987

In addition to overturning specific decisions, right-wing critics like Judge Robert Bork and Attorney General Edwin Meese have advanced a judicial philosophy that challenges basic constitutional premises and doctrines. If adopted, it would undermine the very legitimacy of the courts' efforts to advance constitutional rights.

This strategy purports to rely on neutral principles. It pretends to be objective in that it does not specifically refer to controversial issues like abortion or church-state separation. Attorney General Meese has claimed, for example, that his Justice Department is more concerned with "process" than those of his predecessors, that he is "a more legally oriented attorney general, devoted to legal issues, rather than political issues," and that his arguments from principle were not intended to "imply results." Solicitor General Charles Fried has said, in his somewhat baroque style, that the department "has an important preoccupation with overarching legal principles."[1]

These claims are a smoke screen. The ultimate goal of the conservatives is still to diminish the courts' role in protecting individual rights, for that would be the inevitable result of adopting their philosophical theories.

As his first attorney general, President Reagan appointed his personal lawyer and investment counselor, William French Smith. Smith astounded senators at his confirmation hearing by his ignorance of even the most basic issues he would face as attorney general; *New York Times* columnist Anthony Lewis later described him as a "Rodeo-Drive Warren G. Harding, a society lawyer with a short attention span . . . with rigid ideological views who tunes out when the discussion gets to the hard issues of fact and law."[2]

Shortly after Smith took office, in the fall of 1981 he revealed the philosophic strategy. He announced that his concern was with "the institutional role of the courts" and not just with particular cases. He criticized the courts for "judicial activism" and "political policy-making" and gave notice that the Justice Department would try to raise barriers to people trying to sue in the federal courts. Since the Burger Supreme Court had already been trying to limit access to the federal courts, that didn't sound too radical or ominous.

Smith didn't stop there, however. The Court is particularly suspicious of official actions that impinge on fundamental rights like speech or religion, or that hurt groups that have traditionally been the victims of prejudice and political weakness, such as women, aliens, and illegitimate children. Smith agreed that a high degree of judicial suspicion was justified when racial groups were affected but argued that it should not be extended to laws affecting women and other nonracial groups.

Smith also announced that he was unhappy with the courts' "use of extraordinary equitable decrees" to tell public officials that they must remedy constitutional or other violations of fundamental rights. The power to issue such decrees, a power that goes back many centuries to England, is the basis for judges' efforts to obtain meaningful desegregation beyond the lip service that segregated school systems initially got away with; it is also the basis for the courts' ordering of improvements in unconstitutionally run prisons and mental institutions for adults and juveniles, what Smith denounced as "running . . . state institutions."[3]

Smith's ideas got nowhere. Rehnquist had been unsuccessfully urging since 1976 that only racial and ethnic minorities be given special constitutional protection, and this had been a theme of Robert Bork's since 1971. Despite more Smith speeches, the doctrinal attack seemed to have fizzled—until Edwin Meese became attorney general in the summer of 1985.

Meese had been a law professor for a while and seems especially attracted to conservative theorists, many of whom he hired as assistants or consultants. He was also among the most powerful members of the Administration, and even before he became attorney general, while on the White House staff, he took a very active role in Justice Department business, especially judicial appointments and Supreme Court arguments; Meese was behind the Reagan Administration's effort to force the Internal Revenue Service to give tax exemptions to schools, even if they discriminate against blacks, which the Supreme Court foiled; he also urged abolition of the Legal Services Corporation.

Meese's appointment as attorney general was delayed some ten months for an investigation by a special prosecutor, formally known as an independent counsel, into whether Meese's approval of governmental posts for friends, after receiving financial help from them, violated the law. After the special prosecutor had reported no basis for prosecuting, while carefully refraining from any comment on Meese's ethics, Meese was confirmed.

Within weeks after Meese moved into the attorney general's office, he resumed the broad attack on the Supreme Court that Smith had started. In his first major speech as attorney general, on July 9, 1985, before the American Bar Association, he attacked the sixty-year-old "incorporation doctrine," which is the constitutional basis for making state and local officials honor the essential guarantees of the Bill of Rights. Calling the doctrine "intellectually shaky," he declared that "nowhere else has the principle of federalism been dealt so politically violent and constitutionally suspect a blow as by the theory of incorporation."[4]

The ABA speech provoked intense criticism. Adopting a tactic he was to use often, Meese quickly pulled back, declaring, "I do not have any particular quarrel at this stage of the game with what the Court has done in the intervening [sixty years]." But his spokesman, the Justice Department's director of public affairs, Terry Eastland, promptly added, "There may well be a case in which we might argue that a particular provision of the Bill of Rights does not apply."[5]

The campaign against the incorporation doctrine was part of the broader and more respectable-sounding notion that in construing the Constitution we ought to rely primarily on the original intent of the framers so that judges will not be able to impose their personal views on the law. In that same ABA speech, Meese called for a "Jurisprudence of Original Intent," an insistence that judges "resurrect the original meaning of constitutional provisions and statutes as the only reliable guide for judgment." He followed this a few months later with an address before the Federalist Society, a group of conservative lawyers, in which he criticized judges who engage "in chameleon jurisprudence, changing color and form in each case . . . [who think] that what matters most about the Constitution is not its words but its so-called 'spirit.' These individuals focus less on the language of specific provisions than on what they describe as the 'vision' of 'concepts of human dignity' they find embodied in the Constitution."[6]

A year later, in October 1986, Meese delivered a speech at Tulane University criticizing the Supreme Court's claim that it was the ultimate expositor of the "supreme law of the land"; Gary McDowell, one of Meese's chief theoretician-assistants, described the Supreme Court's claim as "the most pernicious" in our constitutional history. Meese seemed to be suggesting that the Court's decisions bound only the particular litigants in a case. As an example of what he meant, he approvingly mentioned a bill introduced in the Indiana Senate for the explicit purpose of defying a recent Supreme Court church-state separation decision. He also seemed to approve Arkansas Governor Orval Faubus's refusal to obey the Supreme Court's desegregation decision in *Brown* v. *Board of Education;* Faubus's action triggered the 1957 Little Rock school crisis and led to the Supreme Court's insistence that it, not the governor of Arkansas, was the ultimate authority on what the Constitution meant.[7]

The reaction again was one of outrage, and again Meese quickly backed off, writing an article a month later in the *Washington Post* titled "The Tulane Speech: What I Meant."[8]

The theories that Meese and Smith have taken from right-wing judicial theorists would leave Americans with little or no significant protection for their liberties. Consider Meese's earliest target, the "incorporation doctrine," which obligates state and local officials to honor the basic guarantees of the Bill of Rights.

The doctrine was first explicitly "assumed" into being in 1925 by one of the most conservative Supreme Courts in our history, led by Chief Justice William Howard Taft. Six years later, when Minnesota officials obtained a state court order stopping a Minneapolis newspaper exposé of official graft and incompetence, the Supreme Court explicitly said that the First Amendment protected freedom of the press against state interference. During the next half century, the doctrine became so solidly established that in recent church-state decisions that Meese called "bizarre," even Rehnquist agreed that the incorporation doctrine applied.[9]

Despite this apparent unanimity among the justices, conservatives have called the incorporation doctrine "a total fraud" because "state constitutions were intended by the Constitution to be the primary safeguards against the denial of personal liberties by the state governments."[10]

Hardly. Regardless of whether the framers of the original Constitution expected "state constitutions . . . to be the primary safeguards" (Madison certainly didn't trust them, for he tried to have some provisions of the Bill of Rights apply to the states right from the beginning), the Civil War amendments changed everything. Although historians are still fighting over whether the Fourteenth Amendment was supposed to incorporate some or all of the Bill of Rights, everybody agrees that a major responsibility for protecting those rights was taken from the states, who were the targets of those amendments, and given to the federal government because of state abuses against the newly freed blacks.

Nor would our liberties be safe without the doctrine. If we did not have it, what would stop state and local officials from making Protestantism the official state religion, requiring Christian prayer in schools, forbidding the teaching of evolution, removing the works of Kurt Vonnegut, Bernard Malamud, Henry Miller, Langston Hughes, Mark Twain, and Richard Wright from the libraries of schools, stopping newspapers from exposing official dishonesty and incompetence, imposing capital punishment for stealing, denying counsel to someone accused of a serious crime, suppressing a movie like *Carnal Knowledge,* or prohibiting the use or distribution of contraceptives? State and local officials have taken all these and many other actions that violate the Bill of Rights. They were stopped only because the courts invoked the incorporation doctrine, for there is nothing else in the Constitution that expressly deals with such state and local activity.

The "incorporation doctrine" attack is part of a broader theoretical framework that, in Judge Robert Bork's words, "the framers' intentions with respect to freedoms are the sole legitimate premise from which constitutional analysis may proceed." If in the eighteenth century, for example, the framers did not think of making abortions legal, then today the courts cannot. If in 1787 the framers of the original Constitution had a limited view of freedom of speech, then in interpreting the First Amendment today, so should we. If Americans in 1868 were uninterested in equality for women, then that is how we should apply the Fourteenth Amendment today.[11]

This position would keep the Constitution in a powdered wig and knee breeches. It would lock us into the moral vision and limited experience of people centuries ago.

Of course, there has been a basic consistency since 1787 in the American way of doing things. It is reflected in long-standing traditions and customs, in a general adherence to precedent, and in a continuing fidelity to the core ideas and values expressed in the Constitution.

Those expressions are general, not specific, however, and unambiguously answer few contemporary problems. The First Amendment, for example, makes it clear that we put a high value on free speech by deciding that "Congress shall make no law abridging the freedom of speech." But "original intent" proponents, like Judge Bork, really do not believe that Congress can make *"no* law abridging freedom of speech," and he has said so. He is on record as saying the First Amendment protects only political speech, and not speech advocating lawlessness, or literary or artistic expression.* Regardless of whether that is good or bad, the amendment does not say that, for it speaks in absolute terms, nor is there anything in the history of the amendment to support so narrow a view. Judge Bork has insisted that the amendment cannot be read absolutely—which may well be true, though Justice Hugo Black claimed otherwise— but it is only by the exercise of a contemporary judgment, as twentieth-century Americans, that either Judge Bork or anyone else can decide how much the amendment should protect.[12]

The First Amendment also puts a high value on church-state separation and freedom of religion, but that tells us little about released time, remedial reading assistance in parochial schools, or religious practices in prison or the military. The Fourth Amendment requires probable cause for search warrants, but it offers little guidance for deciding when warrants may be dispensed with, or whether the exclusionary rule is necessary. And the Ninth Amendment, which is disdained by Chief Justice Rehnquist, Judge Bork, and other conservatives, despite their claim of adherence to text and history, clearly implies that there are other rights besides those "enumerated" in the Constitution, but it doesn't tell us what they are. There is no escape, in any of these or other constitutional matters, from the exercise of contemporary judgment and wisdom.

Moreover, the framers' intent even on the issues they considered is often difficult to discern. How does one determine the intent of thirty-nine different people, from different backgrounds and with different attitudes, about many of the most important matters? Determining this unitary "intent" is even more difficult with respect to compromises on vital matters to which the framers may have

---

*Judge Bork was not always so enamored of original intent. In 1968 he wrote: "The text of the Constitution, as anyone experienced with words might expect, is least precise where it is most important. Like the Ten Commandments, the Constitution enshrines profound values, but necessarily omits the minor premises required to apply them. . . . History can be of considerable help, but it tells us much too little about the specific intentions of the men who framed, adopted, and ratified the great clauses. The record is incomplete, the men involved had vague or even conflicting intentions, and no one foresaw or could have foreseen, the disputes that changing social conditions and outlooks would bring before the Court. . . ."

agreed with different expectations of what these settlements would achieve.

Furthermore, it is seldom possible to understand what people in earlier centuries meant by certain words without knowing the contemporaneous social and legal context. Historical records are incomplete and confusing. We do not have a verbatim transcript of the debates of the Philadelphia Convention in 1787, for example, only a compilation of notes taken by many people. The editor of the records of the Federal Convention of 1787, Max Farrand, has characterized these records as "carelessly kept," sketchy and incomplete.[13]

The history of the Civil War amendments is no less confusing. Historian Alfred Kelly has observed that the "original intent" respecting incorporation of the Bill of Rights in the Fourteenth Amendment is clouded by "the general aura of vagueness that surrounded the passage of the Fourteenth Amendment in the two Houses. The debate was conducted almost entirely in terms of grand symbolism—that of the Declaration of Independence in particular—and remarkably little in terms of the specific legal implication of the new amendment."[14]

Our understanding of history is also constantly being revised. Twenty-five years ago, Leonard Levy argued in *Legacy of Suppression* that the framers did not intend the First Amendment to repudiate the repressive common law of seditious libel. His conclusions became the commonly held view. Recent research, however, has led Levy to conclude that there was a much greater acceptance of vigorous expression in the eighteenth century than he originally thought. He has accordingly changed the title of his book to *The Emergence of a Free Press.* [15]

Thus it is hardly surprising that lawyers and judges always manage to find some historical support for the result they want. And it is equally unsurprising that few historians consider the "original intent" arguments anything but nonsense.[16]

But even if we could reliably discern the framers' intentions, their views should not be dispositive. They did not adopt the Constitution, they only drafted it. The state conventions adopted the Constitution, and an even larger constituency (two thirds of both houses of Congress and three fourths of the state legislatures) adopted the

Bill of Rights and the Fourteenth Amendment. The constituents' views—in all their multiplicity and uncertainty—are the decisive ones.

Right-wing fidelity to the original-intent doctrine is itself somewhat dubious. *Brown* v. *Board of Education,* which outlawed racial public school segregation, is now so well established that only an occasional disinterested scholar criticizes it, and certainly not a politician like Edwin Meese, who has praised it as an example of loyalty to the original intent behind the Fourteenth Amendment. But it is hardly that. If anything is clear from the murky history of the Fourteenth Amendment, it is that, as one of its sponsors put it, it "was meant to apply neither to jury service, nor suffrage, nor anti-miscegenation statutes, nor segregation." Nor, it might be added, was it intended to gain equality for women, as the Supreme Court made clear in 1873, just five years after the Fourteenth Amendment was ratified.[17]

On the other hand, the historical record is equally clear that the amendment's framers had no objection to racial preferences and affirmative action. The Freedmen's Bureau Act, adopted in July 1866, was bitterly opposed by some because, as one senator complained, it "gives [blacks] favors the poor white boy in the North cannot get."[18]

Obviously the original-intentionalists would not try to justify school segregation or antimiscegenation statutes today, and they certainly are not impressed by the Thirty-ninth Congress's approval of racial preferences. But if there is discretion to pick and choose which original intentions to honor and which to reject, by what criteria are those choices to be made? Except by exercising a contemporary moral and practical judgment, one cannot reject the framers' views on some things but not on others.

The real targets of the original-intent theory are the Court's church-state decisions and the recognition of "new rights" like privacy and abortion. There is historical controversy about the framers' intentions with respect to how much separation they wanted or expected, and "new rights" like privacy are almost by definition not within the original intent. Focus on "original intent" thus could justify much greater religious involvement in official public activities (and, of course, greater state involvement in religious affairs) and a ban on the recognition of "new rights" like a woman's right to have an abortion.

But regardless of the historical controversy, religion and the state in America today are each very different from what they were in 1789–91. Protestantism was all but official then, but today it is just one sect among many. The framers expected that the national government would have a much narrower role and power over the individual than it has come to have. We can never know how the framers would have wanted the broad and expansive language of the Constitution interpreted in these changed circumstances.

As to "new rights," the Ninth Amendment explicitly allows for rights not enumerated in the constitutional text, despite Judge Bork's deprecating it as only "a waterblot on the Constitution." Even Bork agreed that the right of "marital privacy was older than the Bill of Rights," even though it is not mentioned in the Constitution.

The contention that the courts have not shown enough self-restraint and have been illegitimately overactive in protecting constitutional rights is just as dubious. Conservatives insist that their goal is not to weaken individual rights and liberties but to vest their protection in the executive and legislative branches. As one conservative spokesman put it: "The best place to get resolution or redress would be in your legislative offices or in your executive branch offices. The judiciary should be there only to police the outer perimeters which legislators and executive officials have in formulating policy."[19]

Reliance on the popular branches of government for the protection of individual liberty is, however, a contradiction in terms. Justice Robert H. Jackson (a severe critic of what he called "libertarian judicial activists") observed years ago that the Bill of Rights was created to protect the individual and the minority *against* the popular will. The majority, after all, needs no judicial protection, for by definition it controls the legislature and the executive. As Alexander Hamilton wrote in *The Federalist,* the Constitution imposes "certain exceptions to the legislative authority" in order "to guard the rights of individuals from the effects of those ill humors" that can oppress the minority or "injur[e] . . . the private rights of particular classes of citizens by unjust and partial laws."[20]

The Constitution and the Bill of Rights reflect democracy's awareness of its need for self-restraint. Obviously a majority-controlled institution like the legislature is not likely to restrain that same majority, especially when the legislature's own "ill humors" produce the "unjust and partial laws." For that kind of check, an insulated institution is necessary, which is why the courts have the primary responsibility for providing this protection and why federal judges were given the extraordinary privileges of life tenure and an immunity to legislative reduction of their salaries.

The conservative exaltation of "judicial restraint" also seems to be only a sometime thing. Where the protection of property or judicial curtailment of individual rights is concerned, *The Wall Street Journal* and other conservatives urge vigorous judicial activism.

A notorious recent example occurred just a few years ago, in 1985. In 1974, Congress extended the wage-and-hour standards of the Fair Labor Standards Act to state and local employees. Local governments challenged the extension, and in 1976, in *National League of Cities* v. *Usery*, four conservative justices joined uneasily by Justice Harry Blackmun overturned it in the name of states rights. This was judicial activism at its most energetic, for judges rarely overturn congressional action in economic matters.[21]

National League of Cities proved very difficult to apply to other situations. After nine years of confusion, uncertainty, and acrimony, Justice Blackmun joined the 1976 dissenters to overrule it, advising the states to look to Congress for protection against federal action, in accordance with a principle first set forth by Chief Justice John Marshall more than 150 years ago.[22]

One would have expected applause from the right for this judicial deference to the representative organs of government. Instead, conservatives assailed the decision for leaving the states to the tender mercies of "political officials," bereft of a judiciary to "protect . . . the States from federal overreaching."[23]

There are many other examples. Proclaiming fidelity to states rights and localism, the Administration issued a report in November 1986 titled *The Declining Status of Federalism in America*. The report bemoaned congressional and other expansion of federal power over the economy and, despite the Administration's repeated strictures against judicial activism, it severely criticized the Supreme Court for *allowing* Congress to do this without interfering. Suddenly judicial restraint was no longer the cardinal virtue but a mortal sin.

At about the same time that the federalism report was issued, the Administration, *The Wall Street Journal,* and some conservative academics urged the Supreme Court to "incorporate" and adopt an expansive reading of the Fifth Amendment's eminent domain clause to strike down state and local zoning, land use, rent control, and other regulation despite the "intellectual shakiness" and "political violence" to federalism for which Meese denigrated the incorporation doctrine. Meese also suggested that the courts should void the congressionally created independent counsel; nullify application of the federal wage-hour laws to state and local officials; and abolish the independent agencies that regulate business, some of which, like the Federal Trade Commission, had been around since 1914 and whose constitutionality had been explicitly sustained over half a century ago.[24]

A final example of this selectivity in constitutional matters is the persistent effort by Assistant Attorney General William Bradford Reynolds and the solicitor general to persuade the courts to strike down voluntarily adopted state and local affirmative action plans.[25]

The conservatives' selective loyalty to judicial restraint also appears in their interpretation and application of ordinary laws where constitutional issues are not at stake. Although the activism-restraint debate usually focuses on the Court's role in applying the federal Constitution, well over half of the Supreme Court's cases deal with federal statutes. Affirmative action, for example, which affects millions of workers, is largely a statutory matter as is virtually our entire regulatory and social welfare structure.

Although some of these laws are ambiguous or poorly drafted, thereby allowing judges a good deal of leeway in interpreting them, Congress has often made its meaning quite clear. In those cases it is judicial "activism" in the extreme for a judge to ignore this. Yet that is precisely what the current solicitor general, Charles Fried, has been asking the Court to do. One year before he became solicitor general, he called for "a dose of negative activism" to deal with "really silly statutes"—those that impede the Administration's political and social agenda. Since moving into his current position, he has frequently called on the Court to ignore Congress's intent in such matters as voting rights, protection of the handicapped, and state control of health-care decisions.[26]

For their part, in order to favor business, Reagan judges Robert Bork, Richard Posner, Frank Easterbrook, and other right-wing antitrust specialists have encouraged judicial interpretations of the antitrust and other regulatory laws that conflict with the clear congressional intent. Thus Bork said in a November 1986 speech that even if Congress intended the courts to consider social and political values and not just economic efficiency, "it doesn't matter"—the courts can and should ignore the congressional will.[27]

In short, the conservatives are using "judicial restraint," "federalism," "original intent," and all the other ostensibly neutral principles to serve conservative economic and ideological interests. When those high-sounding principles get in the way of those interests, the principles are simply ignored.

4
Judicial Selection, 1793–1980

The President . . . shall nominate, and by and with the Advice and Consent of the Senate, shall appoint . . . Judges of the supreme Court and all other officers of the United States, whose appointments are not herein provided for, and which shall be established by Law.

United States Constitution, Art. II, Sec. 2

"Six years of Republican control of the Senate and the White House have left more despair about conservative policies than pride in the result," complained one unhappy conservative (who insisted on anonymity). Despite two great electoral triumphs, the right failed to overturn the hated abortion, school prayer, or school busing rulings in either Congress or the courts. And even where cases were won, the courts were just continuing an already existing trend rather than responding to new conservative initiatives.[1]

Only when it came to executive enforcement did the conservative cause prevail, and that could turn out to be only temporary. A new administration could quickly reverse that. "Twenty years from now, the Reagan Revolution may be thought of as the Reagan Interlude," worried a former special assistant to the president.[2]

The only way to achieve a true sea change was through changing the composition of the courts; the performance of some of the judges like Richard Posner and Robert Bork in changing the anti-trust laws showed how effective this could be. As the respected nonpartisan *National Journal* put it in July 1985, "growing congressional opposition to the conservatives' agenda has increased the pressure for 'friendly' judges to promote the Reagan Revolution in the legal sphere."[3]

An effort to change basic constitutional principles and rulings is, of course, not unique to Ronald Reagan. Richard Nixon, Franklin D. Roosevelt, Abraham Lincoln, Andrew Jackson, and more than a few other presidents have all tried, often successfully.

What is, however, almost without parallel is the recent court-packing campaign that reaches to so much of the constitutional landscape in such fundamental ways. Only one issue impelled FDR to try to change the judiciary—the Supreme Court's continued in-validation of federal laws to achieve economic recovery. And these, unlike the conservative agenda, were measures that were over-whelmingly passed by Congress and supported by the nation. Theodore Roosevelt's judicial policies were also motivated only by economic problems—the Court's antilabor bias and its refusal to allow either the federal government or the states to respond to the severe problems created by our entry into the industrial age. Lincoln and Jackson also had very limited judicial agendas. And in all these instances the Court had been bucking overwhelming public senti-ment.

Things are very different now. As the preceding chapters show, today's conservatives are trying to turn the clock back in not just a few areas but in much of American life—race and other kinds of sex discrimination, abortion, access to the courts, criminal proce-dure, church-state separation, school prayer and aid to parochial schools, help for the handicapped, economic regulation, free speech and press, national power, welfare, and more. The court-packing campaign is part of a wide-ranging assault on the modern era, for the goal is a return not just to the pre–Warren Court years but to the era of Ronald Reagan's hero Calvin Coolidge.

Conservative spokesmen do not deny this. University of Chicago law professor Richard Epstein, one of the theorists most influential with an administration that listens to theorists and often mentioned as a likely Supreme Court nominee, has proudly written, "It will be said that my position invalidates much of the twentieth century legislation, and so it does."[4]

And unlike prior presidential efforts, the Reagan crusade is not aimed at vindicating the popular will, as expressed in Congress, the courts, or elsewhere. In many ways and in many forums—most recently the Bork confirmation controversy—Americans have expressed either satisfaction with the policies under conservative attack, or mixed feelings. Except perhaps for the school prayer issue, there is certainly no great groundswell of support for the right's social agenda, as there was for FDR's, TR's, and Lincoln's policies.

It wasn't easy for the delegates to the Constitutional Convention in the hot summer of 1787 to agree on who was going to appoint judges. Some, like James Wilson of Pennsylvania, wanted the president to have the exclusive authority. "[A]ppointments by numerous bodies [result in] intrigue, partiality and concealment," said an apprehensive Wilson. Others, like John Rutledge of South Carolina, were fearful of giving the president too much power, warning that "the people will think we are leaning too much toward Monarchy." (He was to rue that opinion later.) Madison was unhappy with giving the power exclusively to either the president or the legislature, though at one point he suggested leaving appointments solely to the Senate. Several plans to divide the authority between the president and the Senate were proposed, and they all initially lost. After months of wrangling, however, the convention agreed on the current division between the president and the Senate, which it finally approved only the day before adjournment. Gouverneur Morris of Pennsylvania summed up the consensus: "As the President was to nominate, there would be responsibility, and as the Senate was to concur, there would be security."[5]

This division inevitably creates controversy. Since senators and representatives are electorally independent of the president, it is not uncommon for the Senate majority and the president to be of different parties, or for the president to have very different views from some members of his own party. Ronald Reagan obviously has far less in common with Lowell Weicker of Connecticut than he does with Jesse Helms. This, of course, makes inevitable both inter- and intraparty disagreements over who should receive these cherished lifetime appointments.

During most of our two hundred years, however, there has been a difference between appointments to the Supreme Court and those to the lower courts. Supreme Court appointments have frequently been subjected to ideological, personal, partisan, and other kinds of attack; one in five nominations has been rejected by the Senate, often for philosophic or political reasons—of some twenty-nine rejections or withdrawals under fire, almost a third were because of the nominee's views on public issues. Lower court nominations, on the other hand, have been relatively free from controversy, and the Senate has turned down very few, usually for incompetency, ethical failings, or just politics.

SUPREME COURT APPOINTMENTS

The Supreme Court didn't amount to much in the national scheme of things before John Marshall became chief justice in 1801. Justices were required to serve on local circuit courts with lower court judges. They had to travel a great deal, frequently on impassable roads, in rough weather, and they often had to stay at uncomfortable inns. A Supreme Court justiceship had so little value that three of the first seven appointees to the Court resigned after serving less than seven years. John Jay resigned the chief justiceship to take the New York governorship, and he refused a reappointment as chief justice in 1800 because the Court lacked "public confidence and respect" as well as "the energy, weight and dignity which are essential to its affording due support to the national government." John Rutledge resigned an associate justiceship in 1791 after just two years, to go on the South Carolina Supreme Court.[6]

Rutledge was willing, however, to go back on the federal Supreme Court as its chief justice, and his nomination for that position offered the Senate its first opportunity to assert its authority in the judicial appointment process.

In 1795 John Jay resigned the chief justiceship and President George Washington nominated Rutledge. The contemporary litmus test for loyalty to the Federalist cause was support for the treaty with England negotiated by John Jay while he was chief justice. After Washington announced the nomination, Rutledge ungratefully made a speech denouncing the Jay Treaty.

The Federalists were outraged. Federalist leaders asked the president to withdraw the nomination, but he refused. Despite Washington's insistence, his immense popularity, and his party's control of the Senate, Rutledge was denied confirmation by a 14–10 vote. Of the fourteen nay-saying senators, three were framers of the Constitution, including Oliver Ellsworth, one of the most respected delegates to the Philadelphia Convention of 1787, author of the Judiciary Act of 1789 that set up our court system, and later the third chief justice of the United States.

Madison was the next president to have a Supreme Court nomination turned down, this time because the nominee, Alexander Wolcott, had been excessively partisan in enforcing the Embargo Act. Thereafter, not many presidents escaped. Andrew Jackson's first nomination of Roger B. Taney failed because Taney had angered both the Whigs and the Calhoun Democrats by approving and following Jackson's orders to withdraw all government deposits from the National Bank. (After Jackson's reelection, Taney was nominated and confirmed as chief justice.) John Tyler had five of six nominations rejected; Millard Fillmore saw even a sitting senator denied confirmation, the only time this has happened; Buchanan's attorney general was rejected because of his proslavery views. A president's popularity availed him little. Had Ulysses S. Grant wanted to break the two-term tradition for president, he could have done so. That made no difference, however, when it came to Supreme Court nominees. The popular Grant lost three of his seven nominations, even though the Senate was dominated by his own party during his entire presidency.[7]

The twentieth century has seen fewer rejections, though in the past quarter century, five nominations have been turned down. Perhaps the most bitter battle in the early years of the century was over Woodrow Wilson's nomination of Louis D. Brandeis in 1916. Anti-Semitism played a role, but at least as great a factor was Brandeis's reformism. Nevertheless, Brandeis was confirmed.[8]

Fourteen years later, however, the Senate did reject a nominee,

Court of Appeals judge John J. Parker, because of several decisions perceived to be anti-union and because he had said during the 1920 gubernatorial campaign, "[T]he participation of the Negro in politics is a source of evil and danger to both races and is not desired by the wise men in either race or by the Republican Party of North Carolina."[9]

Many people felt that Parker had been treated unfairly—overt antiblack sentiments were more respectable a half century ago—but since his defeat made it possible to appoint the saintly Benjamin N. Cardozo two years later, the nation hardly suffered.

Nevertheless, the Parker nomination left a sour taste. Except for the brief flurry over the nomination of Hugo Black in 1938 because of his earlier membership in the Ku Klux Klan, and the racist resistance to Potter Stewart and Thurgood Marshall by Senators James Eastland, Strom Thurmond, Sam Ervin, John McClellan, and a few others—Thurmond announced he could not vote for Stewart because of Stewart's support for *Brown* v. *Board of Education*—there was little opposition to a Supreme Court nominee until the end of the Warren era. The only real fight was not about an individual nominee but over Franklin D. Roosevelt's Court-packing plan. In an effort to overcome the apparently intractable resistance of the Supreme Court to his recovery measures, and buoyed by a huge electoral victory in 1936, Roosevelt tried to enlarge the Court to outvote the five justices who seemed ready to strike down every federal effort to deal with the Depression. The effort, of course, failed, but normal attrition soon transformed the Court.

In 1968 Chief Justice Earl Warren announced that he would retire from the Court. President Lyndon Johnson, who had already said that he would not run for reelection, nominated his close friend and adviser Justice Abe Fortas. Since his arrival on the Court in 1965, Fortas had generally lined up with the liberal majority. Nineteen Republican senators immediately announced that they would oppose the nomination because Johnson was leaving office and should not choose the next chief justice. Conservatives of both parties took off after Fortas for what Arkansas senator John McClellan called the "Warren philosophy" on obscenity, defendants' rights (Fortas had voted for *Miranda*), national security, labor, and speech. Some of the cases for which they berated Fortas had been decided before he was appointed. After a lengthy battle, during which it came out that Fortas had been paid fifteen thousand dollars for a series of law school lectures from funds provided by former clients, he withdrew his name.[10]

The nomination wars resumed the following year. When Nixon nominated Judge Clement Haynsworth of South Carolina in 1969, the judge's stock holdings in companies affected by some of his decisions raised such serious ethical questions that a reluctant Senate rejected him; there was widespread speculation that the rejection also had to do with his votes against unions.

After Haynsworth, the Senate had had enough, and it seemed that almost anyone marginally competent and respectable would sail through. But Nixon then came back with G. Harrold Carswell, a segregationist mediocrity. He was supported by Nebraska Republican senator Roman Hruska, who argued, "Even if he was mediocre, there are a lot of mediocre judges and people and lawyers. They are entitled to a little representation, aren't they, and a little chance? We can't have all Brandeises and Cardozos and Frankfurters and stuff like that there." The Senate was not impressed with Hruska's logic and felt itself compelled to turn Carswell down as well.[11]

The nominations of Robert H. Bork in 1987 and William H. Rehnquist in 1971 for associate justice, and of Rehnquist in 1986 to be chief justice, aroused the most intense controversy. Few nominees had put together so consistently reactionary a record as Rehnquist had when he was nominated for the chief justiceship, but his opponents could not muster a majority against him in the Republican-controlled Senate. Bork had an equally reactionary record, both on the bench and off, and adding him to the Court after the Scalia appointment would have tipped the Court to the far right for many years to come.

Today it seems clear that a Supreme Court nominee's philosophy and ideology are proper subjects for consideration by the Senate. The constitutional text, its history, and a two-hundred-year tradition call for the Senate to play such a role.

The president is, of course, entitled to nominate those in sympathy with his vision of what is good for the Constitution and the country. If that vision plays an important role in his overall policies, and if a nomination could significantly further that vision, then he would seem virtually obligated by his oath to "preserve, protect, and defend the Constitution" to make such a nomination.

But the Constitution entitles the president only to try, not necessarily to succeed. The framers of our Constitution created the judiciary as an independent branch free from executive, legislative, and, indeed, electoral control. That is why they gave federal judges life tenure and immunity from salary reduction. This is also why they divided the judicial appointment powers between the president and the Senate.

A senator thus has the same obligation as the president to ensure that a judicial nominee will further and not undermine the senator's vision of the Constitution. Senators, after all, take the same oath as the president. It is not just a question of whether the nominee did well in law school, or is a competent and honorable lawyer. The nominee's social, political, and judicial beliefs are all relevant, and virtually all constitutional experts—conservatives and liberals alike—agree on this. Conservatives like Professor Grover Rees of Texas, President Reagan's chief judge-picker for several years, wrote in 1981 that "scholars have generally agreed that social and economic philosophy, insofar as they reflect on a judge's likely position on constitutional issues, are legitimate bases on which the senators might vote to confirm or reject Supreme Court nominees." Senator Sam Ervin relied on his aversion to Abe Fortas's philosophy to oppose the Fortas nomination for the chief justiceship, saying, "[T]he 'advise and consent' power is not limited to academic training, experience and character, but extends to the broader question of the nominee's political philosophy." Liberal Columbia Law School professor Charles L. Black, Jr., has written that "in a world that knows that a man's social philosophy shows his judicial behavior, that philosophy is a factor in a man's fitness" to be a judge. The public agrees. A poll taken at the beginning of the Bork nomination controversy found that 62 percent of the respondents believed that the Senate should take the nominee's social and political views into account.[12]

Sometimes it is intimated that the Senate need not be overly concerned with a Supreme Court nominee's philosophy because once on the Court, justices act so unpredictably that presidents do not have the ability to shape the Court. In a speech released a few weeks before the 1984 election, Associate Justice William H. Rehnquist suggested precisely that, though elsewhere he has urged Congress to look closely at the nominee's views.[13]

In fact, despite a few well-publicized exceptions, presidents rarely have been disappointed with the voting records of the people they appoint. The two most celebrated exceptions—Dwight D. Eisenhower's unhappiness with Earl Warren over the Court's desegregation decision, and Theodore Roosevelt's indignation at Oliver Wendell Holmes's dissent in an antitrust case—do not show that, as Justice Rehnquist put it, "even a 'strong' President determined to leave his mark on the Court is apt to be only partially successful."[14]

The fact is that President Eisenhower was not really unhappy with Chief Justice Earl Warren because of the latter's desegregation decision. Eisenhower's biographer Stephen Ambrose reports that during his presidency "Eisenhower never doubted that he had been right in thinking . . . [that] Warren was the best man in the country for the post of Chief Justice." It was only after Eisenhower left office and moved to the right that he became disenchanted with Warren for the Court's communist and criminal law decisions in the early 1960s.[15]

Theodore Roosevelt's indignation at Oliver Wendell Holmes's dissent in an antitrust case was really on a minor issue. On the central constitutional concern of the early 1900s—the Court's veto of social legislation—Justice Holmes fully supported TR's opposition to the Court's rulings.[16]

The disappointments come primarily from issues that emerge after the justice gets to the Court, as with Blackmun and abortion, or that the president does not really think about it, such as Eisenhower and criminal procedure.

The truth is that what a president really wants from his appointees he usually gets. Though not always. The relatively liberal Woodrow Wilson was quite surprised by the generally reactionary performance of James McReynolds, and Richard Nixon certainly did not anticipate Lewis Powell's vote in a major wiretapping case, given statements Powell had made on the issue before going on the Supreme Court. But John Adams was not disappointed with John Marshall's nationalism and concern for protecting property, nor was

Andrew Jackson with Roger Taney's rather different philosophy. When Ulysses S. Grant filled two vacancies after the Court denied Congress the power to issue paper money, his two appointments joined three of Abraham Lincoln's and promptly overturned that ruling. The justices named by Franklin D. Roosevelt voted on the New Deal—his primary concern—just the way FDR wanted. Richard M. Nixon was concerned almost exclusively with criminal justice, and his four appointees have all voted quite consistently to cut back on criminal defense rights. And President Reagan must be quite satisfied with Justices Sandra Day O'Connor and Antonin Scalia, who have shown themselves on most issues almost as conservative as Justice Rehnquist.

Despite the coequal role that the Constitution assigns the Senate in the appointment process, in recent years a presumption in favor of the president's nominee has developed. The question has become whether a nominee's views are "outside the wide range of reasonable constitutional views," in former Solicitor General Rex Lee's words. The philosophical component of this test has baffled and perplexed many liberal senators, as the unanimous confirmation of Antonin Scalia demonstrated. Scalia's record and publicly stated views were almost as conservative as Rehnquist's, yet he was confirmed unanimously, though some of this unanimity is attributable to the senators' lack of enthusiasm for an additional fight—it is the common wisdom that liberal and moderate senators hate the thought of more than one nomination fight at a time or within a brief period, and the Scalia nomination came immediately after the fights over Rehnquist and Court of Appeals nominee Daniel A. Manion.[17]

LOWER COURT APPOINTMENTS

Although the constitutional text and its history do not differentiate between Supreme Court appointments and those for the lower federal courts, the picture is quite different on the lower court level. Ideology has played a much smaller role, and controversy has been relatively rare. Only a handful of the thousands of lower court nominations since 1790 have faced serious opposition and even fewer have actually been voted down, either at the committee stage or on the Senate floor.

Paradoxically enough, the Senate has exercised more of a veto power over appointments to the executive branch, such as cabinet and administrative agency positions, than it has in approving lower court judges. The primary job of executive officers is to execute the president's policies, whereas judges are members of an independent third branch. Therefore it is frequently said that the Senate should allow the president more of a free hand when he chooses a member of his administration than when he chooses federal judges. Nevertheless, the Senate has rejected executive nominations far more often than it has vetoed lower court judgeships.

Here, too, the Senate's insistence on its advice and consent prerogatives goes back to the earliest days of the Republic. The First Congress was in session only three months when Washington nominated Benjamin Fishbourne to be naval officer in Savannah, Georgia. The two Georgia senators had their own candidate, however, and the Senate, in one of its first demonstrations of "senatorial courtesy," supported the Georgians.

Since then almost every president has suffered such rejections for reasons of politics, philosophy, competence, and integrity. John Adams, James Madison, Woodrow Wilson, Calvin Coolidge, FDR— all had executive nominations turned down. Whereas President Reagan lost only three judgeship nominations through 1987, many of his executive nominations were challenged and some defeated: William Bradford Reynolds was rejected for a promotion to associate attorney general, Jeffrey Zuckerman was denied appointment as general counsel of the Equal Employment Opportunity Commission, and Dorothy Strunk was denied confirmation as assistant secretary of labor for mine safety and health, to note but a few. All the rejections and many of the challenges were the result of senatorial disagreement with the views of the nominees. Earlier, Jimmy Carter was forced to withdraw the nomination of Ted Sorensen as director of Central Intelligence in 1977, and Eisenhower lost the nomination of Lewis Strauss for secretary of commerce in 1959, again because of the nominee's views.[18]

But matters have been very different with respect to lower court judgeships. One reason is the senatorial role in judicial selection.

Partly because of the local features of the federal courts and partly because of the president's need to work with friendly senators, for much of our history since 1850, the Senate has played a major role in the selection of lower court judges. Senators have had especially great control over the choice of district court judges, since those courts are entirely within one state. Until recently, senators exercised a good deal of influence on appellate court appointments as well, particularly with respect to judgeships that tradition has officially allocated to their state. Thus, when a Second Circuit judge from New York retired, he was normally succeeded by someone else from New York, and it used to be that if there were New York senators from the president's party, they had a good deal to say about the successor. The Carter Administration substantially reduced senatorial power over appellate appointments.

Senatorial influence is exercised primarily by senators from the president's own party, although if the opposition controls the Senate, the president may have to bargain with opposing senators. If there is a vacancy in a state where both senators are from the opposing party, and if the president is not forced to bargain with the opposition, other political forces, such as powerful congressmen, local politicians, or politically powerful groups, may control the choice. Even when there are senators from the president's party, powerful local politicians may have a voice. During the Kennedy-Johnson years, Chicago mayor Richard J. Daley passed on every federal judgeship in Illinois.

The "give and take" philosophy by which most politicians live has resulted in Senate deference to colleagues, for senators do not like to vote against a colleague's nominee even if he or she is from the opposing party. Moreover, a senator from the president's party can usually veto a presidential choice from the senator's state. In 1939 Roosevelt suffered a stinging 72–9 defeat of a Virginia District Court nomination that Virginia senators Harry Byrd and Carter Glass opposed. The nomination was part of FDR's unsuccessful effort to reduce conservative control of the Democratic Party. Senators Paul Douglas of Illinois and Richard Russell of Georgia blocked several Truman nominees to the district court bench because the president did not accept the senators' recommendations.[19]

Because American parties are relatively nonideological and diffuse, encompassing a wide range of views, American politicians are usually pragmatic types. They generally choose judges from among their friends, associates, and political allies. Before going on the bench, most judges are politically active, often with prior governmental service, and they usually have had many years of law practice; until recently, Court of Appeals judges in particular have usually been lawyers of high professional standing and broad cosmopolitan outlook. Few judicial nominees have seen themselves as ideologues, but rather, like most practicing lawyers whose job is to settle disputes and work out conflicts, as moderate, practical men and women concerned to stay within the mainstream from which almost all are drawn.

For this reason, until recently, ideological challenges to lower court judicial nominees have been rare, and mostly from ideologically oriented conservatives. When President Jimmy Carter nominated Patricia Wald to the Court of Appeals for the District of Columbia, conservatives like Orrin Hatch, Strom Thurmond, and Gordon Humphrey attacked Wald, a mother of five, for being "against the family," and twenty-one voted against her. Abner Mikva, nominated to the same court, was assailed by the gun control lobby, which mustered thirty-one "no" votes (again including Hatch and Thurmond as well as Republican minority leader Robert Dole and Alan Simpson of Wyoming), although the likelihood of Mikva's considering a case involving gun control is small since there are so few such cases. Segregationist senators also challenged Thurgood Marshall and Potter Stewart when they were nominated to lower courts. And conservative senators forced Reagan to withdraw the nomination of Andrew Frey to the local District of Columbia Court of Appeals because he had contributed small sums to abortion and gun control groups.

The diverse political influences and the preference for choosing from among working, politically oriented lawyers have made for a diverse and generally moderate judiciary, even though most presidents give well over 90 percent of the appointments to members of their own party.

This is not to say that presidents prior to Ronald Reagan have paid no attention to a candidate's judicial, social, or other philosophy, particularly on the appellate level. Occasionally senators have also been interested in these matters. As Judge Patricia Wald observed, "After the turn of the century, as the business of federal courts began to deal less with patents and admiralty and more with politically volatile issues such as antitrust, labor disputes, child labor, corruption, and due process challenges to governmental regulation, issue-oriented politics increasingly intruded on judicial selection."[20]

But as noted earlier, the attention to ideology has usually been limited in scope and episodic in operation. And as one student of the appointment process has pointed out with respect to FDR, presidents "never let philosophy stand in the way of a good political stroke."[21]

For the closest historical parallel to the current Administration's preoccupation with ideology, we must go back almost two hundred years, to 1800 and the attempt by the outgoing Federalists to pack the federal judiciary with "midnight judges."

Toward the close of its first decade, the United States experienced some of the most bitter party strife it would ever have. The Federalists and the Jeffersonian Republicans divided along class lines and on international affairs, with at least some of the Federalists eager to join England in its war with France.

To suppress the Republicans and pro-French sympathizers, the Federalists passed the Alien and Sedition Acts of 1798, and many Federalist judges became intensely partisan in enforcing these laws. Supreme Court justice Samuel Chase, who tried criminal cases as part of his circuit riding, was a notorious example. Chase insulted and bullied lawyers for Republican defendants, and announced in advance of one trial "he would certainly punish [defendant] Callender. He would teach the lawyers of Virginia the difference between the liberty and the licentiousness of the press." (Chase was later impeached and narrowly escaped removal.) Other Federalist judges were equally biased, as were the juries and grand juries, who were selected by Federalist United States marshals.[22]

As a result of this partisanship, the Alien and Sedition Acts were enforced very harshly. Newspaper editors and others were sent to prison for up to a year and fined heavily for such comments as charging the Adams Administration with being "a tempest of malignant passions" and Adams himself with being "a professed auto-crat . . . [who] has proved faithful and serviceable to the British interest." Another editor was given six months in prison and a heavy fine for writing "our credit is so low, we are obliged to borrow money at 8 percent in time of peace."[23]

At the same time, the federal judicial system was creaking. Circuit riding by Supreme Court justices was particularly troublesome: Court sessions often had to be postponed or canceled because the justice could not get to the courthouse to hold trial. And if he did get there he would later have to review his own decision if the case was appealed to the Supreme Court.

The Adams Administration therefore proposed a new Judiciary Act to make the federal judicial system more rational. In the process it created sixteen new judges, and many new marshals, clerks, attorneys, and justices of the peace.

In November 1800 the Federalists lost both the presidency and Congress. In January 1801 a lame duck Congress, still controlled by the Federalists, passed the new Judiciary Act. All the new judge-ships and other posts were filled with true-blue Federalists and even former Loyalists, as a last bastion of defense against the victorious Jeffersonians. Up to the last minutes of the Adams Administra-tion—until midnight of March 3, 1801—Secretary of State John Marshall, who had already been appointed chief justice of the United States, signed and delivered commissions. At least four com-missions were not delivered on time, one of which set the stage for the great case of *Marbury* v. *Madison,* which established judicial review over acts of Congress: The newly appointed Republican secretary of state, James Madison, refused to deliver the commission formally appointing William Marbury of Maryland a justice of the peace in the District of Columbia, and Marbury sued him.

The purpose of the midnight appointments was no secret. Gou-verneur Morris, a leading Federalist, wrote that his party was about to experience "a heavy gale of adverse wind; can they be blamed for casting many anchors to hold their ship through the storm?" Jeffer-son wrote in December 1801 that "the Federalists have retired into the Judiciary as a stronghold . . . and from that battery all the works of republicanism are to be beaten down and erased."[24]

The Federalist court-packing produced a bitter fight in 1802 that caused the repeal of the 1801 Judiciary Act and the abolition of all the new judgeships. Federalist leader James Bayard warned that the Constitution would be in jeopardy if the act were repealed and threatened that "there are many now willing to spill their blood to defend that Constitution. Are gentlemen disposed to risk the consequences? . . . the moment is not far when this fair country is to be desolated by civil war."[25]

Despite the threats, the Jeffersonian-controlled Congress repealed the Judiciary Act. To ensure that John Marshall and the Supreme Court would not quickly strike down the repeal and reinstate the act, Congress canceled the 1802 session of the Supreme Court so the new judicial system with its Federalist judges would be fully dismantled before the Court sat again. The Supreme Court ultimately upheld the repeal, but the rancor and bitterness lasted for many years, and the federal system remained substantially unreformed until 1891.[26]

The parallel with the current efforts to preserve the Reagan Revolution through court-packing is obvious. Unfortunately, the parallel extends to the side effects as well: the politicization of the courts, bitter controversy, and great harm to both the substance and appearance of fairness, on which so much of the courts' authority rests.

5
1981–84—Beginnings

Fuse in Administrative Appl. – Tower
Bitterness – partisanship.)
*

I think for a long time we've had a number of Supreme Court Justices who, given any chance, invade the prerogative of the legislature; they legislate rather than make judgments, and some try to rewrite the Constitution instead of interpreting it. I would want a constitutionalist.

Ronald Reagan, 1980

When Ronald Reagan took office in 1981, the federal judiciary was divided about three to two between Democratic and Republican appointees. Although Jimmy Carter had been able to appoint an unusually large number of judges, Republicans had held the White House sixteen of the twenty-eight years since 1953. By December 31, 1987, Reagan had appointed 334 judges, with 28 still pending, and the proportions were reversed, with about 60 percent of the federal bench Republican.[1]

Some of Carter's appointments were well-known liberals. His main goal, however, was putting more minorities and women on the bench, and some of his nominees were quite conservative. Court of Appeals judge Cornelia Kennedy from Michigan, for example, had a record as a district judge that was startling in its almost uniform refusal to rule in favor of a civil rights claim, which had resulted in frequent reversals by higher courts; in 1987 she was on one of President Reagan's short lists of potential Supreme Court nominees to succeed Justice Lewis F. Powell. Mississippi district judge L. T. Senter, another Carter appointee, was bitterly opposed by the civil rights community for indications of racism. And Judge Ruth Bader Ginsburg, usually referred to as a liberal member of the D.C. Circuit, actually has quite a mixed record. Even the minority judges were not substantially more liberal than other Democratic appointees. One careful observer concluded that "there is little empirical evidence to suggest that the voting behavior of black judges diverges from that of white judges—at least in ways other than those associated with party affiliation." The same almost certainly holds true for the female judges vis-à-vis their male counterparts.[2]

This was hardly surprising. Carter's attorney general Griffin Bell, who had the main responsibility for judicial nominations, had long been considered hostile to civil rights, both as a federal judge and earlier, when he was legal adviser to segregationist governor Ernest Vandiver of Georgia in the 1950s and tried to block school desegregation. Because of this history, he had experienced a very rough confirmation hearing.

Democrat or Republican, by 1981 most federal judges shared two basic conceptions of their role: first, that a major function of the federal judiciary was to protect individual rights, and second, that they should interfere as little as possible with economic and other activities not related to civil rights and liberties.

The conservative critics of the courts were clearly unhappy with both of these conceptions, and when one of their own captured the White House and obtained the judge-choosing authority, they promptly set about trying to put reliable conservatives on the bench.

Aware that political power is usually temporary, the right pushed for young judges. Speaking of a thirty-one-year-old he had recommended for the District Court in Texas, Senator Phil Gramm explained that the goal was to pick judges who will "be there for a long time . . . making rulings after I'm dead." White House counsel Fred Fielding acknowledged that the Administration was pursuing such a strategy. During Reagan's first term, 11.4 percent of all his appointees were under forty, a higher percentage than under any recent president; the average age of his appeals court appointees during his first term was 51.5, the youngest average of the past five administrations. A report for the Twentieth-Century Fund completed in mid-1987 found that while less than 2 percent of appellate judges appointed by Eisenhower, Kennedy, and Johnson were under forty, and 3 percent of Carter's, 10 percent of Reagan's appeals judges were in their thirties. Probably because of the inevitable inexperience of these young appointees, over half of them were rated "not qualified" by some members of the ABA screening committee. Overall, 24 percent of Reagan's first sixty-four appellate judges received split "qualified" votes, compared with only 3 percent of Carter's.[3]

Other examples of this youth movement include the early appointment of then-forty-two-year-old Richard A. Posner, a leading conservative theoretician, and thirty-five-year-old Frank Easterbrook, both of the University of Chicago Law School, to the Seventh Circuit (Illinois, Indiana, Wisconsin); J. Harvie Wilkinson, thirty-nine when nominated to the Fourth Circuit (Maryland to South Carolina); Kenneth Starr, an assistant to former attorney general William French Smith, thirty-six when named to the U.S. Court of Appeals for the District of Columbia; Alex Kozinski, thirty-four when nominated to the Ninth Circuit, which covers the West Coast; and Edith Jones (one of Reagan's few female nominees), thirty-six when appointed to the Fifth Circuit (Texas, Mississippi, and Louisiana).

Youth was especially emphasized during Reagan's second term. It was probably the main reason for the ill-fated choice of forty-one-year-old Douglas Ginsburg to the Supreme Court. Reagan was more successful on the district and appellate levels, where his judicial appointees were younger than those of any other president in this century—34.2 percent of his second-term judges were under forty-five, compared to 22 percent for Theodore Roosevelt, who had the second-largest percentage under forty-five.[4]

To obtain ideological purity, the Administration systematically screened the candidates. A nine-member President's Committee on Federal Judicial Selection was established, chaired by Counsel to the

President Fielding and including then-presidential counselor Edwin Meese, Attorney General William French Smith, and other top White House and Justice Department officials. A computer data-bank containing every available publication by a candidate was set up, and day-long interviews were held with the finalists. Many were called for the interviews, but few were chosen.[5]

The Administration also reduced the role of the American Bar Association. Through its Standing Committee on Federal Judiciary, which rated candidates on a four-level scale—"extremely well qualified," "well qualified," "qualified," and "not qualified"—the ABA had come to exercise a great deal of influence over the nominating process, with a monopoly on institutionalized nongovernmental participation in the nominating process.

Founded in 1878 to oppose what it considered liberal decisions by the Supreme Court, the ABA tried from the first to share in the judicial selection process in order to fight the "socialist menace," the "subversion of the judiciary," and "the downgrading of property rights." Its most prominent public effort was against Louis D. Brandeis in 1916, whom it called "not a fit person to be a member of the Supreme Court"; seven ex-ABA presidents, including William Howard Taft, spoke against Brandeis.[6]

The American Bar Association played a major role in Herbert Hoover's nominations but had little influence with the Wilson and Franklin D. Roosevelt administrations. The ABA was associated with conservative Republicans, and Democratic presidents were not inclined to pay much attention to its views.

The ABA's next big chance and the real beginning of its latter-day importance came in 1946, when the Republicans won the Senate. The Standing Committee on Federal Judiciary was formed, and its evaluations of judicial nominees were given great weight, not only by the Eisenhower Administration but also quite often by those of Kennedy and Johnson. Under these administrations, the ABA committee would evaluate those under consideration before the nomination was made.

Jimmy Carter reduced the ABA's influence somewhat by creating special circuit nominating commissions. The Reagan Administration abolished Carter's commissions but also tried to deemphasize the ABA committee's importance by providing it with the name of the nominee only after the Administration had made its choice, thereby allowing the committee only a veto, not a role in the selection.

The Administration's ideological screening was not, of course, foolproof, and passing the ideological litmus test was not always insisted on. Politics and other factors sometimes overrode ideology. Senators, for example, still had a lot to say about district court nominees, and many Republicans, like Charles Mathias of Maryland and Lowell Weicker of Connecticut, were anything but right-wingers.

Senatorial power over judges was considerably weakened, however. The Administration began to insist on at least three to five recommendations for each seat, not just one, as in the past, and ignored some senatorial recommendations entirely. Meese's efforts to see that only very conservative candidates were named angered Pennsylvania senators John Heinz and Arlen Specter, who complained publicly about interference with what they considered their senatorial prerogatives. Senator David Durenberger of Minnesota reported that at one meeting with Attorney General Meese on a Durenberger recommendation that the department was holding up, "there was a big blow up when Ed found out we still thought we had a major role in appointing judges." Conservative Colorado senator William Armstrong's choice of Denver lawyer Carol Welch was vetoed when she told her Justice Department interviewer that while she opposed abortion she thought women ought be allowed to choose whether to have one. And, of course, many of the senators elected in 1980, like Jeremiah Denton of Alabama, John East of North Carolina, Steve Symms of North Dakota, and a good many others, were themselves conservative zealots.[7]

Nevertheless, during most of Reagan's first term, his judge-picking policies aroused little opposition. There were, however, harbingers of the more contentious second term, with examples of what was later to produce enormous controversy: highly qualified candidates rejected by the Administration because of conservative pressure; ultraconservative candidates easily seated; and a controversial nominee who was confirmed, but only after a long battle.

Sandra Day O'Connor

The judgeship wars started off mildly enough with the nomination of Judge Sandra Day O'Connor of Arizona to the Supreme Court in 1981 after Justice Potter Stewart retired.

Liberals feared for the fate of the Supreme Court when Ronald Reagan was elected president. With so many members close to eighty, some departures through death or disability seemed certain. Oddly enough, the first vacancy occurred through retirement by the relatively young and increasingly conservative Stewart, sixty-six; it was later learned that Stewart had been ill. He died in 1985.

Because O'Connor was the first female nominated to the Court, many liberals and feminists promptly supported her. Her only substantial opposition came from anti-abortion groups, who, seeing that she had supported liberalized abortion when she was in the Arizona Senate in 1970 and 1974, thought she was prochoice. At her confirmation hearing, Senators East and Denton hammered away at her, trying to ascertain her views, but in a grueling ten hours in the witness chair, O'Connor evaded all their questions.

Ironies abounded. For one thing, the nomination was a clear example of affirmative action by a president and Administration that has mounted a sustained attack against it. O'Connor's nomination was not based on her legal qualifications or reputation. When nominated, she was an obscure Arizona lower-court judge, with no national prominence, no federal experience, and with no great reputation as either a judge or a lawyer among Arizona lawyers. She would not have made any list of likely nominees combining male and female lawyers. Her assets were primarily her sex, and after that, her conservative and pro-states rights philosophy, her region, and her friendship with Senator Barry Goldwater and Justice William H. Rehnquist.[8]

The other irony is that despite the anti-abortion forces' suspicions that she might be sympathetic to abortion rights, Justice O'Connor became one of the severest critics of the Court's abortion decisions. In most other respects, Justice O'Connor has also been very conservative. In her first six years on the Court she was Rehnquist's most reliable ally, voting with him approximately 87 percent of the time.[9]

Her nomination occasioned no substantial dispute in the Senate, and she was easily confirmed, 99–0.

Judith Whittaker

The Whittaker story ended very differently, and some observers trace that to the Administration's need to placate its very conservative supporters after the O'Connor nomination.

Upon taking over, the Reagan Administration found numerous vacancies on the federal bench. One of these vacancies was in the Eighth Circuit Court of Appeals, which covers seven states in America's heartland, from the Dakotas through Arkansas.

In the fall of 1981 it was reported that the Administration planned to appoint forty-three-year-old Judith Whittaker, associate general counsel of Hallmark Cards in Kansas City, Missouri, to fill the Eighth Circuit vacancy. Whittaker was highly qualified. She had attended the University of Michigan Law School for a year and did so well as to be eligible for the law review. She switched to the University of Missouri in Kansas City, from which she graduated first in her class. She then became the first woman partner in a major Kansas City law firm where she handled complex corporate trials until 1972, when she went to Hallmark. She was a trustee of Brown University and of the University of Missouri at Kansas City. She was rated "well qualified" by the American Bar Association's screening committee, and Chief Judge Donald P. Lay of the Eighth Circuit called her an "outstanding lawyer, possessing the qualities to become a great and gifted judge."[10]

Whittaker had, however, supported the Equal Rights Amendment (as had the 1976 Republican platform), and this offended local right-wingers. The same groups that had earlier opposed the nomination of Sandra Day O'Connor for the Supreme Court turned on Whittaker with a harshness fueled by their defeat on O'Connor. They charged Whittaker with being a closet Democrat, against business, and in favor of abortion, and initiated a massive letter-writing campaign against her. Direct-mail specialist Richard Viguerie aimed his newsletter against her, describing her as a "strong feminist" and a "liberal Democrat." The general counsel of the Senate Republican

Steering Committee charged her with being a "member of the American Civil Liberties Union," "a member of a women's caucus at Hallmark Cards which took fairly liberal stands on abortion and the ERA," and an opponent of a "curb on pornography" in Kansas City.[11]

Almost all of this was false. Whittaker, the daughter-in-law of Charles Evans Whittaker, whom President Eisenhower appointed to the Supreme Court, is a solid establishment Republican and a financial supporter of the Republican Party. She had once belonged to the ACLU but had long since quit. She had represented business interests for over ten years, belonged to no "women's caucus" at Hallmark Cards, and had never been particularly active in "feminist causes"; a friend described her as at most a "moderate" feminist. Her only involvement with the pornography issue was to help Hallmark keep a store selling obscene books *out of* a Kansas City development project. She had served on a legal services board, but so had Reagan's attorney general William French Smith when he was a private attorney. As to abortion, she had never stated her views publicly, and she denied being prochoice.[12]

Her opponents, however, managed to reach Lyn Nofziger, Reagan's political director (who was convicted in February 1988 of illegally exerting influence at the White House on behalf of the corruption-ridden Wedtech Corporation). Nofziger, long known for his own ultraconservatism—he had also fought the O'Connor nomination—and a point man for right-wingers who wanted something from the White House, went to work.

By Christmas the Whittaker nomination was dead. She did not have enough "broad-based support," explained Deputy Attorney General Edwin Schmults. Several years later a White House staffer admitted they had made a mistake on the Whittaker matter, but this was only talk. Even though four new appeals judges have been appointed to the Eighth Circuit since the Whittaker episode, neither Judith Whittaker nor, indeed, any other woman was nominated for any of them.[13]

The Administration's emphasis on the abortion issue resulted in a bias against women. As Fielding admitted to the *Washington Post*, "The abortion issue most often comes up in regard to potential women candidates. I can't comment on why it does. I don't know the answer." By December 31, 1987, Reagan had nominated only 28 women out of 334 appointments to the bench, just 8 percent. By contrast, Carter in his four years nominated 41 women out of 258 judges, or 15 percent, at a time when fewer women had gained the requisite experience; 11 of Carter's 56 appellate nominees were female, but only 3 of Reagan's 76 were.[14]

Richard A. Posner

Conservatives had no problems with Richard A. Posner, a University of Chicago law professor who specialized in economic regulation, particularly antitrust and public utility law.

Posner's academic credentials were dazzling. A *summa cum laude* graduate of Yale, first in his class at Harvard Law School, and president of the *Harvard Law Review,* he had started his legal career by clerking for Justice William J. Brennan. After a few years at the Federal Trade Commission, the solicitor general's office, and as general counsel to President Lyndon B. Johnson's Task Force on Communications Policy, Posner started teaching law, first at Stanford and then at the University of Chicago.

The year with the liberal Justice Brennan apparently left little impact on Posner. In short order he became the high priest of the law and economics movement, writing numerous books and articles applying economic theory to all human problems, from antitrust regulation, where it clearly had a place, to such unlikely contexts as criminal law, social benefit distribution, family law, adoption of babies, abortion, ethics, court administration, privacy, and almost every other facet of human life. For Posner "the economic perspective . . . can be used to understand the problems of utilitarian and Kantian ethics, the social and legal arrangements of primitive and ancient societies and the concept and law of privacy."[15]

These theories were drawn from the libertarian economics-oriented philosophy originally developed by European philosophers Frederick A. Hayek and Ludwig von Mises and elaborated by University of Chicago economists Milton Friedman and Aaron Director. The theories call for minimum state intervention in the so-called free market. In Posner's version, the theory presupposes that human beings function as wealth-maximizing calculating machines in all areas of life. They act according to inexorably working economic principles in free markets, which, if left to themselves, will work out for the best. Posner considers such behavior not only useful but also moral. Economic efficiency—maximum output at minimum cost—is the primary value, and probably the only value, for in Posner's world all the best things in life either result from it or lead to it. Maximizing society's wealth is the ultimate criterion for whether behavior is just or good. "When people describe as unjustly convicting a person without a trial," writes Posner, "taking property without just compensation, or failing to make a negligent automobile driver answer in damages to the victim of his negligence, this means nothing more pretentious than that the conduct wastes resources."[16]

Posner's theories ignore inconvenient realities, such as the fact that even in a truly free market, which is very rare, how one does depends on how much one starts with. To ignore that is to legitimize unhappy outcomes for poor people who don't have very much.

Posner's theories also produce some startling policies. According to Posner, baby adoption, for example, should be subject to auction. He calculates that most babies would cost about $3,000 (in 1978 dollars), and they would be better off if allocated by an auction because "the more costly a purchase, the more care a purchaser will lavish on it." A prisoner blinded by negligent prison doctors should find a lawyer on the open market. If there were no unions, there would not be discrimination against blacks. Racial segregation can be cured by the free market. The government should enforce real estate agreements that discriminate against blacks and Jews. The government may prohibit discrimination by trade unions but not by private business.[17]

For Posner, all choices should be made by one test: Which alternative costs the least and produces the most? Even that calculation, unrealistic as it is, is not based on any empirical reality, for Posner continually makes these cost-benefit judgments on the basis of assumptions, hunches, and speculation, with virtually no reference to empirical data.

The practical result is a pervasive and extreme conservatism that, in Posner's special fields of economic regulation, leads to gutting almost all regulation.

Posner's views have become a significant intellectual force in American law, particularly among those with a conservative bent. *The Wall Street Journal* described it as "the premier topic of debate in academic circles, and it has dramatically changed teaching practices in major law schools." Even a Posner critic like Yale Law School's Bruce Ackerman considers it "the most important thing that has happened in legal thought since the New Deal."[18]

Soon after Reagan became president, he nominated Posner to the Seventh Circuit Court of Appeals, which sits in Chicago. It was a uniquely useful spot for Posner, since that court handles a great many antitrust, securities, and other business cases. Also, it soon would have many more vacancies, which Reagan could fill with judges who would support Posner. It therefore provided an ideal opportunity for Posner to work his views into the law.

When Richard Posner's name came before the Senate in November 1981 as one of Reagan's first Court of Appeals nominees, most members of the Senate had no idea who or what he was. Senator Charles Percy of Illinois, who introduced him to the Judiciary Committee, told the committee that Posner "was originally brought to the attention of the President by an official of the Justice Department and not by myself." The Democrats were still traumatized by their massive loss in November 1980 and by Reagan's total dominance of the political landscape in that first year of his first term. Also, this early in Reagan's presidency, few people realized how much ideological court-packing was being planned.[19] The nomination went practically unnoticed.

Posner's confirmation hearing took place on a Friday afternoon, in a joint session with four other nominees, and with only Chairman Strom Thurmond and the conservative Howell Heflin of Alabama in attendance. Posner's part of the hearing took but a few minutes, and he was quickly confirmed without debate. Although few realized it, the court-packing campaign had begun, and the model Reagan nominee had just been displayed: a young, intellectually strong academic with little trial or other legal experience, with strongly held ultraconservative views based on an economic model, and who was often quite far from the mainstream of American legal thought.

Except for age, the Posner model was followed in other appellate court nominations during the first Reagan term, such as:

- Robert Bork, fifty-four, who had spent most of his professional life as an antitrust and constitutional teacher at Yale (though he had left the school six months earlier to work with a Washington law firm), nominated to the District of Columbia Circuit in January 1982
- Ralph Winter, forty-six, a Yale professor specializing in corporate and election law, nominated to the Second Circuit in New York in December 1981
- Antonin Scalia, forty-six, from the University of Chicago, a specialist in administrative law, who later went to the Supreme Court, nominated to the District of Columbia Circuit in 1982
- J. Harvey Wilkinson, thirty-nine, a law professor at the University of Virginia and former editorial page editor of the *Norfolk Virginian-Pilot*, nominated to the Fourth Circuit in 1983
- Pasco Bowman II, fifty, dean of the law school at the University of Missouri at Kansas City and formerly dean at Wake Forest Law School, a corporate and international trade specialist, nominated to the Eighth Circuit in 1983

This focus on academics enabled the administration to be sure of what it was getting. Each of these men had expressed himself on a variety of issues before being chosen, and there were few surprises when they began to decide cases and write opinions.

Perhaps of equal importance is the nature of the academic function, particularly that performed by critics who are outside the mainstream of prevailing thought. Their function and inclination is to criticize. This induces a readiness—indeed, an eagerness—to correct what the critic considers wrongheaded. There is little respect for precedent and not much for stability, regardless of the lip service to judicial restraint. Posner, for example, declared at his confirmation hearing that he "would be willing to subjugate [his] personal views to the statute or the law" because "I think that kind of subjugation is the judge's duty." Yet in antitrust matters alone, a sympathetic defense lawyer commented on Posner's "almost religious zeal" and lack of "judicial and restrained approach to finding the law." Assistant Attorney General William F. Baxter, a Stanford professor on leave, described Supreme Court antitrust opinions as "rubbish," "wacko." A study on federalism issued by the Administration in 1986 prepared by academics working for the Justice Department lambasted 170 years of Supreme Court precedent, as do the writings of some of the department's most influential academic advisers. Bork's writings on both antitrust and constitutional law are filled with near contempt for four decades of Supreme Court decision making. Scalia's comments on the Court's affirmative action rulings have been equally disdainful. Nineteen eighty-seven Court of Appeals nominee Bernard Siegan, of San Diego Law School, has condemned most of what the Court has done since 1819.[20]

By choosing very conservative academics, the Administration thus ensures an aggressive, uncompromising conservatism that is willing to shake up and overturn.

In only one case during Reagan's first term did his nominee have serious confirmation problems: J. Harvey Wilkinson, the thirty-nine-year-old Virginian nominated to the Fourth Circuit.

J. Harvey Wilkinson

Wilkinson's résumé was impressive except for one thing: He had almost no experience as a lawyer, despite having graduated from law school in 1972, eleven years before his nomination. He had worked for three years as a newspaper editorial page editor and writer, served one year as a law clerk to Supreme Court Justice Lewis F. Powell, and had taught law for about six. His only involvement in any form of law practice was during one year in the Justice Department as an assistant to William Bradford Reynolds, where his job was to review drafts of briefs and memoranda to make certain they furthered the policies of the attorney general. On the few occasions where Wilkinson interjected himself into litigation matters, the trial attorneys found him to be too inexperienced to be helpful. In one case his ignorance of court procedure caused the department to be fined for missing a court deadline; such a fine on the government is almost unheard of. He had never had a private client, written a legal brief by himself, and except for one minor procedural motion while at the Justice Department, had never argued in court. He was not a member of the bar of either the Fourth Circuit Court of Appeals or of any of the district courts that are supervised by the court to which he was nominated. And he was only thirty-nine, hardly the age at which someone has acquired the life's seasoning that one normally assumes a judge should have, particularly a judge who reviews the work of others. American Bar Association rules require twelve years of post–law school experience for judicial nominees and used to require fifteen years.

Wilkinson's lack of experience resulted in an initial determination by the American Bar Association's circuit representative that he was "not qualified." A second ABA representative was brought in—the ABA committee chairman had difficulty recalling another instance when a second representative had been brought in because of a negative vote by the circuit representative—and he came up with a "qualified" recommendation, the lowest level of eligibility. The ABA committee thereupon voted 10–4 to give Wilkinson a "qualified" rating, despite its twelve-years-of-experience rule.[21]

Wilkinson had written books, articles, and editorials, and his views on many of the policy issues facing American courts were developed and known. And they were reliably conservative, particularly with respect to school segregation, affirmative action, bilingual education, capital punishment, and gay and lesbian rights. At the Justice Department he had played an important role in blocking effective remedies for proven civil rights violations and in keeping black parents who insisted on more effective remedies than the Justice Department was willing to urge from participating in desegregation suits. According to one former Civil Rights Division lawyer, for Wilkinson, "the bottom line would always be the most restrictive interpretation possible, one that would afford the people that we were supposed to be representing the least rights possible."[22]

In the Senate, Wilkinson's inexperience became the focus of the controversy, especially since his editorials for the *Norfolk Virginian-Pilot* had stressed the importance of merit selection for judges over politics and personal connections. In a 1979 editorial probably written by Wilkinson and certainly approved by him, the paper praised

Virginia Senator Harry Byrd and the Virginia Bar Association for insisting on "merit" and refusing to bow to Carter's insistence that blacks and women be on Byrd's recommendation lists. Because of his lack of experience as a lawyer, Wilkinson failed his own standards. His former employer, the *Norfolk Virginian-Pilot*, opposed his nomination, concluding, "Obviously he is a bright young man in a hurry, but what's the rush?"[23]

The experience issue also had race and sex discrimination overtones. A lack of experience has frequently been used as an argument against judicial appointments for blacks and women. For example, the ABA had given an "unqualified" rating to Professor Judith Krauskopf, the Carter nominee to the Eighth Circuit vacancy intended for Judith Whittaker, because she lacked trial experience. Wilkinson himself had insisted on such seasoning.

To Elaine Jones of the NAACP Legal Defense and Education Fund, Inc., Wilkinson was "a white male from a privileged background who has connections of power and who does not meet the qualification standards now met by every federal appellate jurist in the country."[24]

When Jones testified, in February 1984, she may not have realized how many "connections of power" had come into play on behalf of this "white male from a privileged background." Shortly after the February hearing, it was learned that the ABA's 10–4 vote in early November 1983 had not been taken in monastic isolation. Committee members had been heavily lobbied by Wilkinson's friends, including Supreme Court Justice Lewis Powell, with whom Wilkinson had very close professional and family connections and for whom Wilkinson had clerked. Powell had called a friend on the committee after being contacted—improperly—by a worried Justice Department official who had learned in confidence from an ABA committee member that the nomination was in trouble. Powell's opinion of Wilkinson had already been made known to the committee twice before, so the call could hardly have been considered just informational. High Justice Department representatives called at least three other committee members, including the chairman.[25]

Wilkinson did not depend only on others to promote his cause. He put together his own lobbying campaign, which included having a black law student at the University of Virginia, where Wilkinson was teaching, contact the black member of the committee. In addition, between November 5, the day after the unfavorable report appeared, and November 7, the day before the ABA vote, Wilkinson made at least sixty calls and contacted fourteen influential people, including law school deans and a newspaper publisher, who in turn contacted at least eight of the fourteen-member committee. Although the campaign may not have been entirely successful—the member contacted by Powell voted against Wilkinson—its overall impact may have been substantial. The black Virginia student whose help Wilkinson had solicited later said that "Jay told me three days later that it helped," though the ABA member the student contacted said, "My mind was already made up."[26]

The Bar Committee members were shocked to learn of the massive lobbying campaign. One member commented that in his six years on the committee, "This is the first time I have ever encountered anything of this kind." And many senators were dismayed. It made little difference, however. After a lengthy floor fight, Wilkinson was confirmed a week after the committee hearing, with thirty-six votes against him.[27]

By the end of Reagan's first term, he had made 129 appointments to the district courts, and 31 appointments to the twelve courts of appeals. Nine women had been appointed to the district courts and only one to the courts of appeals. Seven Hispanics and one black were appointed to the district courts, and one black and one Hispanic to the appeals courts, the worst record on blacks since Eisenhower, who appointed none. A total of 20 percent of the appellate nominees were academics, a modern record.[28]

6
1985—The Campaign Intensifies

It's too long been acceptable for a judicial candidate to be a contributor to the American Civil Liberties Union or the NAACP Legal Defense Fund.
                    Daniel J. Popeo, General Counsel, Washington Legal Foundation

Sometime in November 1984, a few days after the Reagan reelection landslide, I met Nan Aron and William Taylor for lunch at a Chinese restaurant in Washington to talk about the federal courts.

Aron founded and heads the Alliance for Justice, a national organization of over twenty-four public-interest groups, including the Women's Legal Defense Fund, the Children's Defense Fund, and the National Resources Defense Council. The Alliance's mission is to protect the interests of these groups on such matters as legal services, regulatory reform, and restrictions on lobbying and advocacy. Under Aron's direction, the Alliance had stopped many Administration initiatives to cripple the public interest movement.

William Taylor was then head of the Center for National Policy Review, a combination think-tank and activist organization that concentrated on fighting racial discrimination. Taylor, whose specialty is education and school desegregation, had been staff director of the United States Civil Rights Commission during the 1960s and was one of the most experienced and effective Capitol Hill operatives in civil rights matters.

A law teacher for most of my professional life, I had served as counsel to the Senate Antitrust and Monopoly Subcommittee and had been involved in civil rights, civil liberties, economic regulation, and other public-interest issues since the early 1960s as a litigator, writer, and teacher.

What precipitated this lunch was, oddly enough, an unrelated decision the previous June by the Supreme Court. The decision allowed a company that files for bankruptcy to repudiate its labor contract unilaterally. The labor unions sought congressional relief and drew Administration support, but at a price—eighty-five new judgeships, which Ronald Reagan would be able to fill.[1]

The new judgeships, plus the normal forty per year from attrition, gave President Reagan the opportunity during his eight years in office to appoint more than half of the federal judiciary, something no president had done since Franklin D. Roosevelt in his twelve years as president. In addition, five of the nine Supreme Court Justices were over seventy-five and might not last out Reagan's term.

During Reagan's first term, constitutional amendments had been stalled, court-stripping efforts had been killed, reactionary legal theories had failed, and real progress in some areas like voting rights had actually been made. But all of this, together with many of the gains for individual rights so painfully achieved during the past thirty years, might now go down the drain if a court-packing campaign were successful. Right-wing spokesmen like Bruce Fein predicted the greatest changes in direction since 1937, with many if not most of the great civil rights and civil liberties landmarks—abortion, apportionment, *Miranda*—overturned.[2]

There were already signs that the Reagan judges were producing change. A 1984 study issued by the ultraconservative Center for Judicial Studies concluded that during 1981–82 Reagan appointees had fulfilled the Administration's expectations, especially on the appellate level. At the end of Reagan's first term, in October 1984, Jonathan Rose, a former Justice Department official who had been one of the main actors in choosing judges and getting them confirmed (he had been one of the Justice Department lobbyists who saved the Wilkinson nomination when it was in trouble), said that the Administration was "tremendously pleased," particularly with its judges from academia, who had "fully met our expectations of being people committed to the President's judicial philosophy." Judges like Bork, Scalia, Posner, and others were clearly less interested in judicial restraint than they had appeared to be at their confirmation hearings.[3]

With this as a spur, Aron, Taylor, and I got together to decide what to do. There was no disagreement on either the seriousness of the problem or the need for a broadly based, organized effort. It was quickly agreed that the public-interest community should be convened and that as many groups as possible should be involved.

A meeting was held on November 19, 1984. To the organizers' surprise, a very large number of groups attended, including the NAACP, the NAACP Legal Defense and Education Fund, Inc., the Leadership Conference on Civil Rights, and the Women's Legal Defense and Education Fund. All were worried. Under the aegis of the Alliance for Justice, a separate Judicial Selection Project was created, with a staff of its own, to conduct and disseminate research on judicial nominees. Although Senate Democrats had gained a few seats in the 1984 election, they were still in the minority, and Judiciary Committee Democrats had little staff to spare for investigating judicial nominees.

As a matter of principle, strategy, and scarce resources, only the egregious nominees would be challenged, only those who lacked good professional credentials or demonstrated a glaring lack of commitment to fairness and equality under the law. Since few senators have much stomach for such contests, key Democrats and Republicans on the Judiciary Committee would have to be persuaded of both the importance and the feasibility of opposing what one participant called "really terrible" nominees. Nan Aron became chair of the Judicial Selection Project, and a steering committee was formed.

Although the civil rights and other public-interest groups had immediately recognized the seriousness of the problem—twenty-nine groups, including the AFL-CIO and People for the American Way, soon joined the Judicial Selection Project—many others did not. It took many months and a good number of "really terrible" nominees before lawyers and bar groups outside the civil rights public-interest community became alarmed. An article in the *National Journal* in December 1984 had made it very clear that, as presidential counsel Fred Fielding put it, "we have an opportunity to restore a philosophical balance that you don't have right now" and that close ideological screening was being done. But no alarm bells had gone off in the community at large. The usual response among many, including prominent liberal lawyers, was to ask, "Doesn't the president have the right to appoint anyone he wants?" It was difficult to get bar groups and others even to schedule a public discussion of the issue.[4]

By the end of 1985, however, attitudes had changed, and even some conservatives protested. The change resulted not so much from the "really terrible" nominations, none of which had yet gone far enough to come to public attention, but from right-wing efforts to torpedo candidates not considered sufficiently conservative, as in the Whittaker episode. The spring of 1985 saw three such incidents, all of which involved the crudest kind of ideological screening and provoked protests even from those inclined to give the president the broadest latitude. The first of these involved Andrew L. Frey.

BLOCKING THE INSUFFICIENTLY PURE

Andrew L. Frey

Who would ever have thought that a twenty-five-dollar contribution to a gun-control group would cost a law-and-order candidate a judgeship? Yet that is exactly what it did to Andrew Frey.

Andrew Frey was a forty-six-year-old deputy solicitor general when he was first recommended for appointment to the District of Columbia Court of Appeals. The solicitor general's office, which argues on behalf of the United States in the Supreme Court and controls federal appeals in the lower courts, is probably the most elite group of lawyers in the United States. Frey, a Phi Beta Kappa from Swarthmore, had been notes and comments editor of the *Columbia Law Review,* and a law clerk to a federal appellate judge. He also had spent seven years in private practice before joining the solicitor general's staff in 1972. For his work on that staff, Frey earned numerous honors, including the Presidential Award for Meritorious Service from Reagan, and the attorney general's Distinguished Service Award. When he left in April 1986 he had argued fifty-five cases in the Supreme Court and had written over two hundred briefs. His many victories included several landmark decisions.

Frey was not just another able government lawyer, however. He was head of the solicitor general's criminal section and was the chief Supreme Court advocate for the United States in criminal cases. As oral advocate, brief writer, and strategist, Frey played a central role in such prosecution victories as creating exceptions to the exclusionary rule and watering down the standards for probable cause to search. He almost single-handedly persuaded the Court to reshape the law of double jeopardy to allow the prosecution to appeal defeats. He had probably done as much to lighten the prosecution's constitutional obligations as any lawyer in the country.

As part of the home rule granted the District of Columbia during the Nixon Administration, the district was allowed to set up its own local court system, separate from the federal courts. Nominations for the D.C. courts were to be made by the president from among three names chosen by a local seven-member panel, with confirmation by the Senate.

In the summer of 1984, a slot opened on the D.C. Court of Appeals. Frey's name was included on the list of three, and as expected, Reagan selected him. The nomination caused concern among some of the district's civil rights groups. Much of that court's business is criminal, and they feared Frey would be predisposed to favor the prosecution. His experience and intellectual power also would make him especially influential with his colleagues.

That's not where Andrew Frey's troubles came from, however. He had made a few small contributions to a gun-control group and to Planned Parenthood and had successfully defended a conviction under the gun-control law. The National Rifle Association and anti-abortion groups immediately began to lobby against Frey, even though it was very unlikely that he would ever hear a gun-control case—there are very few such cases anywhere—and he wasn't much more likely to sit on an abortion issue. Other right-wing groups like the Conservative Caucus, led by Howard Phillips (whom Nixon had chosen in 1969 to head and destroy the Office of Economic Opportunity), joined the fight against Frey.

This was not the first time the anti-gun-control forces had tried to block a judicial nomination. As noted earlier, they had also come out against Illinois congressman Abner Mikva when he was nominated in 1979 to the United States Court of Appeals for the District of Columbia. Since the Democrats controlled the Senate, and since President Carter backed Mikva strongly, the gun lobby lost, though they managed to get thirty-one votes against the nomination.

This time, with Republicans in control of the Senate, things were different. On March 13, 1985, thirteen right-wing Republican senators, including Denton, East, Helms, and Steve Symms of Idaho, wrote Reagan that because they considered Frey's "political and judicial philosophy . . . very much at odds with your own philosophy and the public positions you have taken" (even though Reagan himself apparently didn't think so), they would have "no choice but to oppose" the nomination. It was also disclosed that Frey had contributed to Helms's reelection opponent, but this was not used against him publicly.[5]

The pressure worked. A few weeks after receiving the senators' letter, the White House withdrew the nomination, the first time a president had turned down a D.C. panel's recommendation. "The judgment was that he would not be confirmed," according to a government source. This mystified observers because the Senate Government Operations Committee, which handles nominations for the local District of Columbia courts, had enough moderate Republicans to join the favorable Democrats, especially if the president made it clear he really wanted the nominee.

The Frey episode is a particularly egregious example of conservative pressure. Few if any gun-control or abortion issues come before the D.C. Court of Appeals, and the grounds for the opposition were completely irrelevant to the job. Moreover, the pressure was able to overcome Frey's obvious acceptability—indeed, desirability—to the president with respect to criminal cases, one of the most important subjects that court does handle. Finally, the nomination was to a local court, of virtually no national significance, so that both the pressure and Reagan's surrender violated basic principles of local-ism and home rule. "If a group of senators went after somebody sitting on a local court in North Carolina, Helms would be the first to complain," protested Frederick Abramson, president-elect of the D.C. Bar Association. But then, Helms and some other senators have always treated Washington as if it were still one of their Deep South plantations. And, as the *London Economist* observed in connec-tion with the Frey nomination, "Reagan's softness in the face of pressure from the right is nothing new."[6]

William E. Hellerstein

"There is a word for the ideological tests for the judiciary which are seemingly now in place in the White House and the Justice Depart-ment. The word is corruption," thundered New York senator Daniel Patrick Moynihan when William E. Hellerstein was turned down for a New York district court judgeship. There was also a lingering stench of McCarthyism about the episode, for the key role in killing the recommendation was played by Roy Cohn, who had been Sena-tor Joseph R. McCarthy's chief counsel.[7]

Hellerstein, forty-four, was chief of the Appeals Bureau of the New York City Legal Aid Society and one of the most respected appellate lawyers in America. Though now bald, bearded, and be-spectacled, he still looked like the star offensive tackle and middle linebacker he had been at high school in the Bronx. Born in poor circumstances, he had made it to Harvard Law School, and in 1964 he joined the Legal Aid Society. He had quickly risen to head the Appeals Bureau, where he became one of the most successful de-fense advocates in the nation, with a string of landmark Supreme Court victories as well as hundreds of appearances in the New York appellate courts, often winning cases that seemed sure losers.

Hellerstein was no left-wing liberal. Though a Democrat, his politics were on the conservative side of the party, particularly on foreign policy. He was also a pillar of the New York legal establish-ment. A member of the Harvard Law School Visiting Committee, at one time or another he was vice president of the Association of the Bar of the City of New York, probably the most distinguished bar association in the country, chairman of its Executive Committee, a member of its Grievance Committee, and on numerous high-level advisory committees. He had taught part-time at New York University Law School, and in 1985 he became a full-time member of the Brooklyn Law School faculty, where he taught evidence and constitutional law, and became a very popular teacher.

In the fall of 1983 a vacancy opened in the Southern District of New York, which covers Manhattan and the Bronx. A seat in the Southern District is one of the most coveted judgeships in the federal system, because of the court's prestige and the importance of the cases it handles. It is also one of the most difficult judgeships to get, because of the many able lawyers in New York. Moynihan and his fellow New York senator, Republican Alfonse D'Amato, had agreed that Moynihan would recommend one of every four appointments. To help him, Moynihan had put together a high-powered bipartisan advisory committee headed by Leonard Garment, a White House adviser to Nixon, Edwin Meese's lawyer in the first independent counsel investigation of Meese in 1984, and Judge Robert Bork's most ardent and energetic advocate during the Senate floor debate.

As expected, many lawyers applied for the judgeship. After an elaborate screening process, Hellerstein was selected. He met for three and half hours in early January 1984 with Moynihan, who enthusiastically approved the choice. A few months later, Hellerstein met with D'Amato, who concurred in the recommendation because of "Hellerstein's fine legal credentials." Everything seemed set.[8]

At this time Hellerstein was working to free Nathaniel Carter, who had been convicted of murder on evidence by his ex-wife that turned out to have been perjured. After an intensive investigation by Hellerstein, Carter was found innocent and released.

On April 18, 1984, a month after receiving D'Amato's clearance, Hellerstein was returning from a party in Queens celebrating Carter's release. He picked up the *New York Post* at the subway and was stunned to read that his judgeship was "dead." According to the *Post*, Roy Cohn had contacted his friends in the White House to tell them to kill Hellerstein's nomination.

The ostensible reason for Hellerstein's troubles was an article written fifteen years earlier on court congestion in which, in passing, he had commented critically on the practice of imprisoning those convicted of minor offenses like minor drug possession, gambling, and prostitution. It also came out that Hellerstein had once talked about having obtained dismissals of minor charges under a New York statutory provision that allows such a disposition for offenses like disorderly conduct, when a judge believes it would be "in the interest of justice." These passages were lifted out of context and used by Cohn and Washington Legal Foundation general counsel Daniel Popeo to brand Hellerstein as "ultraliberal," a ludicrous characterization to all who know him.[9]

Leaders of the New York Bar of both parties rallied to Hellerstein's support. Twenty-four former federal prosecutors, describing themselves as having a "strong commitment to vigorous law enforcement," urged his nomination, describing him as "outstandingly able." Leonard Garment called Hellerstein "tougher than nails" and described his legal views as "mainstream."[10]

The nomination seemed stalled. Then in early 1985, a mutual friend arranged a breakfast meeting between Cohn and Hellerstein at Cohn's apartment. The two lawyers talked largely about Israel and foreign policy, on which they were in substantial agreement. During the course of the breakfast, Hellerstein pointed out that as a defense lawyer his job was to defend the accused and he knew a judge's role was very different. At the close of their meeting, Cohn told Hellerstein, "I guess we agree on more things than I thought." Cohn said he would see what he could do and would make some phone calls. He didn't, nor did he withdraw his opposition.[11]

On March 31, 1985, Administration officials confirmed that the nomination was indeed dead. Former federal judge Harold Tyler, a deputy attorney general in the Ford Administration and future chairman of the ABA Judicial Screening Committee, and Leon Silverman, a leader of the New York Bar Association and the independent counsel in the Raymond Donovan investigation, flew down to the White House to argue on Hellerstein's behalf. It had no effect. Although a White House spokesman acknowledged that Hellerstein was "completely qualified," he had views that were not "consistent with what the committee was looking for." How the White House knew these views never became clear, since they had never spoken to Hellerstein. White House counsel Fielding was more candid. In an interview with National Public Radio legal correspondent Nina Totenberg, he told her that someone "active for defendants' rights" would not make "the final cut."*[12]

Joseph P. Rodriguez

The ultraconservatives did not always win, however. While the Frey and Hellerstein nominations were dying, the President nominated Joseph Rodriguez, a fifty-three-year-old New Jersey Democrat, who was the New Jersey public advocate and also the public defender. As public advocate, Rodriguez represented consumers, poor people, and others not usually considered favorites of the Reagan Administration, and was known as a champion of minority rights. He had previously been chairman of the State Board of Higher Education under a Republican governor, chairman of the State Board of Investigation under a Democrat, and he became public advocate under Republican governor Thomas Kean. A past president of the New Jersey Bar Association, Rodriguez had received the American Bar Association's highest rating, "exceptionally well qualified." He was also Hispanic, and if confirmed he would be the first Hispanic on the New Jersey federal bench. Above all, he was strongly supported by Governor Kean, one of the rising stars in the Republican Party.

The Hellerstein, Frey, and Whittaker victories had emboldened the right, and Rodriguez was a natural target for them. This time, however, they overreached themselves.

In a search for ammunition, Senators Denton, Hatch, and East submitted a lengthy thirty-question questionnaire to Rodriguez. (They had submitted an almost identical questionnaire to Frey.) It

---

*Moynihan's judgeship problems did not end with Hellerstein. Two years later, when Moynihan recommended Columbia law professor Peter Strauss for a district court judgeship, the White House again balked on ideological grounds. This time, however, it was willing to deal. According to a Moynihan aide, the Justice Department offered to approve Strauss if the senator would suggest a "conservative the next time." Moynihan "replied that he doesn't do that—using stronger language, I'm sure," reported the aide.

asked for Rodriguez's views on abortion, school desegregation, church-state separation, affirmative action, capital punishment, the exclusionary rule, labor law, gun control, and other matters. It also asked for all "political contributions" of fifteen dollars or more for the past ten years.

The questionnaire was a serious blunder.

First there was a public outcry. The *Washington Post,* which rarely criticized the Administration's judge-picking, asked, "[I]s it their [Hatch's, Denton's, and East's] intention to oppose any nominee who does not answer every single question to their satisfaction? Will they attempt to pressure the president to withdraw objectionable nominations or block a vote by the full Senate? How will the White House respond to these tactics?"[13]

Much more important, Judiciary Committee chairman Strom Thurmond was furious: Three members of his committee, from his own party, had dared to undertake a separate investigation of a nominee. The autocratic Thurmond angrily rebuked the three senators, informing them that there would be no more such questionnaires.[14]

Democratic senators on the committee, some of whom had been uneasy about opposing judicial nominations, also criticized the questionnaire. Senator Joseph Biden of Delaware, the ranking committee Democrat and a presidential aspirant, was particularly exercised over the questions as to political contributions, saying: "That's like asking whether you're a Catholic, what church do you belong to, do you contribute to your church. What the hell have we become? What's this all about? It's crazy."[15]

Many of the substantive questions were highly inappropriate. For example, some questions—almost all of which were written with a conservative slant—asked for Rodriguez's opinion of specific Supreme Court decisions and opinions, even though as a district judge his views on such matters would be immaterial. For example, two of the many questions on abortion asked:

2. (a) In his dissent to the majority opinion of the Supreme Court in *Roe* v. *Wade,* 410 U.S. 113 (1973), Justice Byron R. White made the following statement: "As an exercise of raw judicial power the Court perhaps has authority to

do what it does today, but in my view its judgment is an improvident and extravagant exercise of the power of judicial review which the Constitution extends to this Court." Do you agree or disagree with Justice White's statement? Why or why not?

3. (a) . . . Do you believe that a "viable" fetus is a human being? If so, do you agree with the Court's finding that the "viable" fetus is not a "person"? If so, on what basis can a valid constitutional distinction be drawn between a "human being" and a "person"?*

Under fire, Denton, Hatch, and East retreated in embarrassment. Although Rodriguez had ducked almost all the substantive questions, the three conservatives professed themselves completely satisfied and indeed "impressed" with his answers. Hatch, however, staunchly insisted that he still "agreed with the substance and merit of the questions. There could have been many more legitimate questions that I would have added." And with a candor that must have dismayed the White House, which had been denying the use of a "litmus test," Hatch added that a nominee's position on abortion "is a controlling question to some of our people on the committee" and that there was nothing wrong with that.[16]

With Governor Kean's powerful muscle behind him, on May 3, 1985, Rodriguez was easily confirmed.

The Frey-Hellerstein-Rodriguez episodes transformed the situation. The insistence on ideological purity was now obvious. An

---

*Other questions were:

10. The Second Amendment to the Constitution states that "a well-regulated militia being necessary to the security of a free State, the right of the people to keep and bear arms shall not be infringed." In light of that constitutional prohibition, to what extent, if any, do you feel that Congress could curtail the right of the people to keep and bear weapons that are of value to common defense?

11. Would you give your present personal position with regards to the Equal Rights Amendment?

15. . . . Keeping in mind that unions are private associations rather than governments, do you think that the granting of exclusive representation powers to unions by the National Labor Relations Act is unconstitutional?

The full text of the questionnaire is in Appendix II.

article I wrote for *The Nation* in May 1985 was widely circulated, and the 250,000-member People for the American Way, which had been created by television producer Norman Lear to defend First Amendment values against the radical right, decided to make the right's judge-packing campaign a major priority. Melanne Verveer, one of the leaders of Washington's liberal Catholic community, formerly with Common Cause and the United States Catholic Conference, and the vice president and public-policies director for People for the American Way, took charge of the latter's organizational efforts.

The Administration denied it was using an ideological "litmus test." Its spokesmen insisted that they never asked directly about the abortion decision or any other specific ruling. "We don't ask anyone their views on abortion or disqualify someone just because they gave to the ACLU," White House counsel Fred Fielding said in an interview in October 1985. But elsewhere Fielding admitted that the Administration tries to choose only "people of a certain philosophy" and that someone "actively prochoice" or "for defendants' rights" would not make "the final cut," as the Hellerstein matter showed. Meese conceded that "we *do* discuss the law with judicial candidates. . . . In discussing the law with lawyers there is really no way *not* to bring up cases—past cases—and engage in a dialogue over the reasoning and merits of particular decisions" (emphasis in original).[17]

The department's mild disclaimers fooled few. When Meese told a Chautauqua audience that politics and philosophy had not influenced the Bork nomination, the audience, apparently used to snake-oil salesmen, roared with laughter. Even before Reagan won in 1980, it was reported he would insist on ideologically sound judges. Herbert Ellingwood, candidate Reagan's legal affairs adviser and Meese's unsuccessful nominee for chief judge-picker in 1985—his name was withdrawn under fire from People for the American Way when it was revealed that he had made appointments to other positions from lists supplied by right-wing religious groups—commented, "It's not only fair but 'reasonable' to ask judges about their political and social philosophies." And Justice Department officials acknowledged in late 1984 that the department often asked prospective nominees their opinion of *Roe* v. *Wade.* Bruce Fein, associate deputy attorney general, who became an unofficial spokesman for the Administration, told *The Wall Street Journal* he knew no Reagan appointee who agreed with *Roe* v. *Wade.* [18]

Also, Senators John P. Heinz and Arlen Specter of Pennsylvania publicly complained about the Administration's refusal to nominate a distinguished conservative Republican state judge whom the department initially considered too "liberal"; after a two-year delay, the judge was confirmed. Other senators also complained that Meese would consider only "highly conservative" candidates.[19]

Some potential nominees themselves protested publicly about the ideological screening, though usually anonymously. One exception to the insistence on anonymity was Lizabeth A. Moody, dean of Cleveland-Marshal Law School and a highly regarded Cleveland lawyer who, among other achievements, was the first female partner in a Cleveland law firm. In 1982 she was recommended by Ohio's Republican establishment for a district judgeship. Some of Ohio's reactionaries did not like her, and in a campaign reminiscent of that against Judith Whittaker, swamped the White House with identically worded letters and telegrams charging her with being pro-abortion. In her interview with Justice Department officials, "one of them a young woman, opened the interview by asking me whether I agreed that the states should regulate abortion," Moody related. "I refused to answer, because I think such questions need to be handled on a case-by-case basis." The judgeship went to another woman. Whether Moody's refusal to answer the abortion question, or some other factor, was decisive is unknown. There was no question, however, about the department's interest in her views on the abortion question, and particularly about a position that the department would urge, in slightly different form, that year in the Supreme Court.[20]

Another aspirant, who preferred to remain anonymous, reported that White House officials had asked some of her associates about her views on abortion. Also, in August 1985, National Public Radio's Nina Totenberg reported that several prominent Republican women being considered for federal judgeships, all of whom had solid political backing, had told her they had been asked directly by Justice Department representatives how each would rule in abortion cases. None had been nominated. "I guess most of us have accepted that we're not going to get these judgeships unless we're willing to commit to a particular position, which would be improper," said one well-regarded state judge, who, like the others, insisted on anonymity.[21]

Another state trial judge, a candidate for a district judgeship, had a more diffuse experience. He was asked for his views of the Supreme Court and his beliefs about the proper role of courts in school prayer, abortion, and school desegregation cases, with particular reference to Judge W. Arthur Garrity's orders in the Boston school case. "I was interviewed by seven people in six interviews," said the judge angrily, "and nobody ever asked, 'What did you do as a lawyer and as a judge?' " The candidate was asked his "favorite Supreme Court decision" and his "least favorite," and though he was never actually asked where he stood on specific issues, "they sure prodded around the edges." And still another candidate, a very conservative federal trial judge, is convinced she was rejected for the Court of Appeals because of her liberal ruling in one case involving federal benefits. Although she, too, was not questioned specifically about the abortion decision, she was asked by Assistant Attorney General Stephen Markman, who took charge of the judge-picking process in 1986, which "three Supreme Court decisions you would overrule if given the opportunity."[22]

Whatever the details of the process, the result was a group of judges an "overwhelming proportion" of whom, as Sheldon Goldman put it, would "have the blessing of Jesse A. Helms or Richard Viguerie." As the *Los Angeles Times* editorialized in October 1985, even if the Administration does not ask potential nominees about specific cases, the selection process is being made with those cases in mind. "The ideological screening that is taking place is demonstrated by the Administration's dismal record on appointing minorities and women to the federal judiciary. Among his appointments so far, the President has managed only one black and 13 women. He cannot find blacks and women who believe that abortion should be illegal, school prayer should be allowed, access to the courts should be restricted, Congress should leave civil rights to the states, the rights of criminal defendants should be cut back and gun control should be outlawed."[23]

Even Professor Philip Kurland of Chicago, a caustic critic of both the Warren Court and of the Burger Court's school desegregation and affirmative action rulings, complained, "Judges are being appointed in the expectation that they will rewrite laws and the Constitution to the Administration's liking." And conservatives like former Attorneys General Herbert Brownell and Edward Levi, who served Presidents Eisenhower and Ford, respectively, called the situation "shocking" (Brownell) and "badly politicized" (Levi).[24]

PUTTING THE FAITHFUL ON THE BENCH

The right was obviously interested in more than stopping "liberals." It also wanted to put its own on the bench. And it did, for a long time with little difficulty except for the Wilkinson episode. The trend was particularly marked on the appellate level, where the Administration can make the choice with little or no senatorial involvement.

Surprisingly enough, this ideological zeal was not particularly noticeable among the Reagan appointments during the first term except for Wilkinson, Pasco Bowman, a protégé of Jesse Helms, and the four (Posner, Bork, Winter, and Scalia) initially approved in 1981–82. But by 1984, the failures in Congress, the courts, and with the public obviously spurred the Administration's search for true believers to put on the bench. During the next three years there were fifteen such staunchly conservative nominees, all but three on the appellate level, many of whom were law professors. This period coincided with Edwin Meese's nomination and tenure as attorney general, which may be more than coincidence.

Most of these nominees had no trouble getting confirmed. Senatorial reluctance to oppose a lower court nominee because of his judicial or political philosophy was still so great that there were no challenges to such very conservative selections as Frank Easterbrook, nominated to the Seventh Circuit, in Chicago, a brilliant colleague of Posner's at the University of Chicago, and so extreme in his views as to be to Posner's right; John Noonan, a Berkeley law professor, one of the leading theorists of the anti-abortion movement (Ninth Circuit); J. Daniel Mahoney, founder of the New York

State Conservative Party (Second Circuit); and Bobby Ray Baldock, whose performance as a Reagan-appointed district judge led one civil rights attorney to call him "death on wheels for civil liberties" (Tenth Circuit).

The District of Columbia Circuit Court of Appeals was a particular target for the Administration's ideological efforts, partly because it was the chief expositor of regulatory law (one of the Administration's top priorities was deregulating business), and partly because so many vacancies became available. To that bench, in 1986–87, the Senate quickly confirmed such "free market" zealots as Stephen Williams, a Colorado law professor, and Douglas Ginsburg, a Harvard Law School professor and assistant attorney general for Antitrust, later to be nominated to the Supreme Court under President Reagan. Also named to the D.C. Circuit were such staunch conservatives as former senator James L. Buckley, brother of William F. Buckley and a pillar of the New York State Conservative Party, and Laurence Silberman, who had some trouble explaining why the Crocker National Bank, of which he had been executive vice president and general counsel, had illegally engaged in a systematic and pervasive failure to report cash transactions to the Treasury, for which it was fined $2.25 million. By mid-1986, the court had a solid right-wing majority.[25]

Apart from the extreme youth of men like Easterbrook (thirty-six), Ginsburg (forty), and Starr (thirty-six), and their almost uniformly strong conservatism, what is striking is how little trial or other lawyering experience the nominees had had. Buckley had last practiced law in 1958, and even then for only four years, during which time he had handled only "a few recalcitrant Yale students before the City Court," as he put it, and a court-assigned divorce case. Noonan had not practiced law since 1960, and Ginsburg had never practiced at all. Having ignored its twelve-years-of-experience rule with Wilkinson, most members of the ABA Screening Committee apparently decided to make a habit of it.

Some members did continue to insist on some substantial experience as a lawyer, however, and the result was that 35 percent of the nominees during Meese's administration of the Justice Department received split-decision "qualified" ratings, the lowest possible passing grade. Under Carter the number of such ABA evaluations was only 6 percent, and it was only 5 percent during Reagan's first term, before the ideological push got into high gear.[26]

There were other nominees who did not escape trouble. By mid-1985 the Judiciary Committee Democrats were becoming apprehensive about both the nominees and the speed with which Judiciary Committee chairman Strom Thurmond was rushing the nominations through. It was also becoming clear that an ideological court-packing campaign was under way. In July 1985, for example, the *National Journal* reported that "Conservatives are gearing up to battle over what many of them hope will be President Reagan's most lasting legacy: reshaping the federal judiciary. . . . [G]rowing congressional opposition to the conservatives' social agenda has increased the pressure for 'friendly' judges to promote the Reagan Revolution in the legal sphere." A few months later, *Congressional Quarterly* also noted that "conservative groups are pressing the administration to populate the federal bench with judges who share their ideology."[27]

On the other side, People for the American Way commissioned me to do a study of the Administration's court-packing; I produced a pamphlet in October 1985 that was widely circulated. Common Cause also began to devote attention to the matter, as did the Leadership Conference for Civil Rights, under the direction of Ralph Neas, an experienced civil rights activist who had played a leading role in the 1982 Voting Rights Act extension.[28]

Judiciary Committee Democrats were especially embarrassed by the Alex Kozinski appointment. Despite serious charges of abuse of office and lack of candor, the Judiciary Committee voted him out unanimously after a single hearing with five other nominees. When the issue got to the floor, Senator Carl Levin challenged the nomination and drew forty-three negative votes. "The Kozinski nomination revealed that there's a very flawed process in the Senate Judiciary Committee for reviewing federal judges," said Common Cause president Fred Wertheimer. "It appears to be pro forma. . . . How did he go from someone who was unanimously approved to someone who was barely confirmed?"[29]

In response to these and other pressures, the Judiciary Committee Democrats first decided to slow down the Administration-Thurmond steamroller. When Senator Edward M. Kennedy was Judiciary Committee chairman in 1979–80, the average time between a nomination and the committee's hearing was sixty-five days, and Kennedy readily acceded to requests by Senator Hatch and other Republicans for more time, even when there was no good reason for the delay. Under Thurmond that period had dropped to twenty-three days, and votes were scheduled an average of ten days after the hearing, twice as fast as under Kennedy.[30]

Thurmond agreed to a stretch-out, but a few months later Common Cause found little real change in the procedure. "The degree to which this agreement improves the confirmation process . . . will depend on the resources, industriousness, and courage of Committee members." Unfortunately, only Kennedy and Senator Howard M. Metzenbaum of Ohio were willing to display those attributes most of the time. Ranking Democrat Biden had given the task of monitoring judgeships to freshman senator Paul Simon of Illinois who, despite the best of intentions and very hard work, lacked the staff, experience, and just plain nastiness to take on the often bullying Thurmond. Biden himself seemed unwilling to get involved.[31]

The Kozinski floor fight in November changed things, however, and it turned out to be the first of many more such battles during the next twelve months.

Alex Kozinski

Alex Kozinski was a refugee from Romania. Born in 1950, he became converted to "free market" conservatism and, when Reagan won in 1980, Kozinski became part of the office of counsel to the president. Bright and very conservative, he quickly became an Administration favorite. From June 1981 to August 1982 he was special counsel to the Merit Systems Protection Board, an office created to protect governmental whistleblowers (those who disclose governmental misconduct) against reprisals. From there, at age thirty-two, he became chief judge of the Court of Claims. Three years later, when he was all of thirty-five, the White House nominated him to the Ninth Circuit Court of Appeals, which covers California and other Far West states.

Kozinski's performance as special counsel to the Merit Systems

Protection Board had aroused much criticism. Agency employees and members of Congress accused him of having subverted the office's mission by ignoring employee grievances and helping agency managers evade the rules. In the first ten months of Kozinski's tenure, the office initiated no disciplinary actions against managers for merit system abuses. Three new requests were filed to halt employee firings, in contrast to twenty during calendar year 1980. Only four investigations of whistleblowing disclosures were ordered by Kozinski. Jesse James, Jr., assistant special counsel for prosecution under Kozinski, wrote: "We no longer provide any protection to federal employees from merit system violations and abuses."[32]

Kozinski had also issued a manual for government managers that instructed them how to use the Civil Service Reform Act of 1978 to fire employees. Titled "How to Avoid Committing Prohibited Personnel Practices in the Reagan Era," the manual used internal OSC investigative materials to set forth what the OSC looked for when it prosecuted cases, providing agency managers with a blueprint for avoiding OSC prosecution.[33]

Kozinski did, however, vigorously pursue several cases against Democrats for alleged violations of the Hatch Act, which prohibits federal executive branch employees from ongoing political activities. In one case, the presiding officer dismissed the charges and criticized Kozinski harshly: "The Special Counsel should have known that he could not prevail on the merits when he issued the complaint. . . . [T]here can be no conclusion other than that the charge was clearly without merit and that the Respondent was totally innocent of any fault or wrongdoing. . . . [There is a] failure to produce any evidence."[34]

At his confirmation hearing for appointment to the Ninth Circuit, Kozinski was questioned about these charges. He responded at length. Although Common Cause and others requested that the hearing be reopened to test his responses, Thurmond refused, and the nomination went to the floor with a unanimous committee vote.

Senator Carl Levin was a member of the Senate Government Affairs Committee, which oversees the Merit Systems Protection Board. Dismayed at the Judiciary Committee's handling of the nomination, he initiated an independent investigation and discovered new and damaging information about Kozinski. More questions were submitted to the nominee, who again responded at length. On the basis of these responses, Levin charged Kozinski with misrepresentation.

Thurmond set another hearing day but gave virtually no advance notice of it, and nothing of significance happened. The full Senate then took up the nomination in floor debate. The new information developed by Levin led Judiciary Committee Democrats to reverse their judgment. On November 7 the nomination was confirmed by a 54–43 vote, the highest negative vote for a lower court judge in recent memory.

Sid Fitzwater

The Kozinski case was just the opening skirmish in a widening war. In the summer and fall of 1985 the White House picked Sid Fitzwater, a thirty-two-year-old Texas judge, to fill a vacancy on the federal District Court in Texas; Jefferson Sessions, the U.S. attorney in Mobile, Alabama, for an Alabama district judgeship; Lino Graglia, a Texas law professor, for a seat on the Fifth Circuit Court of Appeals; Michael Horowitz, former general counsel to the Office of Management and Budget, to the U.S. Court of Appeals for the District of Columbia; and William L. Harvey, an Indiana law professor and Reagan's first choice for chairman of the Legal Services Corporation, to the Court of Appeals for the Seventh Circuit. Still in the predawn stages was Daniel A. Manion, a former Indiana state senator, also for the Seventh Circuit; this precipitated perhaps the most intensely fought lower court nomination of Reagan's entire tenure.

The battle over Sid Fitzwater was led by Ann Lewis, executive director of the Americans for Democratic Action. It began while the Kozinski matter was coming to a head, though the Judiciary Committee Democrats' handling of the Fitzwater nomination seemed little affected by their previously inadequate performance on Kozinski.

Fitzwater's hearing on November 22 revealed that in 1982, the then twenty-nine-year-old Republican judge had posted in three minority precincts Republican-sponsored election signs that were both misleadingly inaccurate and probably intimidating. In big red and black letters the signs warned that it was a crime for which "you can be imprisoned . . . if you influence or try to influence a voter how to vote," which is clearly untrue.[35]

Fitzwater conceded that the purpose was "partisan" and "political," to help reelect Republican governor William P. Clements, who had appointed Fitzwater to the state bench. Even William Bradford Reynolds's Justice Department told the Dallas County Election Commissioner that "we are concerned that no nonracial justification has been offered for placing most of the signs at minority precincts." Texas election officials agreed to take steps to make sure there would be no more such signs.[36]

Despite opposition from black and Hispanic civil rights groups, the Judiciary Committee approved him 10–5—one Senate Democrat was impressed that Fitzwater had tutored a black high school student and paid for his graduation cap and gown—and after a brief filibuster, Fitzwater was confirmed by an even narrower margin than Kozinski, 52–43.

Jefferson B. Sessions III

A nominee's racial attitude is obviously crucial, for we have come a long way from the 1960s, when Senators James Eastland, Sam Ervin, John McClellan, and others would admit to voting against a Thurgood Marshall just because he was black, and outright racists like W. Harold Cox of Mississippi and E. Gordon West of Louisiana could be confirmed. One would have thought that at least this kind of progress would be reflected in the Administration's thinking, but it was noticeably absent in the nomination of Jefferson B. Sessions III, United States attorney from Mobile, Alabama.

Sessions had made his mark by prosecuting black civil rights activists on voting fraud charges. This was part of a campaign by the Justice Department against black civil rights activists that an appeals court later found was targeted at "those counties where blacks since 1980 had come to control some part of the county government." The Administration obtained only one conviction, and even that was later overturned when the appellate court concluded that the prosecution was racially and politically motivated.[37]

The NAACP Legal Defense and Education Fund, Inc., took the lead in opposing Sessions. Assistant Counsel Elaine Jones, one of the ablest and most experienced civil rights advocates in Washington, directed the campaign. Under Jones's direction the fund developed a massive file that revealed that Sessions had called the NAACP "un-American" and "Communist-inspired" organizations that were "trying to force civil rights down the throats of the people," had called a white lawyer who represented civil rights workers "a disgrace to his race," and thought the Ku Klux Klan was "OK until I learned they smoked pot."[38]

Sessions's testimony was so filled with so many inconsistencies and alterations that the very conservative Howell Heflin, from Sessions's own state of Alabama, concluded that Sessions's "admissions, explanations, partial admissions [and] statements about [racially insensitive] jokes" led him to harbor "reasonable doubts about his ability to be fair and impartial." Even though Sessions was something of a hero among Alabama's white racists and was vigorously defended by Alabama's other senator, Jeremiah Denton, Heflin voted against Sessions, and the nomination failed, 10–8, as two Republicans, Specter and Mathias, joined the eight Democrats in opposition. (An interesting postscript is that Denton lost his Senate seat five months later.) Attorney General Edwin Meese angrily blamed "several liberal organizations" and called Sessions "the unfortunate victim of people . . . who appear willing to smear anyone in order to advance their agenda."[39]

BLOCKED NOMINATIONS

Sessions was the first and only Reagan nominee to be turned down by the Senate Judiciary Committee during Reagan's first six years; until then, the committee had approved 269 nominees. But the Sessions defeat was not really the Administration's first loss. Both before and after Sessions, the White House or its nominees quit when it appeared that confirmation was not feasible:

- *William Harvey.* Harvey had been nominated to be chair of the Legal Services Corporation's Board of Directors in March 1982. He immediately set out to end the corporation's law reform and class action activities, and an irate Senate committee refused to confirm him. Shortly thereafter, evidence came to light raising serious questions about expenses and other allowances he claimed from the corporation. He had also attacked the federal administrative agencies as imposing "utterly idiotic and neosocialistic notions of state control upon the society." Moreover, he continually attacked the federal courts. The Administration nominated him to the Seventh Circuit, but he could not get even a "qualified" rating from the normally generous ABA. He withdrew "temporarily" in October 1985. His name was not resubmitted.[40]

- *Michael J. Horowitz.* Horowitz, a former general counsel to the Office of Management and Budget, had earned a reputation for being abrasive, abusive, and intolerant. He had insulted business executives, colleagues, and adversaries, often alienating his own allies with temper tantrums and insults. At a meeting with an executive vice president of the National Association of Manufacturers, he had angrily responded to a question about his checking with a congressman with "you fucking bastard." He responded to another businessman with similar abuse. While at OMB, Horowitz promoted measures to weaken the effectiveness of public-interest advocacy and litigation groups. Many of these measures turned out to be legally and technically flawed. When it was reported that the Administration planned to nominate him to the District of Columbia Circuit Court of Appeals, the Judicial Selection Project prepared a twenty-two-page report on Horowitz, documenting his failings. It was obvious that if he got past the ABA, the nomination would have set off a bitter struggle with probably dim prospects for success. Horowitz decided to withdraw before being formally nominated.[41]

- *Marion Harrison.* A Washington, D.C., lawyer who was counsel to presidential candidate Rev. Marion "Pat" Robertson in 1987, Harrison was also considered for the D.C. Circuit. His name was linked to the milk industry's illegal contributions to Nixon's 1972 campaign, however, and though he was never charged with any wrongdoing, his name appeared frequently in press accounts of the matter. Harrison's name was quietly dropped.[42]

• *Lino A. Graglia.* Graglia is a Texas law professor who opposes judicial review on principle, and especially in civil rights cases. An outspoken foe of busing for desegregation, he urged Austin, Texas, residents to defy a federal court busing order, telling a crowd of eighteen hundred in 1979 that "you are under no obligation to go along with this." Graglia also argued that white parents in Louisiana should be allowed to evade federal court orders by sham custody arrangements, referred in his class to black children as "pickaninnies," and condemned judicially created constitutional safeguards for individual rights as "just bad ideas."

Though Graglia was too extreme for William French Smith to appoint him assistant attorney general for civil rights (William Bradford Reynolds was chosen instead), Meese pushed Graglia for a Fifth Circuit Court of Appeals judgeship. The ABA found him "not qualified," but the Administration persuaded the committee to look again. The committee again rejected him, and the Justice Department asked Carter's attorney general Griffin Bell to review the file. Despite Meese's continuing support, Graglia was apparently too much even for Bell, and the nomination finally died in late spring 1986.[43]

Conservatives were embittered by these defeats, especially of Harvey and Graglia, and they turned on the ABA committee. This was an odd target, indeed, for criticism from the right. During almost its entire existence and until very recently, the ABA had been a stronghold of conservatism of the most extreme variety. It had opposed Brandeis and supported both Haynsworth and Carswell. The committee had almost always been made up of wealthy white males—few others could afford the time—and it generally supported candidates with the same background, especially if they had gone to Harvard, Yale, or some other elite law school. The Carter Administration tried to increase female and minority representation on the bench, and by setting up the circuit judge nominating commission, it diluted the ABA influence somewhat.

The ABA did not change much, however. A study of its evaluations of the Carter nominees showed the same preference the committee had always exhibited.[44]

In the latter part of 1985 it was revealed that in order to obtain a broad range of views, the committee had been providing the names of nominees to the Alliance for Justice, People for the American Way, the NAACP, and other liberal groups before making its evaluation. The conservative Washington Legal Foundation (WLF) also sought the names as well as all the committee's records. The committee refused. The WLF thereupon charged that the "ABA Committee, in cooperation with these select liberal groups, has investigated the political and ideological beliefs of the candidates in such a way as to delay or block the nomination of conservative candidates." It sued the ABA, claiming that the committee was covered by the Federal Advisory Committee Act of 1972, which required that with certain exceptions, groups covered by the act's definition of an "advisory committee" had to be open to the public, along with their records and minutes. Because the ABA committee operated in "secret, star-chamber-like proceedings," according to WLF legal director Paul Kamenar, it was violating the law.[45]

The suit made for strange alliances. Many people had long resented the power over nominations exercised by this unofficial private group. Conservative law professor Philip Kurland of Chicago had criticized the "submission of names for approval to any segment of [the legal] profession, national, state, local, or individual, [as] both inappropriate and undesirable where the Senate is charged with duties of advice and consent. Since the bar is anything but a representative political body, it affords no legitimating function in this regard." Senator Paul Simon of Illinois thought that the Senate was entitled to know the basis for the ABA ratings. Nan Aron, of the Alliance for Justice, commented, "I would love for the process to be open." Liberal Ralph Nader's Public Citizen Litigation Group joined the lawsuit on the WLF's side.[46]

Although the suit is still pending, the committee decided it would no longer release the names of nominees to any groups, something of a victory for the WLF. The ABA's influence remained substantial, however, as its role in the Bork nomination would show.

During these fights over conservative nominees, the right was still exercising its veto on those suspected of a liberal taint. It succeeded in temporarily blocking two district court candidates recommended by Republican senators: David Doty, recommended by Senator David Durenberger of Minnesota; and William Dwyer, recommended by Senator Slade Gorton of Washington State. It also prevented any judicial nomination for Philip Lacovara, a Washington, D.C., lawyer.

Philip Lacovara is one of the lions of the Washington, D.C., bar. A brilliant lawyer and the senior Republican in the Watergate special prosecutor's office in 1973–74, he always considered himself a "conservative Republican." As he wrote in a bitter op-ed piece in *The New York Times* in 1986:

> In 1964 I co-chaired the "Columbia University Students for Goldwater." During the Nixon Administration, I served in the Justice Department as the "law and order" Deputy Solicitor General responsible for handling the Government's criminal cases in the Supreme Court. As one of a handful of registered Republicans living in Washington, I supported Ronald Reagan's election in 1980 and his re-election in 1984. I even think the Supreme Court's abortion decisions are bad law. Indeed, in 1981 Mr. Reagan appointed me as his representative on a panel that screens candidates for the President to name to District of Columbia local courts.[47]

Despite this background, the Justice Department viewed Lacovara as "too liberal" and "not politically reliable" because of his membership in the Washington Lawyers Committee for Civil Rights Under Law and the ABA Section of Individual Rights and Responsibilities, two nonpartisan, solidly establishment groups. In the past, wrote Lacovara,

> political affiliation has provided a source of recognition, not a litmus test for philosophical orthodoxy. Over time,

this pattern has created a Federal judiciary rich in diversity and perspective.

Today the message is quite different: ideology is the primary qualification, and it is a candidate's demonstrated orthodoxy that brings his name before the President and ultimately before the Senate. Unique in our nation's history, the current Justice Department has been processing any judicial candidate through a series of officials whose primary duty is to assess the candidate's ideological purity.[48]

Lacovara also resigned from the District of Columbia Nominating Commission, to which Reagan appointed him twice, because the Justice Department insisted on pushing an "ideological litmus test" for candidates.

David Doty's problem was his wife. Although both were lifelong Republicans, Mrs. Doty had worked for John Anderson in 1980 and was the Republican chairman of the Gender Gap Coalition, a bipartisan group formed to evaluate the impact of Reagan Administration budget cuts affecting women.

To Marlene Reid, vice-chairman of the Minnesota Republican Party, Mrs. Doty's activities were "unforgivable" and showed that *Mr.* Doty was not fit to be a judge. "I've been married for thirty-one years," said Reid, "and if my husband ever asked me to back off a position because it would hurt his career, or even if he philosophically disagreed with me, I'd certainly do it, and I'm sure that if David Doty had taken that approach with his wife, she would have backed off." Although Doty said that he did in fact have political differences with his wife, one White House official said, "There's no evidence that Doty and his wife disagreed," and the nomination languished, though it did not die.[49]

William L. Dwyer's problem was more serious. Though a highly acclaimed lawyer, Dwyer was a Democrat. Also, he had antagonized the powerful right wing of the Washington State Republican Party by representing a state legislator who had sued a prominent conservative Republican for libel. Although this had happened twenty-three years earlier, memories are long in Washington State politics.

Dwyer was supported by both Gorton and his fellow Republican senator, Dan Evans, but the White House refused to make the nomination.[50]

Both Doty's and Dwyer's fate became embroiled in the Manion fight during the summer of 1986, with the Dwyer nomination playing a key role in Slade Gorton's loss of his Senate seat that year; it also may have played a role in the Bork nomination.

7
1986—Manion, Rehnquist, and Scalia

The Administration "is dipping deep into the barrel of suitable talent in their search for ideologically sound judges."

The *(London)* Economist, *May 17, 1986*

DANIEL MANION

The fight over Daniel Manion's nomination to the Seventh Circuit Court of Appeals was a cliff-hanger from beginning to end. Filled with double-dealing and tricky parliamentary maneuvers, it ultimately entangled two other judgeships and probably decided a Senate seat. And though the Administration ultimately won the confirmation battle by one vote, it was so costly a victory, and of so little ultimate benefit, that the Administration might have been better off with a quick loss.

The most interesting thing about Daniel A. Manion, an obscure forty-four-year-old South Bend, Indiana, lawyer, was his name. He was the son of Clarence Manion, a founder of the John Birch Society and a man who had once accused the Eisenhower Administration of "creeping socialism." In 1954 Clarence Manion founded the Manion Forum, which turned out an avalanche of ultraconservative written and broadcast material. Son Daniel was a trustee of the Manion Forum and participated with his father in its weekly radio and television broadcasts from 1971 through 1979.

Like many of the other Reagan appeals court appointees, Manion was extremely conservative. He differed from many of them, however, in one very important respect: He seemed to be a mediocre lawyer. Briefs that he had written turned out to be filled with poor arguments; inadequate expression; and grammatical, syntactical, and other errors. He had almost no experience in dealing with federal or constitutional issues, never having argued a case in any federal appellate court. He had never even run a federal trial, for his practice was basically small personal and commercial litigation, including claims for improper repair of a Volkswagen Rabbit, a few small land condemnation cases, and some minor personal injury suits.

Although the ABA had made an especially poor investigation—it had not looked at Manion's briefs, even though he had no other samples of his writing, and an appellate judge does virtually nothing but write—he still was able to get only a split "qualified" decision in his favor. The Chicago Council of Lawyers, which studied his briefs closely, concluded that he was not qualified because he "would not be able to deal adequately with the difficult legal issues which are routinely presented to the Seventh Circuit."[1]

But his philosophy was sound, and apparently that was enough for the Administration. Though never formally a member of the John Birch Society, Daniel Manion as a state senator in Indiana had written the local headquarters of the society in Elkhart, Indiana, "Your members are certainly on the front line of the fight for Constitutional Freedom. . . . I would be happy to help you in whatever cause you may have before the state legislature." He was also enthusiastic about a book by former John Birch Society president Larry McDonald that condemned *Brown* v. *Board of Education* and the Civil Rights Act of 1964, repudiated the "incorporation doctrine" by which states are bound to observe the Bill of Rights, and approved of stripping the Supreme Court of jurisdiction in obscenity cases; Manion expressed his approval of court-stripping in other forums as well.[2]

While in the Indiana legislature he sponsored a bill to allow posting the Ten Commandments in classrooms, even though he considered it inconsistent with a recent Supreme Court decision. He wanted to register a "legislative protest" against the Court's decision, he said. To many this seemed inconsistent with his oath to support the federal Constitution. And in Manion Forum broadcasts, transcripts of which were unearthed by Ricky Seidman, a lawyer for People for the American Way, he regularly lambasted the Supreme Court for its apportionment, school desegregation, and other rulings.[3]

The philosophical issue may have been a ticklish one for many senators, such as ranking Judiciary Committee Democrat Biden, but Manion's patently inadequate intellectual credentials were something else. Forty-four law school deans, including those from Harvard, Yale, Columbia, New York University, Georgetown, Pennsylvania, Virginia, Michigan, Chicago, and almost every other major law school, came out in opposition to Manion, as did over two hundred other law school professors.[4]

Manion was not, of course, without supporters. (No nominee ever is.) Father Theodore Hesburgh, president of Notre Dame and an old friend of the Manion family, wrote on his behalf, as did the Democratic former U.S. attorney in South Bend. *The Wall Street Journal* commented that "the Seventh Circuit could use a country lawyer like Mr. Manion," noting that Posner and Easterbrook are "not practitioners."[5]

But these few were swamped by a tidal wave of opposition. Newspapers all over the country opposed him. In Florida, the *Orlando Sentinel* was typical, contrasting Manion with Orlando attorney Patricia Fawsett, who "shares the president's conservative views" but has "impeccable credentials" and who was approved by the Judiciary Committee after a few minutes of questioning. "America and the judicial system deserve better," the *Sentinel* concluded. Even so conservative a paper as the *Tucson Daily Star*, in Arizona, urged that "Daniel Manion should be rejected for the Court of Appeals."[6]

Obviously Reagan was not going to back down, and the battle

was joined. The first round ended in victory for Manion. At its meeting in early May 1986, several weeks before the Jefferson Sessions vote, the committee divided evenly, with Republican senators Charles M. Mathias and Arlen Specter voting against Manion. "But then," as the *London Economist* put it, "alarmed at the precedent they were creating, members voted to pass Mr. Manion's nomination on to the full Senate." There the battle resumed, on June 26.[7]

It is likely that no one will ever know what really happened on the floor that day, but charges of deceit, double-crossing, political vote trading, and chicanery filled the air when the day's events were over.

Senator Joseph Biden led the opposition and believed that with Republican votes he had enough to beat the nomination, even though he had lost one likely "no" vote. To get Senator David Durenberger's vote on Manion, the White House agreed to overlook Mrs. Doty's heresies in supporting John Anderson and over budget cuts, and nominate Mr. Doty for the judgeship.

The Democrats started to filibuster against the nomination. Strom Thurmond (who holds the record for the Senate's longest filibuster) protested that "the just thing to do, the reasonable thing to do, is to give him a vote." The opponents seemed in no mood to comply with Thurmond's sudden revelation of "the just" and "reasonable thing," and it looked like a long, drawn-out fight was ahead.[8]

Suddenly the Democratic leaders announced they would agree to a vote. When Majority Leader Robert Dole started to count heads, he realized that Republicans Robert Packwood of Oregon and Paula Hawkins of Florida were out of town and saw defeat staring him in the face. He refused to allow the vote to go forward. Biden grinned at Dole and said, "Come on, Bob, go for it." Dole again refused. Confident of his majority, Biden then offered to pair two Democrat votes with the two absent Republicans on the assumption that both Packwood and Hawkins were for Manion. (By pairing, two opposing senators agree not to vote and thus cancel each other out.) Dole then agreed to a vote.

Earlier in the day, Democrat Metzenbaum of Ohio had gone to Senator Slade Gorton and asked him his position. According to Metzenbaum, Gorton said, "I'm going to vote no." Metzenbaum then said, "If you are going to change, will you let me know in advance?" and believed Gorton had agreed. Nevertheless, thirty seconds into the vote call, Gorton switched without telling Metzenbaum and voted for Manion—the White House had just promised Gorton it would nominate William Dwyer for the district court judgeship it had refused him until then.

Even with Gorton's switch, the vote appeared to be 48–47 against Manion. Senator Dan Quayle of Indiana, Manion's chief Senate sponsor, had been cornering uncommitted senators all afternoon, trying to get them to vote for Manion. One observer reported that at one point Quayle, "red-faced and furious," seemed to be shouting at Republican senator Dan Evans of Washington, who turned white and quickly walked away.

When Quayle saw the 48–47 vote against Manion, he realized that Republican Barry Goldwater of Arizona had not yet voted. He rushed over to Kansas senator Nancy Kassebaum, one of the five Republican votes against Manion, told her Goldwater favored Manion, and persuaded her to pair with Goldwater.

As soon as Biden heard of the Kassebaum-Goldwater pair, he tried to withdraw from his pair, but Byrd told him he had to stick to the agreement.

The Kassebaum-Goldwater pair changed the vote to 47–47, and with Vice President George Bush in the chair and eligible to vote because of the tie, Manion appeared to win, 48–47. To keep the issue alive, however, Democratic leader Byrd quickly switched his vote to a "yes," which enabled him to move to reconsider. Majority Leader Dole promptly ordered a delay.

After the vote it appeared that Goldwater, who was outside in the hall, had not been in favor of Manion and had intended to vote "present." The Quayle maneuver looked deceitful. It also appeared that the absent Packwood, with whom Biden had agreed to pair on the assumption that Packwood also would vote *for* Manion, had told his staff to say he was "undecided." "That is a change from what had been an assertion on the floor immediately before the vote," complained Biden. A Packwood spokeswoman said that as far as she knew, Dole "made no attempt to contact [Packwood] during his travels," to learn Packwood's position, but a Dole spokesman said Dole had tried. Packwood ultimately voted against Manion.[9]

Gorton's switch blew up in his face. He had been facing a rela-

tively easy challenge to his reelection by former transportation secretary Brock Adams, whose campaign seemed unable to catch fire.
Gorton's switch provided the spark. Adams accused Gorton of
"selling out" and "sleaziness." The *Seattle Times* ran a story recalling
that Gorton used to be called "Slippery Slade" and compared him
unfavorably to "Straight Arrow Dan" Evans, who had voted against
Manion. The *Seattle Post-Intelligencer* editorialized that for a senator
there is a time "to deal" and a time to "vote his conscience; take a
stand for what he knows is right and damn the consequences. This
was one of those occasions and Gorton failed the test." Gorton tried
to justify his vote for someone he described as "marginally qualified" by saying Washington deserved a judge as much as Indiana.
But it didn't sell.[10]

Although the White House and Meese denied any deal, Dwyer
was nominated. The nomination was late, however, raising suspicions that the White House was sabotaging this nomination it found
so distasteful. The Democrats refused to waive the time rules, and
the nomination died when Congress adjourned.

Gorton was thus doubly burned. Not only did he look as if he had
sold out, but he could not deliver what he had sold out for. In
November 1986, Gorton was defeated by Brock Adams. A few
months after the One Hundredth Congress convened in 1987, it
was reported that the White House would not resubmit Dwyer's
name, even though Evans wanted them to. The Dwyer story was
not yet over, however.

Manion's opponents faced an uphill battle in trying to get a
motion for reconsideration, for this time it would be much harder
to get Republican votes. Byrd's motion came up on July 23. Even
with Packwood voting against Manion, all the opponents could
muster was forty-nine votes, and they lost, 49–49.

Even then, the opponents nearly did it, for Goldwater again
avoided voting, this time claiming illness. Somehow or other he was
just not going to vote in favor of Manion, though he apparently did
not want to vote against him. This time Goldwater himself arranged
a pair with his fellow Arizonan, Dennis DeConcini, a conservative
Democrat. Though this time it was unnecessary, Bush again voted
to break a tie. The final vote for Manion was 50–49.

In the aftermath there was a good deal of second-guessing about the opponents' decision to end their filibuster and allow a vote. One veteran senator complained privately that opponents should have continued to filibuster. "Even though there might have been some attrition over time, as the Administration turned up the pressure, there were still more than enough opponents for a filibuster, and you can never depend on Republican senators. They're too vulnerable to inducements and pressure." Others, however, pointed out that but for the misrepresentations as to the Packwood and Goldwater positions, the opponents would have prevailed.

The Manion victory cost the Administration dearly. It made it very difficult for Administration spokesmen to insist that their nominees were highly qualified. Indeed, Manion's meager qualifications were an embarrassment, and the Manion nomination became a lasting example of the Administration's preoccupation with ideology regardless of quality or anything else. It almost certainly cost them a Senate seat. And losing the Manion fight would probably not have made the Seventh Circuit less conservative. The Administration could easily have found an equally ideological candidate with more acceptable professional credentials and who could have been confirmed easily.[11]

THE REHNQUIST NOMINATION FOR CHIEF JUSTICE

The nomination of William H. Rehnquist to be chief justice of the United States when Warren Burger retired in May 1986 at first seemed to be the culmination of the conservative court-packing. Few expected any more voluntary departures from the Supreme Court, and the Burger retirement–Rehnquist nomination seemed the perfect symbolic capstone.

It will probably never be known whether Burger voluntarily jumped off the Court a year earlier than expected, or was nudged. He had not been expected to leave until September 1987, when the Bicentennial festivities would reach a high point, with the chief justice in the starring role. Also, Burger himself would turn eighty at that time, making it a chronologically appropriate time to go. The most plausible scenario is that since the increasing probability of a Democratic takeover of the Senate in 1986 reduced the chances of getting a Reagan nomination confirmed in 1987–88, it was politely suggested to Burger that he depart early. Burger, a staunchly partisan Republican, had become increasingly close to the Administration and to Rehnquist. Burger was also finding the dual jobs of Bicentennial chairman and chief justice very exhausting. These two factors may have led him to acquiesce.

His departure was unlamented, for he was one of the least influential chief justices in modern history. Not respected for either his mind or his character, he had irritated many of the other justices by manipulative tactics to control the assignment of opinions, contrary to long-established Court procedures.[12]

Rehnquist was another matter. Personally charming and with a brilliant, swift intellect, he quickly established himself as the most reactionary justice in modern times. On a conservative Court dominated by justices appointed by Presidents Nixon, Ford, and Reagan, Rehnquist was frequently off by himself in dissent from all eight of the other justices, particularly in major civil rights, First Amendment, and criminal procedure cases. This happened so often—approximately fifty-four times, a record—that one year his law clerks presented him with a Lone Ranger doll.[13]

For example, Rehnquist alone voted to:

- give tax breaks to segregated private schools
- allow states to force pregnant teachers to take unpaid leave five months before their due date, regardless of their ability to work
- make servicewomen meet higher standards for obtaining support allotments for their spouses then servicemen
- allow Maricopa County, Arizona, to deny vital medical care to new residents
- allow the federal government to deny food stamps to households in which one of the members is not a blood relative of the others
- allow Arkansas to leave in place some of the worst prison conditions in our history
- allow Texas to deny a Buddhist prisoner a reasonable opportunity to practice his religion

- allow Indiana to deny unemployment benefits to a Jehovah's Witness who refused to work on armaments for religious reasons
- allow northern school districts to maintain segregated schools

and more, much more.[14]

In addition, some eighty-one times Rehnquist was the only vote for hearing a case that the eight others thought unworthy of Supreme Court review. These were almost always lower court decisions that had upheld a civil rights or civil liberties claim.

Rehnquist also developed unique theories limiting individual freedoms that no other justice adopted. He was the only justice, for example, to take the position that the courts may scrutinize official discrimination closely only when it is against blacks and perhaps other ethnic groups. On this theory, discrimination against nonracial or nonethnic groups could be justified by showing a merely plausible reason for the different treatment. Not surprisingly, in a dozen cases he had not voted once in favor of aliens when they were discriminated against with respect to civil service jobs as typists or janitors, or denied the right to become lawyers or even a notary public; the Court upheld such claims eight out of twelve times. Similarly, Rehnquist refused to invalidate special burdens on illegitimate children, such as denying them the right to financial support from their fathers, to inherit equally with other children, to share in their father's workmen's compensation recoveries, or to obtain child welfare and parental disability benefits. Here, too, the Court had frequently lifted some of these burdens, often over Rehnquist's sole dissent. He also voted consistently against women's rights.[15]

Rehnquist also is the only justice to adopt the notion that the Constitution prohibits only preferences for one religion over another, not preferences for religion in general, though there are indications that Justice Scalia will join him in this. Between 1972, when he came to the Court, and 1986, Rehnquist had participated in twenty church-state separation cases and six cases involving a claim that the right to practice one's religion freely was being threatened. On only one narrow issue in all these cases had he voted either for separation or for religious freedom, though the Court had frequently done so. In dissent, often alone, Rehnquist voted to allow the states to provide almost every kind of financial or other support for parochial schools, including tuition grants, tax deductions, and the like. He also voted to allow schools to require a moment of silence for prayer and to require the display of religious symbols.[16]

Only where Congress had passed a statute unmistakably granting a right did Rehnquist vote to uphold it, and even then he tried to limit it. When the Court split on interpreting such a statute, Rehnquist voted to sustain the claim in only three of eighty-one cases, whereas the Court voted for the plaintiff in thirty-five such cases.[17]

Finally, Rehnquist is the only justice to advance the theory that the First Amendment imposes lesser obligations on states than on the federal government. This would produce a multitude of problems, since it would require the Court to work out the specific dividing line between what the states can do and what the federal government can do, with the result that the states would be able to get away with much more suppression of free speech and expression than they do today.[18]

Rehnquist's hostility to civil rights and civil liberties started early. He disliked doing graduate work at Harvard because, he told a friend, "he just couldn't take 'Harvard liberalism.' "[19]

As soon as Rehnquist got an opportunity to put his views into action, he took it. At the head of his Stanford Law School class, in 1952–53 Rehnquist served as a law clerk to Justice Robert H. Jackson. Jackson had been a New Deal liberal but had grown increasingly conservative over the years.

Rehnquist was too much for Jackson, however. For example, Rehnquist urged that Jackson vote against a black challenge to all-white Democratic Party primary elections in Texas. Black voters had been excluded since 1889 solely because of their race, and the primary election was, of course, the only significant election in Texas, then a one-party state. Rehnquist urged that Jackson vote against the blacks because "It is about time the Court faced the fact that the white people in the South don't like the colored people; the Constitution restrains them from effecting this dislike through state action, but it most assuredly did not appoint the Court as a sociological watch dog to rear up every time private discrimination raises its admittedly ugly head." On May 4, 1953, Jackson voted with an 8–1 majority striking down the all-white primary.[20]

The most notorious event of Rehnquist's clerkship was his memorandum to Jackson titled "A Random Thought on the Segregation Cases," initialed "WHR," in which he argued that the separate but equal doctrine of *Plessy* v. *Ferguson* "was right and should be reaffirmed." When the memo came to light in his 1971 confirmation hearing, Rehnquist tried to deflect the criticism by saying "the memorandum was prepared by me at Justice Jackson's request . . . as a rough draft of a statement of *his* views [for presentation at the justices' conference] . . . rather than as a statement of my views." Both Elsie Douglas, Jackson's secretary for many years, and scholars like Jackson's biographer Dennis Hutchinson and Richard Kluger have called Rehnquist's account "absurd." Jackson, a master advocate, did not need Rehnquist to tell him how to argue a position, and the style, content, and context of the memo are that of a law clerk presenting his own ideas to his judge. Jackson, of course, voted with the rest of the Court in *Brown*.[21]

When Rehnquist left the Court, he continued campaigning against civil rights and liberties as a lawyer in Phoenix, Arizona. In 1957 he attacked law clerks and justices on the Court for "extreme solicitude for the claims of communists and other criminal defendants." Commenting on three major civil rights opinions, only one of which involved communism and where the Court ruled either unanimously or 8–1, Rehnquist said, "[C]ommunists, former communists, and others of like political philosophy scored significant victories during the October 1956 term of the Supreme Court of the United States." In 1964 he challenged a proposed public accommodations ordinance for the city of Phoenix with the comment that "the ordinance summarily does away with the historic right of the owner of a drug store, lunch counter, or theatre to chose his own customers." He added in a newspaper letter after the ordinance was unanimously passed, "[I]t is I believe impossible to justify the sacrifice of even a portion of our historic individual freedom for a purpose such as this." Indeed, one witness at his 1971 hearing had heard Rehnquist say, "I am against all civil rights laws." He later retracted his criticism of the ordinance, saying, "I think the ordinance really worked very well in Phoenix. It was readily accepted, and I think I've come to realize since, more than I did at the time, the strong concern that minorities have for the recognition of these rights."[22]

He also attacked efforts to desegregate the Phoenix schools, saying, "[W]e are no more dedicated to an 'integrated' than we are to a 'segregated' society." And in particularly dramatic testimony from over a half dozen witnesses highlighted by James Brosnahan, a former FBI agent and now a distinguished trial lawyer who had flown in from San Francisco, it was charged that in the early 1960s Rehnquist had intimidated minority voters in Phoenix by challenging their eligibility.[23]

One of the most troubling aspects of Rehnquist's anti–civil liberties efforts was an ethical matter during his first term on the Supreme Court.

In 1969 the Nixon Administration adopted an information-gathering and surveillance program against Vietnam War protesters. The program was challenged in a case called *Laird* v. *Tatum,* and in the Court of Appeals in Washington, D.C., the plaintiffs were successful at a preliminary stage. The Supreme Court reversed by a 5–4 vote, holding that the plaintiffs did not have enough of an interest in the action to be allowed to sue, and dismissed the suit without allowing it to get to the merits. Rehnquist participated in the decision, and his vote swung the suit against the plaintiffs.[24]

The plaintiffs had moved, however, to have Rehnquist disqualify himself because of his involvement with the issues that were the subject of the lawsuit when he was at the Justice Department. Rehnquist refused, saying, "I have no recollection of any participation in the formulation of policy on the use of the military to conduct surveillance or collect intelligence concerning domestic civilian activities," and he appended a lengthy memorandum justifying his participation.[25]

It subsequently developed, however, that Rehnquist had had a very significant relationship indeed to this surveillance program, beyond that disclosed in his opinion or revealed in his testimony. As a high official in the department he had sent a key transmittal memorandum that resulted in the policy statement adopted by Nixon that was the subject of the suit, and would probably have been a witness in the case if five members of the Supreme Court, including Rehnquist, had not dismissed it.

Geoffrey Hazard, a Yale law professor who had drafted the ABA Codes of Judicial and Professional Conduct and was the director of the American Law Institute—and, incidentally, a Republican— wrote to Senator Charles Mathias on September 8, 1986, questioning Rehnquist's ethics in participating. "Rehnquist's position as head of the office of legal counsel required him to disqualify himself because he was the responsible lawyer on the matter in question and a potential witness concerning any factual issues. Rehnquist had a responsibility," according to Hazard, to disqualify himself "on his own initiative." Hazard suggested that Rehnquist may have engaged in "a misrepresentation to the parties and to his colleagues on the Supreme Court in his memorandum justifying his actions." Hazard also found implausible Rehnquist's claim to the Senate committee that he had "no recollection of any participation in the formulation of policy on the use of the military to conduct surveillance. . . ." Whether that statement should be accepted is "a matter of judgment," said Hazard, but he pointed out that "it was made by a lawyer of the highest intelligence concerning sensitive state policy over which his office had direct responsibility early in his service in government and about which he had been asked to search his recollection on three official occasions."[26]

This was the man whom Reagan tried to place in the highest judicial position in the nation. And Reagan succeeded. Many senators, knowing the limited judicial powers of the chief justice—his only substantive power is the authority to assign the opinion when he is in the majority—thought it just not worthwhile to fight the nomination and to risk being criticized for voting on ideological grounds. As Senator Biden (who ultimately voted against him) kept asking witnesses opposed to Rehnquist, "why do you think Justice Rehnquist in the role of chief justice would be so much more damaging . . . than as associate justice?" Unfortunately, the witnesses were unable to respond satisfactorily. In fact, who is chief justice makes a big difference in many subtle and not-so-subtle ways.[27]

First of all, there is the obvious symbolism of the choice. The Court is in the forefront of the nation's quest for justice and liberty. Its mission, in Justice Lewis Powell's words, is to afford "protection

[to] . . . the constitutional rights and liberties of individual citizens and minority groups against oppressive or discriminatory government action." To elevate to leadership someone like Rehnquist, who has such a uniquely hostile record to the fundamental mission of the institution, is to mock and disparage that mission. It amounts to saying to the nation—and, indeed, to the whole world—that we really don't take that mission seriously.[28]

The symbolic effect of the appointment is increased by the fact that the chief justice speaks for the federal judiciary as well as the Court to Congress, to the legal profession, and to the nation.

There are also more tangible considerations. The chief justice assigns the writings of opinions when he is in the majority. Like his predecessors, Rehnquist probably will write the most important opinions himself and probably will take on a large number of them. (He reportedly writes easily and quickly.) In the past, when he has spoken for the Court in a decision restricting someone's rights, he has used sweeping and often vague language, as in a recent case refusing to recognize a right to privacy against electronic tracking devices. The scope and ramifications of such opinions are broad and difficult to confine.

Conversely, on the rare occasions when Rehnquist has joined his colleagues in upholding someone's rights—and invariably these have been decisions in which the other eight are unanimous—he has defined the right narrowly, as in a recent case involving the rights of illegitimate children to child support.

As chief justice, Rehnquist's influence will be greater with new justices than with those now on the bench. Because he may serve as chief justice for from ten to twenty years, at least five new justices will join the Court during his reign, and probably more. No matter who appoints them or who they are, they will feel the power of the chief justice, particularly in their early years. Moreover, some chief justices, such as William Howard Taft, influenced appointments to both the lower federal judiciary and the Supreme Court itself. Given Rehnquist's activist history, he may well emulate Taft.

Finally, the chief justice heads a vast administrative apparatus, the federal judiciary. He designates the members of special judicial bodies, including the Temporary Emergency Court of Appeals and the secret Foreign Intelligence Surveillance Act Court, which passes on national security wiretapping. He also presides over the Judicial Conference, a policymaking body that proposes and evaluates rules and legislation affecting the federal courts. He appoints the membership and staff of the conference and of its twenty judicial committees. These groups play a significant role in the administration of justice in this country, for they deal with matters such as class-action rules, discovery, probation, and sentencing. The importance of this authority is magnified by the chief justice's role as the spokesman to the Congress on these and other legislative matters affecting Court administration.[29]

Republican control of the Senate, and the reluctance to impugn a sitting justice, combined to gain Rehnquist confirmation by a 65–33 vote. It was the largest vote against a chief justice in history and greatly exceeded the opponents' expectations. One journalist commented that if the information that emerged about Rehnquist's past had been available in 1971, he would not have been confirmed at that time. But the then Judiciary Committee chairman, James O. Eastland of Mississippi, had refused to order a full investigation, and Rehnquist's 1971 opponents were stymied.[30]

THE SCALIA NOMINATION

Antonin Scalia's views were not too different from Rehnquist's: During Scalia's first term in the Court he voted with Rehnquist 87 percent of the time, more than any other justice, a distinction most recently held by Burger. During his years on the Circuit Court in Washington, D.C., where he was seen as a bright, affable colleague, Scalia had compiled a record almost uniformly hostile to civil rights and civil liberties and favorable to governmental authority.

In First Amendment cases, particularly libel actions, Scalia had voted against the First Amendment claim almost every time. In one of these, a notorious suit by Mobil Oil president William Tavoulareas against the *Washington Post* for a story charging him with nepotism (a suit Tavoulareas ultimately lost), Scalia joined in an opinion that said a newspaper's reputation for seeking "hard-hitting investigative stories" could be used as evidence of the paper's recklessness about the truth of the story. In another case he tried to limit constitutional protection to speech and not to include any expressive action.[31]

In race/sex discrimination cases, Scalia invariably voted against the plaintiffs, often in dissent. All of his criminal-law decisions were in favor of the prosecutor, and he ruled again and again that plaintiffs trying to get into federal court have no standing. And in public statements before he went on the Court, he mocked affirmative action, spoke out strongly for capital punishment, and attacked both the state and federal courts for their development of constitutional civil rights that do not have a long-standing historical basis. "If it contradicts a long and consistent understanding of the society . . . it is quite simply wrong," Scalia said, causing doubts about his views of the legitimacy of overturning *Plessy* v. *Ferguson*'s quite widely accepted separate-but-equal doctrine. He was particularly hostile to judicial supervision of unconstitutionally run prisons, schools, nursing homes, and other institutions. Not surprisingly, the far right was very happy about Scalia since, as ultraconservatives Patrick McGuigan and Jeffrey P. O'Connell wrote, "it was clear that his jurisprudence was similar to Rehnquist's."[32]

Nevertheless, Scalia was unanimously approved. Potential Democratic opponents were preoccupied with the simultaneous Rehnquist nomination, and it was felt that no major changes would result from Scalia's election—he was simply replacing an almost equally conservative Burger. Even though it was likely that Scalia's brains and charm would make him more influential than Burger, this was too subtle to consider and would, in any event, make only a marginal difference.

8
1987—Bork, Ginsburg, and Kennedy

We are standing at the edge of history. Our efforts have always stalled at the door of the U.S. Supreme Court and [Judge Robert Bork's nomination] may be our last chance to influence this most important body.

Rev. Jerry Falwell, Moral Majority leader

In November 1986, the Democrats won the Senate by a surprisingly large margin, picking up eight seats. The president had campaigned hard to keep a Republican Senate, often raising his concern about what a Democratic Senate would do to his campaign to move the courts to the right. In one speech he charged that Democratic senators would allow "drugs, thugs, and hoodlums to pervade society by placing a bunch of sociology majors on the bench." The defeat thus weakened him considerably in the judgeship wars. How much did not become apparent until the Robert Bork nomination. Among the missing were such hard-shell right-wingers as Jeremiah Denton, John East (through suicide), James Abdnor, and Paula Hawkins. Their replacements included Tom Harkin, Brock Adams, Wyche Fowler, and other liberals.[1]

Most important, the Judiciary Committee returned to Democratic hands. Senator Edward M. Kennedy, who could have resumed the chairmanship, chose instead to take the Labor Committee chair, and Joseph Biden became the Judiciary Committee chairman.

Biden had not wanted the job. An all-but-announced presidential aspirant at the time, Biden needed time away from Washington to campaign, and a chairman's duties interfered with that. Also, the Judiciary Committee is a difficult and thankless assignment. It provides very little control over money or patronage and gets most of the difficult social issues. Constitutional amendments for school prayer, abortion, and busing, court stripping, civil rights legislation, and capital punishment are just a few of the controversies that come to the committee. The large increase in controversial judgeships added to both the weight and the delicacy of the committee's responsibilities.

The chairmanship posed an especially difficult problem for Biden. Since his early years in the Senate he had tried to distance himself from liberals like Kennedy and Metzenbaum and from liberal positions. But he was also to the left of many conservatives on these issues. Apparently he was quite satisfied with this uneasy quasicentrist position, but it was risky. The Judiciary Committee chairmanship heightened the risk, for it forced him constantly to make hard choices, with the danger of alienating either the right or the left. Indeed, civil rights groups had been quite unhappy with Biden's failure to come out against Rehnquist early enough, as well as in other nomination battles.

But a politician asking to lead the country cannot turn down an opportunity to show how good a leader he is. And the very exposure that made the spot so dangerous also made it inviting. Being chairman offered a spotlight that would provide a presidential candidate who started with a low recognition factor outside Washington with invaluable publicity.

Biden therefore agreed to take the Judiciary Committee chairmanship. To deal with judgeships, he created a special task force with its own staff to screen the nominations. The task force was headed by Vermont's Patrick Leahy, a highly respected former prosecutor and a senator who knew how to ask sharp questions, a skill not too common among senators. Biden also put Metzenbaum and the conservative Howell Heflin from Alabama on the task force. The result was that troublesome lower court nominations would be flushed out and developed by others before Biden would be faced with them, leaving him plenty of time to figure out exactly how to react. As events turned out, Biden's other troubles made all this unimportant.

On January 30, 1987, the President nominated Bernard Siegan for a seat on the Ninth Circuit Court of Appeals in California. The nomination languished for a while as the Senate took its time reorganizing itself after the Democratic victory. By midspring the Judiciary Committee was ready to go to work on the Siegan and other nominations.

Siegan's writings showed that he opposed almost everything the federal courts had done since 1819. An advocate of judicial activism on behalf of property rights, he had made his reputation by arguing that the Supreme Court went wrong in 1937, when it decided it would no longer override legislative judgments on economic and social matters. On civil liberties and civil rights, however, he was a judicial-restraint zealot. In his 1987 book *The Supreme Court's Constitution,* he condemned the Court's decisions against race and sex discrimination and for separation of church and state and the expansion of free speech and congressional power; he also challenged the government's issuance of paper money. All of these, he claimed, have "eroded the rule of law" and were worthy of impeachment. Another battle seemed in the offing.[2]

But not just yet.

On June 26, 1987, Justice Lewis F. Powell, Jr., the Court's most crucial swing vote and probably its most influential member since he joined it in 1972, shocked almost everyone with an announcement that he planned to retire immediately.*

Five days later, on July 1, Reagan nominated D.C. Circuit Court of Appeals judge Robert H. Bork to succeed Powell, setting the stage for the most significant judgeship fight of the Reagan Administra-

---

*But not everyone. On June 2, 1987, at a luncheon given by the Alliance for Justice in his honor, civil rights leader Joseph L. Rauh predicted that Powell would retire at the end of the current Supreme Court term. The general reaction was disbelief that Powell, a Democrat, would hand President Reagan such an opportunity. (One lawyer muttered, "What's Joe been smoking?") When I later asked Rauh how he had known, he replied, "Straight logic. I was absolutely certain they had pushed Burger off, and of the remaining nine, Powell was the only one to push."

tion and perhaps the most important domestic controversy of Reagan's eight years.

THE BORK NOMINATION TO THE SUPREME COURT

When Reagan became president, many anticipated that the Supreme Court would soon disappear as a protection for individual rights. Many justices were very old, and at least a few of the liberals, enough to tip the balance for many years, were likely to leave during the Reagan presidency.

Through June 25, 1987, however, only two justices left, and both were from the conservative wing. Since all the remaining justices seemed relatively healthy, it looked as if the conservative effort to reshape American law would fall short.[3]

The unexpected retirement of Lewis Powell on June 26 and the swift nomination of Bork were thus a staggering one-two punch to civil rights and other public-interest groups. If Bork were confirmed, a moderate, humane conservative would be replaced by a rigid, hard extremist.

Lewis Powell was an unlikely hero for liberals, and to some extent their admiration for him was excessive. He was a wealthy Virginia lawyer, and a former president of the American Bar Association. Appointed to the Court by Nixon in 1971, he had quickly established himself as conservative, independent, and flexible. During his fifteen years on the Court he was probably its single most influential member. Although Supreme Court periods usually are identified by the name of the chief justice, the 1972–87 Court could more appropriately be called the Powell and not the Burger Court.

The conservative side can be shown statistically. The annual *Harvard Law Review* statistics indicate that Powell voted most often with Chief Justice Burger in ten of Powell's fifteen years on the Court. In other years, his closest alignments were with Rehnquist (five years) and O'Connor (one year). Conversely, the justices with whom he voted least were Marshall (eight years), Douglas (five years), and Brennan (two years). In his final year, Powell voted most often with Rehnquist, in almost seven-eighths of the cases, and least frequently with Marshall—55 percent. Powell voted consistently for the prosecution in criminal cases, and for business interests in business, labor, and antitrust cases.[4]

The independence, however, is equally obvious. Time and again Powell separated himself from his more conservative colleagues. In free speech cases, for example, he sometimes wrote separately to emphasize his concern for First Amendment values, as in a case denying a reporter the privilege to keep information confidential. In other cases he actually dissented, as in a case denying the press a constitutional right to access to prisons.[5]

Many of Powell's characteristics appeared in an important opinion he wrote at the close of his first year on the Court. In a case growing out of the upheavals caused by the Vietnam War, the Court struck down Attorney General John Mitchell's claim that a president has an inherent power to wiretap Americans without prior judicial approval if the attorney general thinks it necessary to gather intelligence about threats to our domestic security.[6]

Before joining the Court in August 1971, private citizen Powell had written a widely circulated article supporting the attorney general's claim, without even a glance at the Fourth or First Amendment values at stake. *Justice* Powell, however, voted to rebuff the attorney general, and in writing the Court's unanimous opinion (Rehnquist did not participate) delivered an eloquent discourse on the relationship between free speech and freedom from arbitrary intrusions.[7]

Even here Powell's basic conservatism came out. His opinion did not simply deny the attorney general's claim but went on to suggest that because intelligence gathering necessarily was less specific than investigations to solve specific crimes, Congress could authorize looser requirements for intelligence gathering than for conventional law-enforcement searches.*[8]

Justice Powell's conservatism was most prominent with respect to access to the courts for constitutional challenges. He was a leader

---

*Congress has not seen fit to provide such an authorization, however, partly because the Justice Department has never even asked for it. It is a bad idea anyway, because in any politically tinged criminal case, the authorities would be tempted to use that authority to evade the more stringent law enforcement requirements.

in reversing the Warren Court's efforts to open the federal courts to people hurt by official abuses. In cases ranging from taxpayers trying to force disclosure of the CIA budget, to welfare recipients trying to prevent the elimination of tax incentives for hospitals to serve poor people, Powell led the fight to keep people out of court, no matter how blatantly unconstitutional the official conduct. Even here, however, Powell showed flexibility: Where Congress had authorized such suits, as, for example, in legislation against housing discrimination, Powell broke from the Rehnquist-Burger group to allow the suit to go forward.[9]

It was in the human rights area that Powell became most influential and endeared himself to civil rights advocates. The best known example is the *Bakke* case, which involved a medical school's plan to set aside a certain number of places for minority applicants. Powell's opinion upholding voluntarily adopted affirmative action laid down the legal principles that governed most of the cases that came up afterward, even though the opinion was joined by no other justice. It also provided relief to the particular white applicant who challenged the plan in question, who was himself highly qualified and may well have been wronged. Although it was easy to find analytic flaws in the opinion, it was a brilliant compromise that kept affirmative action alive within manageable limits, as did his concurring opinion two years later in a case upholding a minority set-aside in federal public works programs.[10]

By the time Powell retired, the legal acceptability of affirmative action within certain limits was fully established. And it was because of Lewis Powell. He was the only justice to be on the winning side of every affirmative action on which he sat (he disqualified himself from one suit) and was the swing vote on many of the 5–4 decisions so common in this area.

Because the Court was so polarized into two nearly equal blocs, Powell was frequently the swing man in other civil rights and civil liberties contexts as well. He was on the winning side in every church-state separation case during his time on the Court, despite the many confusing turns this area of the law took. His views also prevailed in every case granting rights to illegitimate children, on every abortion-related issue, and in many decisions affecting education, food stamps, welfare, and capital punishment. On the other hand, he made the fifth vote denying constitutional protection for homosexual activity. In 1986–87, his last term, there were forty-two 5–4 decisions—far more than usual—and Powell was on the winning side in thirty-four, a third of which went for the Court's liberal wing. In eleven First Amendment cases during that term, in which government action was invalidated seven times, and six of the eleven decisions were 5–4, Powell was in the majority in all eleven.[11]

Powell's departure was thus greeted with shock and dismay by civil rights and other liberal groups. At the eleventh hour it offered a weakened lame-duck president and his scandal-enveloped attorney general a chance to obtain with one stroke what they had not come even close to achieving in the preceding six and a half years.

Bork was chosen to succeed Powell because he was what one White House aide called a "right-wing zealot" who, in Bruce Fein's words, on "the fighting issues—abortion, affirmative action, free speech, church-state—will make a difference," and give "the entire docket of the Court . . . a conservative hue." Bork's appointment "may be our last chance . . . to ensure future decades will bring morality, godliness and justice back into focus" proclaimed Christian Voice, an evangelical organization; Jerry Falwell and other conservatives were equally joyful.[12]

However, Bork's handlers—White House chief of staff Howard Baker and Washington lawyer Lloyd Cutler, a Democrat—did not think that the Democratic-controlled Senate would confirm such an ideologue. Therefore they tried to package Bork as a "moderate conservative" in the tradition of John M. Harlan, Felix Frankfurter, Robert H. Jackson and Powell—Cutler actually likened Bork to Louis D. Brandeis and Hugo Black.[13]

The strategy was revealed early in a little-noticed incident. When Reagan announced the Bork nomination, Attorney General Edwin Meese, Bork's biggest booster aside from the president and a key figure in selecting Bork, stayed in the next room, out of sight.[14]

The Bork fight ended with a latter-day version of the post–World War I German excuse: The losers had been robbed. Judge Bork had been "lynched" by what Reagan called "an ugly spectacle, marred by distortions and innuendoes and casting aside the normal rules of

Tower parallel

honesty and decency." *The Wall Street Journal* railed against a "bloody campaign" of "brazen lies," "smears," "distortions," and "Mc-Carthyism." Bork's opponents had politicized what should be apolitical and had misled the American people. To Reed Irvine of Accuracy In Media, "there is no doubt that the communists played an important role" in blocking the Bork nomination. The fifty-eight senators who voted against Bork, including six Republicans, apparently were cowards, knaves, fools, or worse.[15]

The campaign to transmogrify Bork into a "mainstream jurist" may well have been doomed from the start. Bork had written a major book and scores of articles, speeches, and judicial opinions for over a quarter century. On almost every important issue likely to come before the federal courts, he had spoken and, almost invariably, come down on the far right.

Robert Bork had started out as a liberal who passed out leaflets for Adlai Stevenson on street corners and was attracted to Eugene V. Debs. At the University of Chicago Law School, however, he underwent what he later described as "a little bit like a conversion experience" under the influence of free-market conservative economist Aaron Director and swung sharply and permanently to the right. In 1954 he began to practice law in Chicago and wrote some articles applying Chicago School economics to the antitrust laws. In 1962 he left practice and joined the Yale Law School faculty, where he established a national reputation with a series of powerfully reasoned articles that called for loosening antitrust-law restrictions and overturning almost everything the courts had done to put teeth into those laws.[16]

While at Yale he turned his attention to constitutional law and developed his thinking in a seminar with distinguished constitutionalist Alexander Bickel. This culminated in a 1971 law journal article where Bork set out a theory of constitutional interpretation from which he never diverged and that became the focal point of the confirmation controversies.[17]

Bork's theory insisted that constitutional doctrines must be derived from and defined by "neutral" sources and principles, for otherwise judges would be acting as undemocratic moral dictators. The only truly neutral sources of constitutional doctrine are the text, the original intent of the framers, and implications from the governmental processes established by the Constitution. "Where constitutional materials do not clearly specify the value to be preferred," he wrote, "there is no principled way to prefer any claimed human value to any other. The judge must stick close to the text and the history, and their fair implications, and not construct new rights."[18]

On the basis of this theory, Bork proceeded to castigate as "unprincipled" and illegitimate much of what the Court had done for the protection of individual liberty since 1923. He concentrated his fire on three areas: privacy, equality, and free speech.

Privacy. Because he could find nothing in the text of the Constitution or its history from which to derive a right of privacy, Bork attacked the Court's 1965 birth-control decision in the *Griswold* case as well as the precedents it had relied on, including the 1923 case affirming a right "to marry, establish a home, and bring up children" and the 1925 decision establishing a parent's right to send a child to a private school. In later years he broadened his attack on privacy law to include the 1973 abortion decision, calling it "an unconstitutional decision, a serious and wholly unjustifiable usurpation of state legislative behavior." Although he had suggested in a 1968 article that the Ninth Amendment might provide some basis for protecting individual rights not specifically enumerated in the Constitution, he later declared that judges "should" treat [the amendment] as nonexistent and ignore it."[19]

Equality. "There is no principled way in which anyone can define the spheres . . . in which equality is required. These are matters of morality, of judgment, of prudence . . . [for] the political community" and not for judges, wrote Bork. He condemned the Fourteenth Amendment equal protection clause decisions outlawing the poll tax (he later said it was just "a very small tax") and the decisions establishing the one-person, one-vote principle, abolishing school segregation in the District of Columbia, barring courts from enforcing racially restrictive housing covenants, preventing a state from sterilizing certain criminals or interfering with the right to travel, and prohibiting discrimination against illegitimate children. As late as June 1987 he declared, "I do think the Equal Protection Clause probably should have been kept to things like race and ethnicity," thus excluding women, aliens, illegitimate children, and others from meaningful judicial protection under the clause. Five years earlier, in 1982, he had remarked that "the identification of favored minorities [other than racial or ethnic groups] will proceed according to current fads in sentimentality." The only equal protection decision he explicitly supported was the now-sacrosanct *Brown* v. *Board of Education,* though his effort to square this with his original-intent theory, given what we know about the segregationist views of the framers of the Fourteenth Amendment (see Chapter 2), was unpersuasive.[20]

Bork's hostility to governmental action on behalf of minorities including blacks did not stop with his critique of court action. In 1963 he criticized a section of the proposed Civil Rights Act of 1964 that required white businesses to serve blacks as resting on a principle of "unsurpassed ugliness." He also condemned the Supreme Court 1966 decision *allowing* Congress to use the Voting Rights Act to bar literacy tests. "At almost every critical turning point in the civil rights movement," testified William T. Coleman, Jr., Gerald Ford's secretary of transportation, Bork had "turned the wrong way."[21]

Free Speech. In his 1971 article, Bork also propounded a theory that would have the First Amendment protect only "explicitly political" speech, which he defined as limited to "criticisms of public officials and policies, proposals for the adoption or repeal of legislation or constitutional provisions and speech addressed to the conduct of any governmental unit in the country." He explicitly excluded from constitutional protection literary, artistic, scientific, moral, or other forms of expression, as well as pornography and public vulgarity, even if political. He repudiated the Court's long-established clear and present danger test and would have denied protection to any speech urging violation of the law. In later years he expanded the protected class to include scientific or moral discourse that "directly feed[s] the democratic process," but as late as June 1987 he did not think "courts ought to throw protection around . . . art and literature."[22]

In 1973 Bork became solicitor general of the United States, and at his confirmation hearing made the first of many "confirmation conversions," this time repudiating his 1963 views on the civil rights law. Shortly thereafter he became embroiled in the Watergate controversy when, as acting attorney general, he fired Special Prosecutor Archibald Cox for demanding the Nixon tapes after Bork's superiors, Elliot Richardson and William Ruckelshaus, had refused to do so.

In later years Bork's supporters would try to make much of the fact that as solicitor general he had often presented arguments favoring civil rights. In many of these cases Bork was presenting positions with which he personally disagreed, for as he acknowledged, his job was to represent the Administration, regardless of his personal views, and in many of these instances the Administration's position was quite liberal. Generally, however, Bork tried to present the conservative side on such matters as capital punishment, busing, and criminal justice.[23]

He went back to Yale in 1977 and continued to speak out forcefully. He criticized the Court's school prayer and other church-state separation decisions, and its affirmative action rulings. He also advocated strong executive power.

In 1978 Bork published a book on antitrust law in which he assailed congressional action in the antitrust sphere as ignorant and misguided. Despite his frequently proclaimed insistence on judicial deference to legislative action, Bork urged that judges pay no attention to what Congress intended, no matter how clear, if it is inconsistent with what he considered the correct economic principles. In that book, as he had elsewhere, he called for the courts to overturn most current antitrust law, and to loosen the restrictions on business to permit almost all mergers and restraints on distribution.[24]

In 1982 Bork was appointed to the Court of Appeals in Washington, D.C. There he quickly established a reputation for ingenuity in denying litigants access to the courts and for great deference to executive authority. A study released by the AFL-CIO during the confirmation controversy found that in seventeen of seventeen access cases in which the judges disagreed, Bork had voted to keep the plaintiff out of court. Even in decisions that were unanimous as to the result, Bork often wrote separately, urging more stringent tests for access. Despite his repeated calls for judicial restraint, he continually tried to erect technical barriers to judicial redress, often despite established precedent. Thus Bork tried to prevent congressmen from challenging what they considered an illegitimate use of the pocket veto; Haitian refugees from challenging a program to stop refugees from coming to the United States; Medicare patients from challenging an effort to prevent the courts from reviewing claim denials; American hostages from suing Iran; survivors of a terrorist attack from suing Libya; and organizations, which often have the resources, from suing on behalf of their individual members, who usually don't.[25]

Bork also seemed particularly sympathetic to business. In the one big antitrust case that came before him, he went far beyond what was necessary to decide the case and wrote his own restrictive views into the law.[26]

Despite this public record, Lloyd Cutler, who headed the confirmation effort, threw himself wholeheartedly into the job of peddling Robert Bork as a moderate.

Cutler launched the campaign with a *New York Times* op-ed piece in which, after describing himself as a liberal Democrat and a civil libertarian, he insisted that Bork was just another mainstream conservative who believed in judicial restraint, civil rights, and the First Amendment. He focused on a prominent libel case in which Bork had written eloquently about the dangers to press freedom posed by the increasing frequency of libel suits, and had called for increased constitutional protection for the press in political controversies. (The year before, Cutler had used Judge Scalia's opinion in the same case to demonstrate *Scalia*'s liberalism—even though Scalia and Bork were on *opposite* sides in that case.)[27]

Republican Minority Leader Robert Dole weighed in with a floor speech a week later arguing that the Senate should focus on the "nominee's fitness and merit" and ignore ideology and philosophy. This position was also pushed vigorously by President Reagan and Bork's leading Senate supporters, Orrin Hatch, Gordon Humphrey of New Hampshire, and Assistant Minority Leader Alan Simpson of Wyoming. The senators were not too persuasive, for all had invoked ideological arguments to oppose both Carter and Reagan appointees, and few in the Senate or elsewhere took this argument seriously. The issue virtually disappeared after early polls revealed that a majority of the public believed that the Senate should indeed consider the social, political, and philosophical views of a Supreme Court nominee, especially since everyone realized Reagan had nominated Bork for political and ideological reasons.[28]

The right also rolled out its money raising and public-relations artillery. Bill Roberts of the Dolphin Group in California, who had led the successful fight against California chief justice Rose Bird in California in 1986 and was a former Reagan campaign manager, was brought in to raise $2.5 million for an advertising campaign, and to target some twelve senators who seemed important; Jerry Falwell's Moral Majority delivered 22,200 postcards to the Senate Judiciary Committee; and senators were continually bombarded with orchestrated pro-Bork mail and phone calls. By September 23, 1987, four days after Bork had concluded his testimony, Republican Senator Arlen Specter, a key swing vote, had received 45,000 pieces of mail, running three to one in favor of Bork. The National Conservative Political Action Committee announced it would spend $1.2 million and mail out 3 million pieces of mail; Richard Viguerie called 100,000 people, mailed several million letters, and sent out over $1 million worth of direct-mail solicitations on Bork's behalf; Concerned Women for America, a conservative group, planned pro-Bork ads in Pennsylvania and Alabama, the home states of Judiciary Committee members Arlen Specter and Howell Heflin, respectively, and sent op-ed pieces to every newspaper in the country.[29]

Conservative groups were not happy, however, with the moderate strategy. They complained bitterly that the White House and Reagan should be selling Bork for what he was. "Since when do conservatives want to fight and bleed and die to get moderates on the Supreme Court?" demanded Richard Viguerie. "The problem is that the White House doesn't want to approach this as an ideological contest," lamented Daniel Popeo. The Justice Department, led by Meese and William Bradford Reynolds, who was also kept out of sight but played a major role in the fight, also favored a hard sell.[30]

Cutler and others, however, pointed out that "there weren't enough conservatives left [in the Senate] to win." And Bork himself joined in the strategy. He made dozens of calls on senators and gave an unprecedented series of press and other interviews in which, while disclaiming any intention to discuss issues, he insisted that he was neither a liberal nor a conservative, telling the *Washington Times*, "I don't consider myself a conservative."[31]

The final element in the strategy was Bork himself, described by White House strategists as their "secret weapon." With happy memories of Lieutenant Colonel Oliver North's crowd-rousing performance at the Iran-Contra hearings, they were certain that the brilliant, charming, and articulate Robert Bork would do as well.

For their part, Bork's opponents immediately began organizing. All saw it as an uphill battle, though some were convinced a filibuster could succeed if the Democrats would be willing. Nan Aron of the Alliance for Justice, Ralph Neas of the Leadership Conference on Civil Rights, Melanne Verveer of People for the American Way, and Bill Taylor, serving as a key strategist, began to organize the opposition.

The very first meeting after the nomination was announced was a happy surprise: So many organizations showed up that the large conference room at the Leadership Conference on Civil Rights was nowhere near large enough. Ultimately over three hundred groups came out against Bork, ranging from consumers and environmentalists to the American Jewish Committee. Key roles were played by Planned Parenthood, Common Cause, and the American Civil Liberties Union. This was the first time the ACLU had actively campaigned against a judicial nominee, and its influence was particularly great on the local level. It may well have been the first and only time that the entire liberal and public-interest community joined together on an issue.

The first order of business was to make it clear that the nomination would be fought vigorously, regardless of the odds. Task forces for lobbying, research, media relations, and grass-roots organizing were set up. A Bork nomination had been a possibility in 1986, and a start on analyzing his record had already been made by a group called "Supreme Court Watch," under the auspices of *The Nation* magazine's Nation Institute. The results of this and other early analyses were quickly disseminated, especially to key senators, to forestall their early endorsements of Bork.

Among the most important elements of the opposition were Bork's own colleagues in the academy and at the bar. Over two thousand law teachers, more than 40 percent of the total at accredited law schools, signed letters against him, including the deans of Harvard, New York University, Michigan, Georgetown, Northwestern, and many other schools. The normally very conservative Philip Kurland of the University of Chicago, a longtime and caustic critic of the Warren Court, wrote a widely circulated article in the *Chicago Tribune* in August in which he described "Bork's entire current constitutional jurisprudential theory [as] directed to a diminution of minority and individual rights." Laurence Tribe of Harvard, America's leading constitutional lawyer, and many other prominent constitutional experts also came out against Bork. And the Association of the Bar of the City of New York, representing seventeen thousand lawyers, and probably the most prestigious bar group in the country, joined the opposition.[32]

Of particular importance, five of the fifteen members of the American Bar Association Committee on Federal Judiciary refused to give Bork a "qualified" rating, the first time the ABA had not been unanimous in favor of a Supreme Court nominee since it had begun evaluating candidates.

There were other signs of unexpected opposition to the nomination. To the delighted surprise of the opponents, money poured into their offices, often unsolicited. Before the battle ended, the anti-Bork groups had raised and spent over $2 million. By contrast, the pro-Bork groups had trouble in fundraising. Bill Roberts's ambitious plan to raise millions was scrapped, as were many other ideas by the Bork supporters.

One reason for the pro-Bork moneyraising troubles was revealed by the public-opinion polls, which consistently showed no great enthusiasm for the nominee. Prior to the hearings, these polls reported that most people had no opinion, and of the small percentage who did—only 27 percent as late as the week before the hearing—14 percent supported his confirmation and 13 percent were opposed. A survey by the Cambridge Survey Research Center, which helped shape the strategy of Bork's senatorial opponents, found that "two-thirds or more of white southerners said they were less inclined to support Bork because of his opposition to various civil rights measures for blacks."[33]

The polls contained other bad news for Bork. A *New York Times/*

CBS poll found that whereas 39 percent thought the Senate should consider only a nominee's legal qualifications, 52 percent thought it should also consider his stand on major issues before the Court. And 70 percent trusted the Senate more than the president with respect to who should sit on the Court.[34]

The anti-Bork groups also managed to arrive at joint strategy decisions, some of which were not easy for them. Early on, it became clear that the public was most concerned about Bork's views on privacy, minority rights, and sympathy for big business. The opposition, nevertheless, believed that the confirmation battle should not turn into a referendum on abortion or on any other single issue. The prochoice groups like the National Abortion Rights Action League, led by Kate Michelman, a relative newcomer to the Washington political scene who learned quickly, agreed not to press their special concerns to the forefront, though the abortion decision probably was the most threatened by the Bork nomination.

The gay rights groups also had good reason to fear Bork. He had written a decision allowing the Navy to fire a nine-year veteran cryptologist and linguist for homosexual conduct. Furthermore, in 1978, while at Yale, Bork had opposed the decision to bar on-campus recruiting by law firms that discriminated against homosexuals. Nevertheless, the gay groups also agreed not to take a publicly prominent role for fear that this could be used by Bork's right-wing supporters against the opposition. At a massive gay rights rally in Washington on October 11, anti-Bork placards were discouraged.

In perhaps the most significant exercise of self-discipline, all the groups decided to refrain from testifying at the hearing and to rely solely on the forty-two lawyers and academics who testified in opposition. Charges that the opposition to Bork was inspired by "special interests," charges that were similar to those that had been used so damagingly against Walter Mondale in 1984, had already surfaced, even though the "special interests" in this case represented virtually every sector of American life. Also, some of these groups had not made a very good impression at the Rehnquist hearings, and most had been relegated to evening slots when nobody was watching. When Lane Kirkland, president of the AFL-CIO, decided that the unions would not testify, the other groups agreed to do likewise.

The Bork opposition was centered in Washington, where "Stop Bork" buttons depicting a photograph of the nominee with a red bar cutting diagonally across it seemed everywhere. But Washington was not unique. There was an astonishing outburst of hostility to Bork's views throughout the country. Anti-Bork rallies were organized on college campuses; local disability and environmental groups undertook letter-writing campaigns.

Judiciary Committee senators were equally busy. Arlen Specter, a moderate Republican from Pennsylvania and probably the key undecided vote on the committee, spent the summer poring over Bork's voluminous writings and speeches. Possessed of a first-class analytic mind and knowing that he would be under intense pressure from both sides, Specter absorbed and analyzed everything Bork had written and said.

Edward Kennedy also was working furiously. He had been the first to announce his opposition to Bork within hours of the announcement in a speech some criticized as intemperate. Intemperate or not, the speech sent a signal that there would be a real opposition, and it was crucial to encouraging the opposition in what was inevitably going to be an uphill struggle.

Kennedy did not stop with speeches. Not only did he and his staff study Bork's work carefully in preparation for the hearings, but Kennedy also urged southern blacks like Mayor Richard Arrington of Birmingham, Alabama, and Mayor Sidney Bartholomey of New Orleans to organize other black leaders and to contact the southern senators, the single most critical bloc in the battle. In a conference call in September he also energized some forty state and regional AFL-CIO leaders.

The central figure among the senators was Judiciary Committee chairman Joseph Biden of Delaware, a 1988 presidential candidate. This was his big chance to make a national reputation for himself, to jump from being a virtual unknown to becoming a household name.

The risks were equally high. Considered by some to be glib and shallow, Biden had a reputation for verbal gaffes, which had gotten him into trouble in the past. Moreover, there was a great deal of skepticism as to whether he would be able to stand up to an articulate and brilliant legal expert like Robert Bork on the latter's turf.

Columnist George Will—who was later revealed to have been an usher at Bork's wedding—was sure Biden would not. The day after the nomination was announced, Will wrote that "the bad news for Biden is that . . . [Bork] will be more than a match for Biden in a confirmation process that is going to be easy."[35]

Will could not have been a worse prophet. Biden not only bested Bork in the legal exchanges, but also he and his staff brilliantly orchestrated much of the opposition.

Biden was particularly instrumental in generating southern opposition, which turned out to be the key to Bork's defeat. A strategic memo prepared for Biden in early September concluded on the basis of extensive polling data that "the potential for the development of intense opposition to Bork is perhaps greater in the South than in any other region. . . . Bork poses the risk of reopening race relations battles which have been fought and put to rest. . . . Bork flouts the southern tradition of populism. And (perhaps most surprisingly to some) Bork poses a challenge to a very strong pro-privacy sentiment among southern voters," particularly conservative white women.[36]

Armed with this information, Biden spent weeks cultivating Senator J. Bennett Johnston, Jr., of Louisiana, who had early on worried that the nomination might reopen old civil rights wounds. Biden sent him reams of material and convinced Johnston, who wanted to be the Democratic Senate leader, that this was a golden opportunity to exercise leadership, especially since Majority Leader Robert Byrd seemed unwilling to take a position.

Johnston organized a series of seminars for newly elected southern senators in which he pointed out that they had been elected only with the support of the black vote and that Reagan had campaigned very hard against them in 1986. Ultimately every southern Democrat except Ernest Hollings of South Carolina followed Johnston's lead and voted against Bork.

Biden also called southern Democratic governors and, in perhaps his most important stroke relating to the hearings themselves, devoted many hours to a successful effort to persuade former transportation secretary William T. Coleman, Jr., a respected Republican, and former congresswoman Barbara Jordan, both of whom are black, to testify. Both were initially reluctant, and the two were probably the most effective witnesses at the entire hearing.

In addition, Biden devoted many intensive weeks to analyzing Bork's writings, with the assistance of Harvard's Laurence Tribe and others. Whereas Bork had refused to participate in more than two of the "murder boards" scheduled for him as mock hearings, Biden and Tribe had a six-hour session in which Tribe played Bork.

It all paid off. Biden focused on exactly the right issues, questioned brilliantly, and received kudos from Republicans as well as Democrats for the courtesy and fairness with which he conducted the eighty-seven hours of testimony.

The hearings themselves were an unprecedented event in American history. In the Bicentennial year of the Constitution, Americans were treated to an intensive two-and-a-half-week public seminar on the most important constitutional issues of the day. The confirmation fight became a great national referendum on the Constitution.

Bork, of course, was the center, more so perhaps than any nominee before him. Never before had a judicial candidate been willing to answer so many probing questions on so wide a range of constitutional issues. In sharp contrast, Antonin Scalia had refused to answer most of the questions he was asked, irritating some senators.

For thirty hours, over five days, Robert Bork sat in the witness chair, patiently and courteously, rarely giving way to anger or the sarcasm to which he was prone, and answered questions covering everything from his role in Watergate to his views on dirty talk in public. After Bork left the stand, 110 lawyers, professors, and other experts testified, 62 in Bork's favor and 48 against, plus 2 members of the American Bar Association. Privacy, antitrust, administrative law, free speech, abortion, voting rights, poll tax, executive power, Bork's free legal work for public-interest causes (or, rather, lack of it), his progression from liberal to conservative, the Senate's role, the president's foreign policy powers—few topics escaped detailed scrutiny.

These hearings were Bork's downfall. As Lloyd Cutler put it right at the beginning, "[T]he confirmation will turn on whether Judge Bork is able to satisfy the members of the Senate and the general public that he is not, in fact, a right-wing ideologue, but is, in fact, a judge much closer to the center and . . . Justice Powell, than he is to the justices over on the right." But Bork's writings were in fact those of "a right-wing ideologue," and he faced the problem of remaining true to what he had previously said and yet appearing moderate.[37]

Bork therefore began to shade and back off from some of his more extreme positions on equal protection and the First Amendment's speech clause. He insisted that he accepted "settled doctrine." He refused, however, to recede significantly from his views that the Constitution contained no basis for a right of privacy. He thus wound up with the worst of all possible worlds: He looked shifty and unpredictable on some of his unpopular positions and intractable on the others. As Biden put it later, "Every time I could get him to recant, I won." Senator Patrick Leahy called the recantations "confirmation conversions," and the label stuck.[38]

Bork's public personality and demeanor also did him little good. Though witty and affable, he came across as cold and intellectual, showing little compassion or sense of injustice. When asked why he wanted to be a Supreme Court justice, he answered, for "the intellectual feast," hardly a good reason for giving someone the enormous responsibility and power available to a Supreme Court justice to affect the lives of 240 million Americans, for better or for worse. He rarely mentioned justice, equity, or mercy. The White House hopes that Bork would charm his way to the Supreme Court were never realized. The portly sixty-year-old ex-professor and judge with a Mephistophelian beard, who was given to subtle, often unpersuasive distinctions, could not do for the cause of judicial conservatism what the trim, uniformed Marine lieutenant colonel wearing a chestful of combat ribbons had done for right-wing patriotism.

Public-opinion polls taken immediately after Bork's appearance showed that his testimony had hurt him. Now most people in all sections of the country were against him, and of those who said they knew a lot about him, most were opposed. The most surprising of these surveys was in the *Atlanta Journal,* which revealed that he had very few supporters in the South, the most conservative region in the country.[39]

Senators responded in the same way and swiftly came out against Bork. On September 30, the day after the hearings ended, Bennett Johnston and Arlen Specter announced their opposition, and soon after so did conservative Lloyd Bentsen, a Texas Democrat. The following Tuesday, October 6, the other undecided votes on the Judiciary Committee—conservative Democrats Dennis DeConcini of Arizona and Howell Heflin of Alabama—also voted against Bork, and the Judiciary Committee wound up 9–5 against him. For all practical purposes the fight was over.

Nevertheless, Reagan refused to give up. He switched to the law-and-order theme, though Bork had testified he had no special expertise in criminal law. Reagan and Bork's other supporters charged that Bork had been victimized by a "lynch mob" who had distorted Bork's words and smeared him as someone opposed to privacy, women's rights, and free expression. The outrage reached a particularly high pitch against the ABA, for its 10–5 vote had made opposition respectable. The Reagan tactics, however, were as much a smear and a distortion as anything he charged the opponents with. As North Carolina Democrat Terry Sanford complained, "We are tired of having our integrity impugned . . . our sincerity questioned . . . our intelligence insulted. . . . The senators who are voting for Judge Bork have no monopoly on honesty."[40]

The ads and public statements of the Bork opponents were in fact occasionally guilty of hyperbole. An ad featuring actor Gregory Peck implied that Bork was against privacy and voting rights, whereas he was actually opposed only to *constitutional* protection for these rights—there was no evidence he had opposed *legislative* protection for them. But these exaggerations are inevitable in any hard-fought struggle, and opinion surveys showed that the ads played a very minor role in the public mind. It was how Bork had come across at his hearing that was decisive.

Nor was it Bork's personal views about abortion, privacy, or civil rights, whatever they were, that counted. Bork was not rejected because, as he bitterly complained, he had been falsely painted as "a racist, a sexist, and probably a fascist." All the senators and the many law professors who opposed him, many of whom knew him personally, certainly did not believe that. It was his narrow view of the Constitution and the role of the judiciary in protecting constitutional rights that were the issues causing his downfall, and most people recognized that.[41]

The signs of impending defeat accumulated as more and more

Republicans and southern Democrats declared themselves against the nominee, and it was widely believed that Bork would withdraw. To almost everyone's amazement, he insisted on a floor vote.

The debate didn't begin until October 21. By then it was not only yesterday's news but also was completely overshadowed by the stock market crash, an escalation of Persian Gulf hostilities, temporarily dashed hopes for a summit between Reagan and Soviet leader Mikhail Gorbachev, and Nancy Reagan's cancer surgery. When the debate began, fifty-four senators had already declared against Bork, with four undecided. Ultimately all four, including the very conservative Mississippian John Stennis, voted no. The only big surprise was Republican John Warner of Virginia, who also joined the opposition, making six Republicans who had abandoned Reagan to vote against Bork, as did all but two Democrats.

On Friday, October 23, after two days of desultory debate, the Senate voted 58–42 to reject the nomination. The most contentious confirmation battle in American history was over, and the Senate had rejected a Supreme Court nominee for the twenty-seventh time.

The Bork confirmation struggle became a national plebiscite on what Americans wanted from their Constitution and their courts. The most significant lesson from that experience was that despite the great popularity of a president eager to realize the right-wing social agenda by tilting the Supreme Court, Americans approved of what the courts had done to promote social justice and individual liberty. This was particularly true with respect to privacy and equality, the two areas on which the Supreme Court has concentrated in the past twenty years and where it has changed American life the most. These were also the areas, together with freedom of expression, on which the confirmation battle focused and where Bork's long-standing hostility to almost all the Court's most significant rulings was most prominent. The Senate, reflecting the national consensus, overwhelmingly refused to risk putting someone in a position where he could threaten these achievements.

Also, it was again shown that a nominee's social and constitutional philosophy is an ineradicable factor in the appointment process, both for the president, who makes the nomination, and for the

Senate, which must vote on confirmation. And appropriately so. Arguments that the Senate should consider only a nominee's brains and moral character fell on deaf ears, as they always have. No one questioned Bork's brains or integrity, but nobody believed that they were all that mattered.

The Bork controversy may also have demonstrated that although a nominee's philosophy and views are crucially relevant, having the nominee explain them is both unnecessary and unreliable, and that we should return to the system under which we operated for some 135 years prior to 1925. Fifty years ago, Supreme Court nominee Felix Frankfurter, a man who had expressed himself on important contemporary issues as much as Bork had, told the Senate Judiciary Committee, "I think it improper for a nominee no less than for a member of the Court to express his personal views on controversial political issues affecting the Court. . . . I should think it not only bad taste, but inconsistent with the duties of the office for which I have been nominated for me to attempt to supplement my past record by present declarations."[42]

Frankfurter was clearly correct. It is rare that someone will be nominated to the Supreme Court without having given quite reliable indications of what he or she thinks about the major pertinent issues. Justice Scalia refused to discuss what he thought in any detail, but his positions on many issues were quite clear, and there were few surprises in his voting pattern during his first year on the Supreme Court. Little was learned about Judge Anthony Kennedy's position on key issues from his appearance before the Senate Judiciary Committee that was not already known from his decisions and speeches. Kennedy "walk[ed] a fine line between liberal and conservative senators concerned about where his views fit on the political spectrum," reported *The Wall Street Journal* the day Kennedy completed his testimony, and despite prehearing declarations by some senators that the nominee would have to divulge his views in great detail, "his ambiguous answers to questions raising the most controversial issues left unclear what Judge Kennedy would actually do on key issues like abortion, affirmative action, and religion."[43]

It sometimes happens, as with the nomination of Douglas H. Ginsburg after Bork lost, that a candidate's position is unknown with respect to almost all major issues. (In Ginsburg's case, that was partly because of his youth and inexperience, which were themselves a problem for his nomination.) But what is unknown can rarely be determined with any reliability at a hearing, since there is a natural and very human temptation for the nominee to shade his views to suit what he thinks is wanted by the senators, who control something the nominee wants very much. Bork showed that. Once on the Court, the nominee can ignore what he said, and properly so. It was inappropriate, for example, for Bork virtually to pledge that if confirmed he would not deviate from the views he had expressed at his confirmation hearing. Had he been confirmed, his oath of office as a justice would be to the Constitution, not to the Senate, and were he to conclude in a case before him that a precedent, settled or otherwise, should be overturned, he would have a constitutional obligation to vote that way regardless of what he told the committee.[44]

A nominee should, of course, be given an opportunity to present facts about his or her background, such as Bork's firing Cox during the Watergate investigation, or the charges against Chief Justice Rehnquist that he had intimidated prospective voters, or Kennedy's club memberships. This is quite different, however, from a lengthy explanation by the nominee of his views on complex legal issues that often require subtle, nuanced answers and that induce the nominee to indicate a future vote.

The foregoing is, however, almost certainly a futile suggestion. The ground rules have now changed, and it appears inevitable that future Supreme Court nominees will be questioned on the specifics of their philosophy.

The political implications of the Bork fight were also significant. Black concerns were now important and perhaps even crucial for southern Democrats, who would henceforth have to navigate between those concerns and the danger of antagonizing too many white voters. As *National Journal* columnist William Schneider pointed out even before the nomination struggle heated up, racial issues would continuously present southern Democrats with the dilemma of choosing between an indispensable black vote and an equally indispensable slice of the white vote.[45]

Finally, one is struck again by the bitter ironies that pervade public life. The Bork nomination presented presidential aspirant Biden with one of the greatest challenges of his political life. If he handled himself well, he would be catapulted from relative obscurity to national celebrity; if he failed, his presidential ambitions probably would fail also.

Biden succeeded beyond anyone's expectations. He handled himself superbly at the hearings, both in the exchanges with Bork and in his overall leadership. He probably deserves much of the credit for the 58–42 outcome, a victory that was not only against the odds but also by a margin that nobody would have thought possible.

Nevertheless, when the battle ended, Joe Biden's 1988 presidential ambitions were dead. Early in the hearings it was revealed that he had copied other people's speeches without attribution, and he had misrepresented his law school performance. A few days after the disclosures, he felt compelled to withdraw from the race.

As for Robert Bork, the *Washington Post* noted that Bork's own *Ollman* v. *Evans* libel opinion, cited so often by his defenders, contained the appropriate epitaph to his lifelong ambition. There he had written: "Those who step into areas of public dispute, who choose the pleasures and distractions of controversy, must be willing to bear criticism, disparagement, and even wounding assessments. Perhaps it would be better if disputation were conducted in measured phrases and calibrated assessments. . . . But that is not the world in which we live, ever have lived or are ever likely to know."[46]

On January 13, 1988, Robert Bork resigned from the Court of Appeals and announced that he planned to answer what he called "a campaign of misinformation and political slogans."

THE GINSBURG FIASCO

"Spoiling for a Second Round" is how *Newsweek* described the president's decision to nominate Washington, D.C., Court of Appeals Judge Douglas H. Ginsburg, forty-one, to the Supreme Court after the Bork nomination was defeated. It never got to that, for it ended as surprisingly and as quickly as it began. Nine days after his nomination was announced, Ginsburg was pressured into withdrawing because he had smoked marijuana several times in the 1960s and 1970s, even though most people, including those who normally would be his opponents, considered the incidents irrelevant to his qualifications.[47]

As soon as Bork's defeat appeared certain, White House chief of staff Howard Baker had tried to prepare the way for a more moderate, more confirmable appointee than Bork. To no avail. The president did not want anyone more moderate. Although a prepared speech on the Bork defeat was toned down by his staff, Reagan couldn't help departing from his text to lash out at the Senate and promise he would send up someone "they'll object to as much as they did to that one." (He later claimed it was a "facetious remark.") And with the encouragement of Senator Jesse Helms, Edwin Meese, and Robert Bork, he did just that.[48]

Names of successor nominees soon were floated. A list of fifteen serious contenders was pared down to two: fifty-one-year-old Ninth Circuit Court of Appeals judge Anthony Kennedy, a former protégé of Reagan and Meese, and forty-one-year-old Douglas H. Ginsburg of the D.C. Court of Appeals, a former Harvard Law School professor.

On the surface, Kennedy seemed quite confirmable. Although he was a conservative judge with a strong law-and-order record, he had a reputation for pragmatism and relative moderation. He was Howard Baker's first choice and was flown to Washington on Wednesday, October 28, for interviews. He seemed set.

And he was, until Edwin Meese, who had been away, returned to Washington and got to work. According to Mitchell E. Daniels, a former White House political director, Reagan and Meese were looking for "someone close enough to Bork's philosophy to keep faith with his supporters but perhaps someone obscure enough to be immune from caricature."[49]

Ginsburg fit. An ardent free marketeer, he had written almost nothing outside economic regulation and antitrust, his specialties. Justice Department true believers were nevertheless sure he was "one of us," a "son of Bork," as Patrick Buchanan happily dubbed him. Ginsburg and Bork had voted alike in every case they sat on together. One judge on their court commented that Ginsburg followed Bork "like a Saint Bernard."[50]

Ginsburg was also Jewish, and according to one Administration official, there were early plans that this might be a selling point that would neutralize Jewish liberal opposition.[51]

And he was very young, perfect for the Administration's youth strategy. At only forty-one, he might serve forty years or more, into the second quarter of the twenty-first century.

In contrast with what Meese, Helms, and Meese's lieutenants William Bradford Reynolds and Charles Cooper seemed to know about Douglas Ginsburg, Judge Anthony Kennedy upset Helms and Hatch. Kennedy had indicated some sympathy for homosexuals fired by the Navy and had even suggested there might be a constitutional right to privacy for intimate relations.[52]

Reynolds set up shop in the White House and mobilized Helms, Hatch, Gordon Humphrey, and other ultraconservative senators for Ginsburg and against Kennedy. Helms responded by reportedly threatening to filibuster if Kennedy were nominated. "No way, José!" warned Helms. "I will publicly and privately and actively oppose the [Kennedy] nomination." The martyred Bork also got behind Ginsburg.[53]

Reagan was scheduled to announce the nomination on Thursday, October 29, at 2:00 P.M. At 10:30 A.M. the media were still sure it would be Kennedy. According to some reports, at 12:30 P.M. or so, Reagan decided on Ginsburg.

Within days the nomination began to crumble. Although opponents were cautious, questions were immediately raised about Ginsburg's inexperience. He had never practiced law, and he had been a judge for only a year, during which he sat on very few cases and wrote no important opinions. Also, his record was hardly distinguished enough to make up for his lack of experience. Unlike William O. Douglas, who had been chosen for the Court at age forty, but had been chairman of the SEC and elected dean of the Yale Law School by then, Ginsburg had briefly held only three middle-level jobs in the Reagan Administration and had not been a particularly distinguished scholar at Harvard.

The very lack of a record that had commended Ginsburg to Reagan also created problems. What was there about this man that so pleased Helms, Meese, and Bork? Would senators be willing to take a chance on a question mark? A questionnaire Ginsburg had filled out when up for his Court of Appeals judgeship provided some of the answers. In it he indicated he shared both Bork's original-intent views and his opposition to ready access to the federal courts for people protesting official abuse.[54]

A particularly telling revelation of Ginsburg's overall philosophy was in his answer to a question asking what he had done to show his "concern for equal justice under the law." He responded that he had taught and acted on the conviction that the law should not exclude anyone from trading in a free market, unfettered by government regulation on behalf of "special interests." Racial injustice, sexism, poverty—these apparently played no role in his thinking about justice, but only the opportunity to make money without government interference.[55]

In addition, Ginsburg's ethical sense seemed blunted. Three days after his nomination, it came out that while briefly heading the Antitrust Division, he had actively participated in at least three cable regulation matters even though he owned almost $140,000 worth of stock in a cable company. He had also grossly exaggerated his court experience on his Court of Appeals questionnaire—he had only argued one case, not thirty-four, as he said. The day after he withdrew, *The New York Times* also reported that he had sat as a judge on a case involving action he had taken while an administrator.[56]

Ginsburg's record at the Office of Management and Budget, where he apparently blocked safety regulations, was also a potential source of trouble. In one case a federal court had branded his behavior as illegal.[57]

And Jewish groups were offended by suggestions that they would be reluctant to oppose him because of Ginsburg's being Jewish.[58]

Rumblings also came from the ABA. Because of his inexperience, it had given Ginsburg only a "qualified" rating when he had come up for his Court of Appeals judgeship the year before, despite a cursory investigation, and there was no reason to think he would do better this time. In early November it was reported that the committee was "poised to deliver yet another blow: a split decision on Ginsburg's credentials for the Court."[59]

All of this was ammunition for his natural opponents on the left. But none of it mattered, for it was his natural allies on the right who did him in. And ironically, it was because of events that were almost inevitable, given the very youthfulness for which he was chosen.

A week after Ginsburg was nominated, on Thursday, November 5, National Public Radio reported Ginsburg had smoked marijuana several times, most recently in 1979 while a law professor.

Conservative senators were stunned and outraged. The Reagan Administration, particularly Mrs. Reagan, was on an antidrug crusade. "Just say no," she urged at every opportunity.

The president's first instinct was to defend the nominee, as did Hatch, who was masterminding Ginsburg's Senate strategy. A "youthful indiscretion," Reagan called it, in marked contrast to his normally less tolerant judgment on those who had used drugs in the 1960s. The remark was also inconsistent with a Justice Department policy that barred the employment of anyone who had used drugs after college. To R. W. Apple, Jr., of *The New York Times,* it was "for Reagan, an old trap—rhetoric vs. reality." Other observers wondered how the prenomination investigation by the FBI could have missed so much.[60]

On Friday, November 6, Secretary of Education William J. Bennett, one of the most conservative members of the Administration and an ardent antidrug crusader, asked Reagan whether he could urge Ginsburg to withdraw. Despite Reagan's public show of support for his nominee, Reagan did not say no. Bennett took it as approval and telephoned Ginsburg. The nominee was reported to be "not inclined" to quit. The pressure from the right was too great, however. On Saturday, nine days after the nomination was announced, he withdrew.

In the aftermath, some wondered whether Ginsburg had been pressured to withdraw because at least some conservatives had concluded he was not confirmable and the losing battle would take so long that Reagan would not be able to get another nomination through.

Ginsburg's supporters, however, were very angry. Hatch, who had fought strenuously for Ginsburg, condemned the "gutless wonders" at the White House for not supporting the nominee. Meese denied any responsibility for the selection of Ginsburg, saying it was the president's choice. Reagan denied having anything to do with Bennett's telephone call. And conservatives were bitter. "It's just amazing to contemplate," lamented Michael P. McDonald, an official of the Washington Legal Foundation. "We were so close to locking in a conservative majority in the Court into the next century."[61]

The last word belongs to *The Wall Street Journal.* Under the headline "The Ginsburg Marijuana Mudball," the *Journal* bitterly condemned those at Harvard who had breached Ginsburg's "privacy" by revealing his drug use when asked, and concluded: "Washington, D.C. is a city of lying in the gutter, wallowing in hypocrisy. It has become a bizarre sinkhole of character assassination and smirking self-righteousness. It will eagerly cast not only the first stone, but any other rocks it can lay its hands on."[62]

How the Babylon of the Potomac wound up responsible for the conservative reaction to Ginsburg's indiscretions was not made clear.*

Fearful that further delay might jeopardize his chance to get someone on the Court, on November 11, four days after Douglas Ginsburg withdrew, a chastened president announced he would nominate Anthony Kennedy, saying, "The experience of the last several months has made all of us a bit wiser." And in response to a suggestion that Meese had "blown" Ginsburg's background investigation, Reagan snapped, "He didn't blow the last one," wrapped his arm around Meese, and strode from the room.[63]

At this writing, Anthony Kennedy still is an unknown quantity. Clearly he is a conservative judge, particularly in criminal justice. His rulings in a number of race and sex discrimination cases also show an insensitivity in these areas, though he seemed to support some affirmative action programs. His views, if he has any, on other controversial issues such as abortion, privacy, church-state, economic regulation, and executive power are largely unknown.

---

*That wasn't quite the last word. Shortly after Ginsburg withdrew, the Justice Department opened an inquiry into the legality of the possible conflict of interest involving his cable activities and stock holdings, which could result in the appointment of a special prosecutor. The Department cleared him in February 1988.

Though his speeches show grave doubts about the use of judicial power, he does not seem to be an ideological crusader like Bork and Ginsburg.[64]

The Judiciary Committee, pleased that Kennedy did not come across as an ideological zealot, and fearful of another nasty fight, "played pattycake with him," in Joseph Rauh's words, and asked him very few probing questions. It also scheduled the hearings to take place very early, before much work could be done on his record. On February 3, 1988, Kennedy was unanimously confirmed.[65]

And Bernard Siegan? That battle was for 1988.[66]

9
The Impact of the Conservative Court-Packing Campaign

The President has done exceedingly well at the appellate level and fairly well at the district level.

James McClellan

By December 31, 1987, President Reagan had appointed 76 court of appeals judges out of 168 authorized appellate positions, and had 9 more pending; he had appointed 258 district court judges out of the 575 authorized, with 19 more pending. Of the 334 appointments, 28 were women and 20 were black, Hispanic or Asian-American.[1]

What difference has this spate of ideological appointments made? Are the Reagan judges far more conservative than others? Have they been able at least to begin the conservative revolution in the courts? Have there been any other consequences from this kind of appointment?

Answers to these questions at this time are not easy. A fundamental shift in judicial direction can come only from the Supreme Court, and until the Powell retirement provided an opportunity for such a change, that had not happened. If anything, the 1986–87 term was one of the Court's more liberal years because of Justice Powell's votes on affirmative action and church-state issues. At this writing, Justice Antonin Scalia has been there but one full year, and though he sided with Chief Justice Rehnquist in some 87 percent of the cases that year, Chief Justice Burger, whom Scalia replaced, voted with Rehnquist at about the same rate during his last few years on the Court. Justice O'Connor seems to be to the right of her predecessor, Justice Potter Stewart, at least judging by their relation to Rehnquist: O'Connor has lined up with Rehnquist about 86 percent of the time during her first six years, whereas Stewart was with Rehnquist an average of only 60 to 65 percent. But on such issues as women's rights, O'Connor is actually less conservative, though on abortion and the rights of criminal defendants, much more so. In any event, the change to O'Connor from Stewart has not made much of a difference. If, as some suggest, Justice Kennedy is somewhat to the right of Justice Powell, then that change will also make just a marginal difference.

Ronald Reagan has thus failed in his desire to be the president who pushes the Supreme Court to the far right, despite the opportunity to replace three members of the Court, including two moderate conservatives. The immediate effect of his three Supreme Court additions may be only a marginal shift to the right.

Reagan has, however, ensured that for some time to come it will be very difficult to move the Court substantially to the left, even if future appointments are made by Democratic presidents. Unless all future appointments are quite liberal—an unlikely prospect, in light of history, even if it is a Democratic president who replaces the older justices—there will be a hard core of four quite conservative justices to block a significant tilt to the left. And, as will be discussed more fully below, if a Republican wins the White House in 1988, that president will be able to add justices who are like Scalia and Rehnquist and will move the Court much farther to the right than the Reagan appointees could.

On the trial court level, the differences so far do not seem great, partly because many of the likely changes are in the fact-finding and management of specific trials, and such matters take time to become noticeable. Civil rights lawyers have complained about some Reagan judges and been pleasantly surprised by others, which is true for the judges selected by most presidents.

Moreover, despite the White House's effort to control the choices, continuing senatorial and other influences have often forced district court nominations quite different from the kind the Administration would have liked. New Jersey Governor Thomas Kean's choice, Judge Joseph Rodriguez of New Jersey, was certainly not Edwin Meese's idea of an ideal judge, nor is William Dwyer, on whom Senator Dan Evans insisted.

The most significant changes are at the Courts of Appeals, where law is made for blocs of states by "regional Supreme Courts" and where the Administration has had the freest hand. It is here that the truly ideological appointments have been made, with special emphasis on ideologues and law professors like Robert Bork, Alex Kozinski, Richard Posner, Laurence Silberman, Stephen Williams, Daniel Manion, Frank Easterbrook, Douglas Ginsburg, and Pasco Bowman. And it is on this level, too, that as of December 1987, Reagan appointees had become a majority on many of the circuits—the Second Circuit in New York, the Sixth and Seventh in the Midwest, and the Washington, D.C., Circuit—and were near a majority elsewhere. Together with Nixon-Ford appointees, on most Courts of Appeals, the conservatives were in command.

Obviously, the decisions of these judges have not been uniformly hostile to individual rights. Obedience to the Supreme Court or strong circuit precedent, regardless of unhappiness with these decisions, and even the judges' own beliefs or their objective legal analysis have sometimes produced surprisingly liberal results. Ralph Winter in New York, for example, has been relatively sympathetic to criminal defendants, and Posner has not tried to reduce access to the courts with standing and similar devices. Also, some of the decisions against individual rights were legally sound, for neither the Constitution nor other law provides a remedy for all the world's ills and injustices, and judges do not have a roving commission to right every wrong.

But many of these new judges have ignored precedent or unambiguous law, or, when choices were available, have chosen the side of authority in order to reject a claim that rights were violated. Creating and expanding court-shutting devices like standing, government immunity to suit, and political questions, rewriting the antitrust laws to virtually eliminate concern about economic concentration and the preservation of small business, and narrowly interpreting Supreme Court precedent have been among the most common techniques. In the process, these judges have transformed at least two of the circuits—the Seventh and the District of Columbia—into forums hostile to civil rights or civil liberties claimants.

Some observers have already concluded, however, that the court-packing campaign has had no effect. *U.S. News & World Report* wrote in February 1987 that "Reagan's Court revolution [had] come up short. The President's judges were supposed to advance a right-wing agenda [but] instead they've often stymied conservativism." The magazine noted that abortion restrictions, silent prayer, anti-pornography laws, and mandatory drug-testing programs have all been struck down by Reagan appointees. And though most of these decisions were by district judges, where ideological purity in choosing judges has been enforced much less, two academic studies of rulings by Courts of Appeals judges also try to minimize the impact. Both studies conclude that most Reagan appointees are no more conservative than other Republican appointees, who are, however, more conservative than Democratic judges.[2]

These studies are premature. One analysis, by a political scientist, was of the 1981–84 period, and the other, by a *Columbia Law Review* team, is of 1985–86. The conservative court-packing campaign did not really get under way until mid-1985, however, after the creation of the 85 new judgeships. Before then, Reagan had appointed relatively few of the approximately 85 to 90 appellate judges he could be expected to name; during his first term he appointed only 31. By December 31, 1987, he had appointed an additional 45, or a total of 76 of the 168 authorized appellate judges, with 9 more pending. It was not until mid- to late 1985 that most of the ideologically chosen judges were appointed; four of the six current Reagan appointees on the District of Columbia Circuit did not join the court until November 1985. Since appeals court judges usually do not begin to issue opinions until about four to six months after they are appointed, very few opinions by these judges were included in these studies.*

Furthermore, two specific findings in the Columbia study actually showed a very real impact. First, the study found that in discrimination cases, the Reagan appointees were significantly more conservative than other Republican appointees. With respect to cases involving government benefits such as Social Security and disability payments, and in government regulation, Reagan judges were also more conservative, but the cases were too few for statistical significance.†[3]

The Columbia study also found that although most Reagan appellate judges voted like other Republican appointees (except for the areas mentioned), four of the strongly ideological judges in-

---

*The Columbia study is limited to the nonunanimous appellate decisions. This also understates the impact of the Reagan appointees, for there is no reason to think these judges would promote their views any less vigorously in unanimous opinions than where they have only a majority.

Also, the studies cannot consider the principle of law that is being applied, for they deal only with outcomes. Posner, Bork, Scalia, and others have frequently written in very far-reaching terms when they had a majority or unanimity as to outcome. In the antitrust case discussed earlier, the court was unanimous as to the result, but Bork rewrote the antitrust principles in defiance of precedent, drawing a protest from Judge Wald, who concurred in the result but refused to join in the opinion. This case would not get into the study. In a nonunanimous case that was included, Bork rewrote public utility law on behalf of stockholders against consumers.

Concurring opinions are also omitted from consideration, and these often show very radical departures from established principles. Of Bork's 136 Court of Appeals opinions, 25 were concurrences, many of which called for major changes in the law.

On the other hand, outcome statistics may somewhat overstate the differences. In some cases, all the judges in a divided court may agree on the governing law, but they may disagree on the facts or on how the law is to be applied in that case.

†The other study found that during an eighteen-month period from July 1983 through December 31, 1984, Reagan appointees were marginally more conservative in civil liberties and civil rights cases, though the differences were very small. And a third study found more conservatism among Reagan appointees in criminal appeal cases, and more in sex discrimination at the trial level.

cluded in the study—Bork, Easterbrook, Scalia, and Winter—had much more conservative records than the other Republicans. "As a group," noted the study, "Judges Scalia, Bork, Easterbrook, and Winter voted on the liberal side of the case only 12 percent of the time, far less than the 34 percent rate for the rest of the Reagan judges and the 35 percent rate for the other GOP appointees." Bork, for example, voted on the conservative side almost 90 percent of the time, in contrast with the overall Republican average of 65 percent. These four judges are more typical of the many appointed in 1985–87, when the ideological campaign was intensified.[4]

Apart from measurable factors, there are also more subtle influences. A judge who is locked into a minority on a circuit must limit his disagreements in order to avoid being written off as an automatic dissenter. A minority judge may even refrain from dissenting at all in a case, even though he disagrees. For the same reason, a minority judge who is writing for a panel majority favoring a civil rights plaintiff or a criminal defendant must write quite narrowly. Otherwise the judge may lose the panel majority, or the case may be *en banced*—that is, reheard by the full court. Many cases in the District of Columbia Circuit were *en banced* because the conservative majority on the circuit led by Judge Bork was unhappy with the decision, and there are indications that this is happening in other circuits as well.

To assess the actual impact on the law, it is necessary to make qualitative studies of the developing law in the circuit in certain crucial areas and of the rulings of specific judges. The importance of the first is obvious. The second is important, because even if the overall circuit has not shifted, a litigant still may be faced with a hostile panel.

Although almost no systematic studies of the first kind have been made, a preliminary study of the performance of individual Reagan appointees by ultraconservative James McClellan's Center for Judicial Studies was made in 1984, and it indicates a shift to the right. Craig Stern, author of the study, analyzed all decisions by Reagan appointees during the first two years of the Reagan Administration for conformity to the letter and spirit of the Republican Platform of 1980. The results were surprisingly consistent:

> President Reagan's appointments are redefining the role of the Federal Judiciary . . . the President has, in general, kept his pledge to appoint men and women to the bench who exercise restraint.

> Of the sixty-two judges evaluated in this study under the standards specified [adherence to the Republican Platform of 1980] . . . thirty-one judges exercised restraint in all of their significant cases without exception . . . sixteen exercised restraint in nearly all their significant opinions . . . nine . . . exercised restraint in no more than half of their significant cases . . . and six published no [pertinent] opinions. . . . The conclusion is inescapable that the Reagan judiciary, so far, has lived up to expectations.[5]

Although the language for "the standards specified" was of "restraint," what Stern discussed and commended was the dismissal of any kind of statutory and constitutional challenge to public or private authority, such as suits by Medicare patients whose funding was terminated without a hearing, by public assistance claimants, by handicapped people, by antitrust plaintiffs, and by anyone suing under a Civil Rights Act provision.

The study was, of course, very early. But it did try to analyze every one of the early rulings by the initial Reagan appointees, and it is at least suggestive of their inclinations.

More intensive studies have been done of the early Reagan appellate choices, particularly Bork, Scalia, and Posner, the first two because of their nomination to the Supreme Court, and Posner because of his patently extreme views and his astonishingly prolific pen—he averaged ninety opinions a year, far above the average.

Bork's record has already been discussed. Posner's and Scalia's are different only in emphasis.

Richard A. Posner

Whereas Bork focused on shutting the courthouse door—partly because such issues often arise in litigation against the federal gov-

156

ernment, a staple of the D.C. Circuit's case load—Posner seemed quite uninterested in such arguments. He concentrated instead on antitrust and similar economic issues, the kind Bork rarely got a chance to deal with. In this area Posner went at the law with a zeal that even a sympathetic corporate lawyer described as "almost religious," marked by the absence of "a judicial and restrained approach to finding the law." About one Posner opinion, the lawyer commented, "Judge Posner is too much of a legal scholar to believe that the opinion is a judicial and restrained approach to finding the law as opposed to getting it to where he is convinced it should be—without delay."[6]

Posner's basic idea, as one expert put it, was to "narrowly construe the antitrust laws" to allow a great deal of anticompetitive behavior, and to get around inconsistent Supreme Court decisions. In 1986 a group of twenty-one state attorneys general attacked Posner and the Seventh Circuit for ignoring Supreme Court rulings and condoning such practices as allowing competitors to form group boycotts designed to exclude other competitors; permitting a manufacturer to prohibit advertising price reductions; and allowing a manufacturer to insist that if a customer wanted a very desirable product, the customer had to take a second and less desirable item.[7]

Antitrust law was not the only arena in which Posner justified the conservatives' pleasure at his appointment. His opinion that prisoners who are injured by prison doctors should look for a lawyer in the open market without assistance from the court has already been discussed. He called for changes in the law of habeas corpus, which allows state prisoners to go to federal court to challenge their convictions on constitutional grounds, a call in which Easterbrook joined. With the concurrence of another Reagan appointee and over a vigorous dissent, he overturned a district judge's ruling against a high school basketball association rule that prevented Jewish players from wearing *yarmulkes,* even though the district court found that the skullcaps created no safety hazard; Posner required the Jewish ballplayers to come up with alternative headgear even though the basketball association had made it clear that its "no headgear" rule was quite absolute.[8]

Antonin Scalia

Both on the D.C. Court of Appeals and on the Supreme Court, Scalia has vindicated Reagan's faith in his conservatism. On the Supreme Court he was in a three-justice minority with Rehnquist and White in the March 1987 decision that allowed voluntary affirmative action for traditionally segregated jobs, and he wrote a blistering dissent. He was in a two-member minority with Rehnquist on a case in which the Court ruled that a Louisiana statute that required the teaching of "creationism" if evolution were taught was religiously motivated and therefore violated the First and Fourteenth amendments to the Constitution. In the seven 1986–87 cases in which the Court invalidated official action because it conflicted with the First Amendment, Scalia dissented vigorously in three. In both the creationism and affirmative action cases, as in at least three others during his first year on the Supreme Court, he showed little deference to precedent, explicitly urging the Court to overrule or reexamine five solidly established doctrines, one of which went back as much as thirty-seven years, and another, the affirmative action case, has been relied on by hundreds of thousands of employers.[9]

On the Court of Appeals, he had consistently voted with Bork to reduce access to the courts. Scalia developed some restrictive notions of his own, particularly in limiting the right to challenge action by regulatory agencies. He rarely voted in favor of the press or for any other First Amendment claim. Instead, he joined in a decision that condemned the *Washington Post* for its vigorous investigative reporting of alleged nepotism by the president of Mobil Oil Company, and upheld a $2 million libel judgment against the paper; the *Post* ultimately won that case, over Scalia's dissent. In another case, he read Supreme Court precedent in the narrowest way possible in order to deny journalists access to certain documents.[10]

Scalia showed himself especially deferential to executive power at the expense of the other two branches, both in the decision striking down the Gramm-Rudman-Hollings Budget Act (he is thought to have written the opinion in that decision) and elsewhere. And he continually ruled against blacks and women who claimed they were discriminated against; in case after case, often in dissent, he refused to find that illegal discrimination had been proven.[11]

For most of the other ideological appointments, there are relatively few opinions to consider because all these appointments are recent and the record is thin. Nevertheless, some signs of these judges' predispositions are available, although it is still too early to discern more than tendencies.

J. Harvey Wilkinson

"Conservatives couldn't be happier with Judge Wilkinson," concluded *The Wall Street Journal,* in February 1988. "He's as good as we anticipated he would be," rejoiced William Bradford Reynolds.

And no wonder. In one split decision in July 1987, for example, Wilkinson used the 1984 Supreme Court decision that struck down an affirmative action employment plan because it called for layoffs, to kill a Richmond City plan that set aside 30 percent of municipal construction contracts for minority businesses. The dissenting judge pointed out that the City Council had evidence before it that between 1978 and 1983, only two thirds of 1 percent of past city contracts had gone to minorities, and that, as one city councilman put it, "the general conduct in the construction industry in this area, and the State and across the nation, is one in which race discrimination . . . is widespread," a point disputed by no one at the hearing, noted by the Supreme Court in another case, and virtually beyond dispute. The Supreme Court has agreed to review the case. Wilkinson has also favored the prosecution in criminal cases and usually opposes civil rights claimants.[12]

On the other hand, Wilkinson tried to have the full Fourth Circuit rehear a case in which Larry Flynt was ordered to pay damages to Jerry Falwell for invading his right to "privacy." *Hustler* magazine did a parody of a Campari Liqueur ad in which Falwell allegedly committed incest with his mother as his "first time." Except for Wilkinson, the circuit lined up on ideological lines. Some observers have suggested that Wilkinson's eloquent concern for First Amend-

159

ment values resulted from his three years as editor of the *Norfolk Virginian-Pilot.* The Supreme Court unanimously agreed with Wilkinson.[13]

Frank Easterbrook

Easterbrook has been on the Seventh Circuit since only the spring of 1985, but during that time he has established himself as a brilliant manipulator of legal doctrine, usually to keep litigants from suing public officials.

In a prison case, where a prisoner was kept in solitary confinement for 289 days because his Muslim religious beliefs kept him from handling dishes on which pork had been served, Easterbrook not only wanted to rule against the prisoner but also to open up and overrule rulings in the case made eight years earlier and not even challenged by the prison administrators.[14]

In another case, Easterbrook was willing to allow Social Security Administration judges who ruled against beneficiaries to refuse to make specific fact findings, even though this was required by the statute; other members of the court refused to go along with him. And in still other cases he tried to create procedural barriers against Social Security recipients and others claiming government benefits.[15]

Easterbrook has also tried to protect local governments against someone beaten up by the police, by narrowly defining "excessive force." One commentator concluded that Easterbrook was "as 'result-oriented,' 'unprincipled,' and 'nonneutral' as the liberals he and his colleagues have so often criticized on these very grounds."[16]

Alex Kozinski

Affirmative action was a target not only for Wilkinson but also for Alex Kozinski in California. In a case involving a system of preferences in municipal contracts created by the San Francisco Board of Supervisors for minority (10 percent), female (2 percent), and local businesses, Kozinski applied a very restrictive interpretation of the

Supreme Court's racial preference cases to strike down the minority preferences, though he upheld the other two. Even though he admitted that the city had made a very careful analysis of the problem and that no witnesses had spoken against the preferences, he concluded there had been no finding of prior discrimination by the board, a prerequisite to such relief, despite lower court findings and evidence to the contrary. He, together with another Reagan appointee and a conservative Carter judge, nullified the ordinance and reversed the lower court, which had upheld the plan.

Robert L. Harris, attorney for the San Francisco Black Chamber of Commerce, commented, "San Francisco's ordinance is a very mild one compared to others. If its ordinance is invalid, then there really is no hope for remedying the situation, and there's no way minority businesses can break into the system."[17]

Kozinski also seems to have ignored governing Supreme Court decisions in ruling that a 1984 Santa Barbara, California, regulation that controlled mobile home park rents might be what lawyers call a "taking," requiring the city to compensate the mobile home landlords for the reduced value. As three judges pointed out, at least three Supreme Court cases and numerous other courts had rejected rent regulation challenges, often without even bothering to hear arguments. Kozinski relied on a lone dissent by Rehnquist in a 1983 case that the Court had refused to hear "for lack of a substantial federal question."[18]

Kenneth Starr and Laurence Silberman

Judge Laurence Silberman of the D.C. Circuit quickly established himself as one of the most zealous ideological appointees, whereas Judge Kenneth Starr, an early appointee, was something of a centrist. On affirmative action, however, such distinctions vanish, and both took aim at it in a case reconsidered after the Supreme Court's 1987 rulings and decided in August 1987. In a 2–1 decision, with Judge Abner Mikva in angry dissent, the two Reagan appointees brushed aside substantial evidence of discrimination at the D.C. Fire Department and read the Supreme Court 1987 decisions upholding affirmative action very narrowly. They reversed the approval of a voluntarily adopted affirmative action hiring plan by a lower court judge, who had overridden an inherent hostility to race-conscious employment decisions—he struck down the promotional provisions—because he found the evidence of past hiring discrimination to be so strong.[19]

John Noonan

In a case growing out of California's Medfly problem, Terrence Allen, an entomologist employed by the California Department of Food and Agriculture, was removed from the Medfly Eradication Project after he publicly criticized the project management. A majority of the appellate court panel ruled that he was entitled to try to show that the removal was because of his criticisms, which were constitutionally protected. Reagan appointee Judge John Noonan read the preliminary papers in the case in such a way as to deny Allen the chance even to begin to prove his case, and would have thrown the case out immediately, even though, as the majority pointed out, the case turns on motivation, something that is notoriously difficult to prove until the parties have had a chance to examine each other's files.[20]

Stephen Williams

For over fourteen years, efforts had been made to compel the secretary of labor to issue standards for access to drinking water and toilets by several million farmworkers. As Chief Judge Patricia Wald of the D.C. Circuit wrote:

> The rulemaking record demonstrates beyond dispute that lack of drinking water and toilets causes the spread of contagion, bladder disease, and heat prostration among farmworkers. Yet resistance to issuing the standard, a counterpart of which is already in place for every other OSHA-covered type of employment, has been intracta-

ble. An arsenal of administrative law doctrines has provided the justification for ricocheting the case between the agency and the courts for over a decade: a decade in which field workers have gone without benefit of drinking water or the most rudimentary sanitary facilities.[21]

After many court battles, in 1979 the D.C. Court of Appeals insisted on some timetable for the rule. An agreement was reached for February 1985. In March 1984, however, the secretary of labor decided to review the matter again. A year later, in April 1985, he concluded that while a federal regulation was clearly necessary, out of concern for federalism, he would give the states still another chance. He therefore decided to delay the federal regulation for yet another two years.

Once again the farmworkers went back to court, but this time the court refused to allow any more delays. Pointing out that Congress had already decided that the federal government should take the lead because the states had failed to do so, the majority ruled that the secretary had no authority to postpone federal standards any further "simply because he would prefer state governments to take over the responsibility."

Reagan appointee Stephen Williams dissented. The fourteen-year delay apparently didn't bother him, nor did the fact that very few states seemed willing to adopt the necessary standards.

Obviously it is difficult to make definitive judgments about so subtle a matter as impact, for it is still very early. As Stephen Markman, who took over as the Justice Department's point man in judge-selection, said in May 1987, "It will take five to ten years before the full impact of the process is felt." That seems a bit pessimistic (or optimistic, depending on one's perspective), but the basic point is correct: It is still early, and at this writing, the single most important factor, the future direction of the Supreme Court, has not yet been decided.[22]

Furthermore, a large group of judges, even if all of them are appointed by the same president, will inevitably vary in outlook and activism on specific issues. There must be a certain critical mass of them, as well as the major shift at the Supreme Court level discussed earlier. This is why, as students of the 1930s found, "the overall liberalism score of the Roosevelt judges is not *radically greater* than the liberalism score of the justices appointed by Hoover, Coolidge and Harding."[23] It takes time.

But the trends are clear, and changes in the circuits have already taken place, particularly in those circuits like the D.C. Circuit and the Seventh, where ideologically selected judges together with other conservatives have a solid majority. "Shaping a circuit in the Chicago School image" is how the *National Law Journal* described what was happening to the Seventh Circuit. According to Chicago lawyers, by July 1987 Posner and Easterbrook were "increasingly . . . showing signs of dominating the court."[24]

In Washington, D.C., a local legal journal, the *Legal Times*, observed in May 1987 that "litigators [have] had to revamp their strategies to suit [the] 'Reaganized bench.' " "There definitely has been a new direction," said Rex Lee, Reagan's first solicitor general. Employment discrimination lawyers, for example, were filing all their suits in the local courts. Said one lawyer, "[T]he D.C. Circuit Court has swung in the past six years from being probably one of the most liberal courts in the country in the area of employment to now, more often than not, one of the most conservative." And that held for most other areas as well, especially environmental suits where the Reagan majority's new restrictions on access to the courts are excluding challenges to the Administration's laxer environmental policies.

As the *Legal Times* concluded: "While the Court has by no means given conservatives and the administration everything they want, the D.C. Circuit has moved far closer to the Reaganite ideal: hesitant to overrule administrative agencies, grant nontraditional plaintiffs standing, create new rights, and exercise its judicial powers."[25]

A comparison with another circuit is revealing. A survey of employment discrimination law in the Eleventh Circuit during 1985 found that plaintiffs frequently won. With respect to issues as diverse as theories of liability, burden of proof, and procedural rules, and in contexts as disparate as race, sex, age, and handicap discrimination, the appellate court frequently ruled for plaintiffs. A glance at the judicial roster gives at least one indication of why: There were no Reagan appointees on this court until May 1986.[26]

Another illustration of the difference between most of the Reagan appointees and others appears in a decision by the full Fifth Circuit, which covers Texas, Mississippi, and Louisiana. In that case, all but one of the Reagan judges joined in a decision rejecting a challenge to their deportation by Patricio and Maria Hernandez-Cordero and their children, a Mexican family who had lived in the country for twelve years and who were being expelled for illegal entry and overstaying their visa terms. The law allowed exceptions to deportation for people of good moral character who would suffer "extreme hardship" if deported. Everyone agreed that the Hernandez-Cordero family was of very good moral character and would suffer greatly if deported. The immigration authorities, however, had ruled that this did not constitute "extreme hardship."

Concluding that the Immigration Bureau authorities had virtually unfettered discretion in determining whether the deportees would be allowed to stay because of the "extreme hardship" provision, the majority, in an opinion by Reagan appointee W. Eugene Davis, allowed the deportation order to stand virtually without review.

The five dissenters, all but one a non-Reagan appointee, criticized the majority for its almost unmeetable criterion for "extreme hardship" and its readiness to abandon control of such vital decisions to low-level officials "in the depths of the bureaucracy. . . . The administration appraisal of the suffering that would be endured by this family was piecemeal, devoid of compassion and wrong," wrote one of the dissenters. The majority did not disagree, but that made no difference.[27]

There are other impacts from the conservative court-packing campaign, apart from the specific case outcomes and shifts in substantive and procedural law: the effects on how Americans perceive the courts and on the internal workings of the institution.

The conservative campaign to tilt the courts in a new direction is not illegitimate. Those in a position to produce such a tilt and think it necessary are constitutionally and otherwise entitled to do so.

Such a concentrated effort introduces an intensely partisan and divisive note into the selection process, however. Although partisan politics are inevitable to some extent, such considerations usually have played a very minor role in lower court appointments and only a slightly greater role in Supreme Court nominations. Senator Patrick Leahy of Vermont once said that "National Pickle Week has been as likely to generate spirited debate as the selection of a federal district or appellate judge with life tenure," and though that is far from an ideal situation, it means that less attention can be paid to partisan political and ideological considerations.[28]

The conservatives' crusade to pack the courts with ideological zealots has induced more rather then less partisanship. The name-calling, acrimony, and recriminations generated by the Bork, Manion, Ginsburg, Rehnquist, and other controversies are hardly consistent with the choice of men and women whose task it is, if confirmed, to do justice evenhandedly, without regard to friendship or party. Regardless of who is primarily responsible, such bitter conflict is inevitable when a very controversial nomination is made.

The effect on how the courts are perceived by the public and the bar is especially disturbing. It is not hard to imagine the uneasiness of a lawyer arguing a case before a judge whose appointment he publicly opposed, and the nervousness his client must feel. On the other side of the bench, it takes a remarkably mature and selfless person to forget who tried to deny him a highly coveted prize. Disqualification is a solution but hardly an ideal one.

The polarization that such controversies create can also make it more difficult for judges to work together, to seek common ground, and to narrow differences. It may harden positions that were far apart to begin with.

Finally, the determination with which the conservatives have pursued their goal of putting reliably staunch conservatives on the courts could well produce a mirror-image determination in a liberal administration. Such a reaction would be particularly understandable if there is widespread public support for such a move, as there was for FDR, except when he tried to tamper with the Supreme Court's independence. Roosevelt encountered no widespread public opposition to his efforts to appoint liberals in the normal course of events. This kind of action and reaction can only damage the courts even further.

All of this can impair the aura of objectivity and fairness on which the authority of our courts ultimately depends. That would be the gravest harm that the conservative court-packing would inflict.

10
The Future

The next presidential election could be one of the most important turning points for the Constitution in our history.

James McClellan

Whoever lives by the crystal ball soon learns to eat ground glass.
Laurence Tribe, Tyler Professor of Constitutional Law, Harvard Law School

CRITERIA FOR JUDICIAL APPOINTMENTS

What, then, are the appropriate criteria for the selection of judges? High intelligence, integrity, experience, distinguished credentials as a lawyer—these are the obvious standards on which everyone agrees, and are matters of fact that, when disputed, can be resolved by the record. The only point that needs to be emphasized is that on these matters the burden of proof is on the candidate to demonstrate that he or she has these traits. A candidate for a lifetime position on the federal judiciary is not entitled to a presumption in his or her favor on these matters.

The hard question is whether something more must exist. In particular, what articles of belief or philosophy must the nominee have, and who must show that? Are the criteria different for the president, who has the authority to nominate, than for the Senate, which must give "advice and consent"?

At the Supreme Court level, the answers are relatively easy. As discussed in Chapter 3, a president who has a vision of the Constitution has the right and indeed the duty to nominate candidates who will further that vision. If President Ronald Reagan did not think the Supreme Court's abortion and school prayer decisions were consistent with the Constitution, then just as President Franklin D. Roosevelt was authorized to nominate justices who would overturn the pre–New Deal Court's narrow vision of federal power over the economy, President Reagan was authorized to name justices who would overturn the abortion and school prayer decisions.

By the same token, and for the same reasons, a senator has the same obligation as the president to ensure that the nominee will further and not undermine the Constitution as the senator sees it. The respective roles of the president and the Senate in the appointment process are firmly established by the text of the Constitution as well as by two hundred years of history.

It is much more difficult to set criteria for lower court appointments. They have less power to innovate and to impose their views on the law than Supreme Court justices do. The overwhelming proportion of their cases, unlike those on the Supreme Court's docket, are noncontroversial. Their jurisdiction is not the whole nation but only a region and always subject to review, though the odds for such review are very low.

On a more practical level, senators play a greater role in choosing them, especially for the district courts, so that fellow senators are not inclined to give a nominee a hard time. Therefore, some think that setting standards for what views are acceptable is virtually impossible.

A few negative guideposts may, nevertheless, be available, qualities and ideas that a nominee should *not* have, drawn from the cases in which nominees have been rejected.

Perhaps most obvious is a lack of fair-mindedness and an unwillingness to listen. Although this criterion is not very specific when stated in the abstract, it was evidence that Michael Horowitz lacked such fair-mindedness that doomed his chances. Where such evidence does exist, it should disqualify a candidate.

Similarly, any sign of bias toward racial, ethnic, sexual, or other groups that are likely to come before the court in matters where group identity may be relevant should also eliminate a candidate. This was Jefferson Sessions's and G. Harrold Carswell's fatal flaw.

Related to this as a disqualifier is a demonstrated and active hostility to generally recognized rights, such as the right to vote. If proven, the charges that Chief Justice William H. Rehnquist tried to intimidate Hispanic voters in Phoenix, Arizona, in the early 1960s and that Judge Sid Fitzwater tried to frighten black voters in Dallas in 1982 should have doomed their nominations.

Beyond these negative criteria is a criterion that might be called part of the job description, one that flows from the very nature of the federal courts in our society, and indeed, to an increasing extent, in every free society: a belief that the federal courts have the responsibility and authority to protect and promote the rights of individuals and minorities. As Justice Lewis Powell once put it, "the irreplaceable value of [judicial review by the federal courts] lies in the protection it has afforded the constitutional rights and liberties of individual citizens and minority groups against oppressive or discriminatory government action." That is why the Bill of Rights was added to the Constitution—to protect individual rights "by the legal check which it puts into the hands of the judiciary," in Thomas Jefferson's words. If a nominee believes that the federal courts have only a negligible or a minor role to play in this task, then the job is not for him or her. This is one of the main reasons Robert Bork was rejected by so overwhelming a vote.[1]

Obviously this doesn't mean that a nominee must agree with every prior ruling favoring individual rights. A nominee need not approve the rule excluding illegally obtained evidence, but he or she must show a recognition that the Constitution puts a great value on privacy. A nominee need not think *Roe* v. *Wade* was properly decided, but there must be a recognition that the Constitution protects a right of intimate relationships, of marital and other privacy. There must be an acceptance of the fundamental proposition that state officials are bound by the Bill of Rights, even though there can be differences as to specifics. There must be a recognition that free speech is fundamental to any free society and that any restriction on speech must meet a heavy burden.

Nor is it enough that the nominee gives lip service to these principles at the confirmation hearing. There should be a demonstration that the nominee is committed to them. The nominee need not have marched in civil rights demonstrations, nor worked for a civil liberties group, but he or she must have done something to try to combat injustice, whether through service on a legal aid board or some free *pro bono* work for those who could not otherwise afford a lawyer.

There should be nothing startling about this latter requirement. Even the questionnaire used by Strom Thurmond's Judiciary Committee asked, "What actions in your professional life evidence your concern for equal justice under the law?"

Judge Robert Bork's answer in 1981, when nominated to the Court of Appeals, was as follows:

> Equal justice under the law is the general phrase used to describe the rule of law and the requirement that the law's distinctions not treat as different persons and things which are alike. I believe that any lawyer—whether in the capacity of legislator, judge, practitioner, or scholar—who formulates his viewpoints with intellectual honesty and who applies legal principles consistently and without favoritism evinces a concern for equal justice under law. To allow personal feeling for or against a party to vary the operation of the law is the antithesis of equal justice. I have attempted to follow these principles in my career in government, as a teacher, and in practice.[2]

This response is clearly inadequate. It is very rare that someone with a real "concern for equal justice" can live fifty-four years and have nothing more to answer than this.

Judge Douglas Ginsburg's answer is just as unsatisfactory. As noted earlier, in 1986 he gave this statement to the committee, as evidence of how his actions "evidence [his] concern for equal justice under the law":

> I have taught and acted upon my deep conviction that in a democracy such as ours the law should not be used to exclude would-be participants from entering markets,

> pursuing their trade, and competing to serve consumers and thereby to gain a place of respect in the economy and our society. The effort to eliminate unnecessary economic regulation, to which I have contributed both as an academic and as a government official is, in my view, preeminently intended to restore the principle of equal justice under law where it has been driven out by special interests with disproportionate influence over the apparatus of the state.[3]

No comment seems necessary.

The absence from a nominee's life and career of any actions that really further equal justice should be a disqualification, for it shows a lack of commitment to one of the primary functions of a federal court: to afford "protection . . . [for] the constitutional rights and liberties of individual citizens and minority groups." In the words of conservative senator Howell Heflin, for a nominee to be confirmed he or she must demonstrate "a passionate love of justice, the great cement of a civilized society, the guardian of all life and liberty." If there is no sign of any concern about injustice, a basic prerequisite for the job has not been met.[4]

The other side of the coin is also important, though its predictability is very difficult: The nominee should not consider the judicial commission a mandate or permit to ignore established law, precedent, and the limitations of the judicial function. The line between adjudication and legislation is often thin and even invisible. Over 250 years ago, a Bishop Hoadly in England sermonized that "whoever hath an absolute authority to interpret any written or spoken laws . . . is truly the lawgiver. . . ." But there are limits imposed by logic, precedent, and the imperatives of democracy that assign primary policymaking authority to the elected branches and require self-discipline and self-restraint on the part of so unaccountable a branch of government as the judiciary. In Judge Learned Hand's words, the judge "must not enforce whatever he thinks best, he must leave that to the common will expressed by the government." Whether this requirement is enforceable at the nomination stage is another matter, but where there is a track record, as with a lower court judge nominated for higher judicial office, it should play a role.[5]

The best criteria mean little, however, unless the screening improves. The Douglas Ginsburg and Daniel Manion nominations show how poor the screen is, even with respect to nonideological matters like competence and integrity. The ABA is supposed to focus on competence, but it failed dismally in this regard where Manion was concerned, for it was left to a private group, People for the American Way, to come up with the briefs and memoranda that demonstrated his weakness.

And why, at both the Court of Appeals and Supreme Court level, did neither the FBI nor the Judiciary Committee discover Ginsburg's quite frequent marijuana use? The possible conflict of interests revealed on the face of his Court of Appeals questionnaire, where he listed both his cable TV stock holdings and his participation in a major cable TV case in the Supreme Court? And why did no one point up the inherent implausibility of his claim, on the face of this same questionnaire, that he had "tried to judgment and verdict" thirty-four cases during his two years at the Justice Department? It was not hard to discover that he had appeared in court only once during those two years. As *Legal Times* commentator Kenneth Jost observed, "It is remarkable that a lifetime seat on the federal bench can be gained with only limited review of the nominee's background," especially on a court that is generally considered second only to the Supreme Court in importance.[6]

Common Cause has suggested that the Senate Judiciary Committee enlarge its investigative staff and devote more time for committee review; obtain more detailed information from the ABA, including the basis for its evaluations; give prompt and adequate notice to outside groups; limit the number of nominees considered at a single hearing; and share responsibility among more senators for monitoring the nominees.[7]

Though these suggestions obviously have a good deal of merit, even they will not help if the committee majority sees its role as a rubber stamp for the Justice Department, as the committee did when Strom Thurmond was chairman.

Apart from the committee there are few effective screens. The

Justice Department obviously cannot be trusted when it is eager to push a nominee. The ABA committee has lost credibility by its performance in the Manion nomination as well as its reliance on confidential information and secret processes. The ABA also is fearful of antagonizing whatever administration is in office by being too aggressive, for that might jeopardize the committee's favored role in the selection process.

Legal Times commentator Jost has suggested forming an independent commission to evaluate competence, integrity, experience, and other nonideological considerations. It is a useful idea but impractical, for it will almost certainly be opposed by all the present participants in the process.[8]

For the near future, therefore, the Common Cause suggestions seem the most realistic and could do some good, especially if the Judiciary Committee minority is provided adequate time and resources.

THE FUTURE OF THE FEDERAL COURTS

The future of the federal judiciary will be determined by the outcome of the 1988 presidential election. If a Republican is elected president, and if he chooses justices the way President Reagan has tried to do, then the probability that the Supreme Court and the lower courts will continue to promote individual rights vigorously is almost nil, now and for many decades to come. The Burger Court's pragmatic conservatism is no precedent, for there may be no liberal or even centrist bloc to offset the conservatives and force moderation.

And it is very likely that a future Republican president will in fact appoint judges like those that Reagan has tried to nominate, especially to the Supreme Court. He or she will have to, because of the right's continued dominance of the national Republican Party.

That dominance, and with it the effort to tilt the courts to the far right, did not begin with Ronald Reagan, and it will not end with him. It responds to powerful political and social forces: those who have never forgiven the Supreme Court for *Brown* v. *Board of Education*

174

and all that flowed from it; the religious fundamentalists who see the Court as the "secular humanist" incarnation of the anti-Christ; the anti-abortion groups and individuals who believe the Court is condoning murder; the many others of an authoritarian cast who believe the Court's effort in the past thirty-five to forty years to provide more protection for the individual against the state is fundamentally and dangerously misguided.

These groups have played a dominant role in Republican politics ever since 1964, when Barry Goldwater won the Republican nomination for president and the moderately liberal Nelson W. Rockefeller was booed by the Republican National Convention. To get the Republican nomination and to ensure enthusiastic support and effort in the general election, Republican presidential candidates, formerly considered politically moderate, have therefore bent themselves out of shape to woo the right, to make up for past sins, and to remove all doubt as to their conservative purity. In 1987, for example, Robert Dole, the Senate minority leader, joined Jesse Helms in a shameful attack on the State Department by refusing to confirm a nomination for ambassador to Mozambique because Helms wanted to support a murderous terrorist rebellion against the Marxist government, even though the Administration supported that government, and Dole was the Administration's point man in the Senate. George Bush's embarrassing self-debasement and posturing for the far right are too well known to need discussion. The pressure from the right is so strong that when the Republican Mainstream Committee, a moderate Republican group, invited the party's presidential candidates to address it, only Pierre du Pont IV showed up, and he lectured them on the group's heresy. And at this writing (February 1988), the Pat Robertson bid for the Republican presidential nomination has also pushed the Republican candidates to the right, as has the conservative bitterness over the Bork and Ginsburg defeats.[9]

In order to govern, however, a Republican president, even one as "right-minded" as Reagan, must disappoint the true-believing conservatives, whether as a matter of policy, as with arms control, Central American policy, trade and other agreements with the "evil empire," and domestic measures like catastrophic-illness health insurance or taxes, or because he cannot deliver what they want, such as constitutional amendments or legislation on abortion, school prayer, affirmative action, and busing. Howard Phillips's furious outburst that Reagan was a "useful idiot for Soviet propaganda" for signing the Intermediate-Range Nuclear Forces Treaty is obviously extreme, but it accurately reflects the ultraconservatives' bitterness at their hero's betrayal in dealing with the "evil empire." Even so loyal a solicitor general as Charles Fried, who antagonized the Court by his aggressiveness on behalf of the Administration's social agenda, has disappointed James McClellan. And when Reagan initially tried to depict Robert Bork as a moderate centrist, solely for tactical reasons, Washington Legal Foundation head Daniel Popeo exploded that "the problem is the White House doesn't want to approach this as an ideological contest." Popeo, Richard Viguerie, and their friends blame Bork's defeat on Howard Baker because he tried to sell the nominee as a moderate conservative and not for what he really was.[10]

The one thing a president can do for these supporters—and this will ultimately be just as effective on the social issues—is to give them the judges they want. It is no accident that Moral Majority leader Rev. Jerry Falwell hailed the Bork nomination, saying, "We are standing at the edge of history." He knew that a Bork on the Court would move the Court to the right for decades to come.[11]

The 1988 election offers Falwell, Viguerie, Popeo, Robertson, and company another chance. If the Democrats lose the presidency again, they probably will not be able to stop such nominations, even if they retain control of the Senate, which is unlikely if they don't win the White House. Even in 1987, when the Democrats controlled the Senate, Reagan lost no lower court nominations. If they lose another presidential election, Senate Democrats will be too shell-shocked to offer much resistance to whoever is nominated.

Should the Supreme Court be reduced to relative insignificance, protection for individual rights would shift to Congress and to the state courts and legislatures. State legislative protection is spotty at best, usually ineffective, and often nonexistent. Many state legislatures have been dominated by very conservative elements.

A few state courts have looked to their own state constitutions to provide protection for civil rights and liberties that the federal courts have refused. This is particularly true for some protections for the criminally accused, and equalization of the amounts that states spend on school districts. But most state judges are elected and are fearful of the kind of hostile reaction at the polls that Chief Justice Rose Bird of California and two other colleagues encountered in California over capital punishment, which ejected them from office.

Congress can and has done much. Indeed, most of the law against discrimination is statutory. But both the stimulus and the primary guarantor of our rights, as Lewis Powell observed, is the Supreme Court. Also, what Congress does must be interpreted and applied by the courts, and conservative judges have not really limited their effort to roll back rights and liberties to constitutional questions. Frequently they have construed civil rights statutes very narrowly, and in some cases would even deny Congress the power to act. Judge Bork, for example, criticized the Court's decision upholding Congress's power under the Fourteenth Amendment to enact certain parts of the Voting Rights Act striking down English-language literacy tests in order to allow those educated in Puerto Rican schools to vote. Other judicial conservatives have interpreted "judicial restraint" to include narrow construction of civil rights statutes and other laws granting rights and benefits against official authority and private power.

Judicial review to preserve and advance individual rights is one of the glories of the American system of government. It has not, as some have suggested, impoverished political democracy. On the contrary, judicial rulings on behalf of individual rights have directly or indirectly stimulated much of the civil rights legislation on the books; they have certainly not discouraged such legislative initiatives.

Other countries have come to recognize this, and judicial review is being adopted throughout the world, even by many nations traditionally hostile to judicial power, such as France and Germany. Nations as different as India, Italy, Zimbabwe, Japan, Argentina, and the Philippines, to name but a few, have adopted some kind of judicial review of legislative and executive acts to ensure protection of constitutional rights. International courts like the European Court of Human Rights are imposing additional obligations to honor those rights, even on countries with a tradition of parliamentary supremacy, such as Great Britain. They have all come to realize what the framers of our Constitution understood and the American people continue to believe: A vigorous, independent judiciary is indispensible to a free society. It is no accident that dictators like Adolf Hitler, Augusto Pinochet in Chile, and Juan Perón in Argentina always move quickly to bring the judiciary under their control.[12]

In 1944, a year when freedom was still just a faint hope in much of the world, Judge Learned Hand addressed a group of new American citizens. "Liberty lies in the hearts of men and women," he told them. "When it dies there, no constitution, no law, no court can save it; no constitution, no law can even do much to help it. While it lies there, it needs no constitution, no law, no court to save it."[13]

There is some truth to the first point but very little to the second. Even where, as in the United States, liberty does indeed "lie in the hearts of men and women," the nation still needs a vigorous judiciary dedicated to nurturing and protecting human rights. In times of trouble, judges can stand in the way of what Alexander Hamilton called the "ill humors" of the majority until the troubles pass; in calmer times it can shore up and expand those rights so they can be available even when things get worse.

Without judicial review to protect our rights and liberties, without courts willing and able to make the majestic generalities of the Constitution respond to the ever-changing necessities of the times, our heritage of liberty and justice is in jeopardy. This is the danger that is posed by the conservative court-packing campaign.

APPENDIX I

The Conservative Agenda in Civil Rights, Antitrust and Economic Regulation, and Criminal Procedure

CIVIL RIGHTS

School Desegregation

The repudiation of school segregation by a unanimous Supreme Court in *Brown* v. *Board of Education* is so sacrosanct today that no respectable (or at least politically sensitive) official would dare attack it frontally. The attack is instead on what seem to be subsidiary or technical issues, such as a particular remedy like busing, or methods of proof, which turn out to be crucial to whether the *Brown* decision will have anything more than symbolic impact.

Even with this oblique strategy, desegregation opponents continue to be relatively unsuccessful, despite strong public hostility to busing. Although the Supreme Court has been far from uniform or even consistent, it has generally continued to insist on meaningful desegregation. The issue has not faded away, however, for America's schools are still largely segregated, new problems are on the horizon, and the judiciary's prominent role in school desegregation offers an especially convenient target.

The first decade after *Brown* saw almost no desegregation, as southern officials used sympathetic local judges to stall and evade. The 1964 Civil Rights Act changed this, however, by giving the Department of Health, Education, and Welfare (HEW) a major responsibility for enforcing school desegregation, with the power to cut off federal funds to school districts that refused or stalled.

Southern school officials immediately responded with "freedom of choice" plans allowing children to go to any school they wanted to. Not surprisingly, white children chose to remain in white schools, and black children knew they had better stay in the black schools—not too many

179

were willing to take on the danger and terror endured by the black students who tried to go to previously all-white schools in Little Rock and elsewhere.

HEW quickly saw that freedom-of-choice plans would not desegregate the schools and insisted that southern school districts adopt more realistic plans; after a 1965 fiasco in Mayor Richard J. Daley's Chicago, however, HEW stayed out of the North.[1]

The stepped-up governmental activity produced an immediate outcry from politicians. Starting in 1966 and every year through 1981, the House of Representatives passed antibusing legislation. At times Senate liberals were able either to defeat a Senate version or to water the bill down, but ultimately the opponents prevailed and HEW finally was removed from the school desegregation process. This did not have much practical significance, because politics and presidential policies had accomplished the same result as soon as Richard Nixon became president in 1969. The symbolism and political significance were obvious, however: Being against busing was good politics.

The 1968 presidential campaign was the first in which desegregation and busing played a major role, as both Richard Nixon, adopting a "southern strategy," and George Wallace, with his attacks on "pointy-headed professors" and "overeducated ivory-tower folk," lashed into the federal government's desegregation efforts.[2]

Before the southern caucus of the 1968 Republican Convention, Nixon attacked both the courts and HEW, saying it was "dangerous" to use federal funding to "force a local community to carry out what a federal administrator or bureaucrat may think is best for the local community." The issue was fueled by the Supreme Court's landmark decision in *Green* v. *County School Board of New Kent County* (1968), in which the Court unanimously rejected a freedom-of-choice plan in a Virginia community that had no residential segregation, was roughly half black and half white, ran one white combined elementary and high school and one black combined school, and in which twenty-one school buses rode overlapping routes over which white children were driven past the black school, and black children past the white. For the first time since *Brown,* the Court made it clear that if a school board had created a segregated school system, it had an obligation to "convert to a unitary school system in which racial discrimination would be eliminated root and branch"—in other words, to integrate, not just to stop discriminating. The Court threw out the board's freedom-of-choice plan and insisted on a "plan that promises realistically to work and promises realistically to work *now.*"[3] (Italics in original.)

Upon Nixon's election, the federal effort to desegregate slackened. In the fall of 1969 the Department of Justice opposed school desegregation in the Supreme Court. It was the first time the department opposed civil rights groups, and the government lost.

That was not the only government loss. In a 1971 case from Charlotte, North Carolina, *Swann* v. *Charlotte-Mecklenburg*, the Court again unanimously came out for vigorous desegregation efforts, including busing where necessary; again the Justice Department supported the losing school board. Although the opinion was by Warren Burger, his own choice for chief justice, Nixon continued to attack the Court and offered a constitutional amendment to ban busing. It did not come even close.[4]

Nevertheless, the public seemed to hate busing, even though most people said they were in favor of integrated schools, and many American schoolchildren did go to school by bus for reasons having nothing to do with desegregation. Fears of poor schools, violence, and costs, whether justified or not, dominated public opinion and impelled some normally liberal northern congressmen and senators to take the lead in opposing busing.

Desegregation foes in the North suffered an even greater defeat in a 1973 Denver case, *Keyes* v. *School District*, the Supreme Court's first northern school case. In that case the Court relieved plaintiffs of the need to prove that a school board had intentionally segregated *every* part of a school district, once the plaintiffs proved that there had been intentional segregation in one significant part of the district. Only Rehnquist dissented on this point, insisting that northern schools were obligated to do nothing more than allow freedom of choice.[5]

The following year, however, the Court began to retreat. First it ruled that a court could not order that desegregation include the suburbs unless the suburb was itself guilty of intentionally segregating the schools, a ruling that doomed the increasingly black cities to permanent racial isolation. Two years later, in 1976, the Court ruled that in order to show a constitutional violation, plaintiffs had to prove that the school board had *intentionally* segregated the schools, which is very difficult—it was not enough that the *effect* of the board's actions was to create or maintain school segregation.[6]

The 1976 decision seemed to strike hard at school desegregation. Nixon and Ford officials had almost entirely abandoned the effort anyway, and the newly elected Jimmy Carter, and his attorney general Griffin Bell, a former chief of staff to segregationist governor Ernest Vandiver who helped Vandiver thwart efforts to desegregate the Georgia schools, seemed no more eager to push the issue. This left school desegregation to the financially strapped and modestly staffed private civil rights organizations, and the increasingly stringent proof requirements imposed by the Supreme Court seemed to make their task almost impossible.[7]

And the end of the school desegregation crusade seemed near when the Court ruled in 1977, in a Rehnquist opinion, that the federal court could order Dayton, Ohio, to eliminate only the specific segregation resulting from a proven segregative act. Because of proof problems, this would effectively block substantial desegregation in any locality that did not have a recent law mandating segregation—every place but the South, which had had such laws.[8]

That was the low point. Two years later, the Court switched again. Perhaps because it realized the consequences, the Court pulled back from its 1977 decision and swung over to the other side. In two cases from Ohio, Justice Byron White built on the 1973 Denver case to ease the proof requirement and to make it relatively easy to show that the entire school system had been deliberately segregated and warranted a busing order. With that, the Court concluded its school desegregation rulings, at least for a while.[9]

The 1979 victory for the civil rights forces was of surpassing importance. Like so many other such victories, however, it is fragile, for the rules developed by the majority were approved by only five votes (not including Justice Powell's), making them vulnerable to just a slight shift in the Court's future composition.

Ronald Reagan was obviously opposed to busing. Indeed, he opposed all the landmark civil rights legislation of the 1960s; during the 1980 primaries he announced that he had changed his mind about the Civil Rights Act of 1964 "because I recognize now that it is institutionalized and it has, let's say, hastened the solution of a lot of problems." In the 1976 campaign against Gerald Ford for the GOP nomination, for example, he called for a constitutional amendment outlawing busing and repeated that call in 1980, where it wound up in the Republican Platform. A 1979 effort to adopt such an amendment by Ohio Republican Ron Mottl had failed to muster even a majority of the House of Representatives, but 1981 looked to be different.[10]

The Reagan Administration's assault on civil rights was led by William Bradford Reynolds, head of the Civil Rights Division at the Justice Department. Reynolds, a Washington, D.C., lawyer, had no background in civil rights, but that didn't quench his zeal. He quickly made it clear that he had nothing but disdain for the Supreme Court civil rights decisions.

The school desegregation cases were among his first targets. In the 1968 *Green* case, the Court had ruled that "if . . . other ways . . . promis[e] speedier and more effective conversion to a unitary, non-racial system, 'freedom of choice' must be held unacceptable." Nevertheless, Reynolds announced that "we are not going to compel children who don't choose to have an integrated education to have one." In the 1971 Charlotte, North Carolina, case, the Court had approved busing because "desegregation plans cannot be limited to the walk-in school"; Reynolds declared that the department was against all busing. In *Keyes,* the 1973 Denver case, the Court allowed the plaintiffs to take advantage of certain presumptions to justify a desegregation remedy throughout a school system, but Reynolds announced that "in deciding to initiate litigation, we will not rely on the *Keyes* presumption."[11]

In litigation that the department was already involved in, he immediately set to work to undermine the desegregation efforts. In Chicago he reversed the department's position and accepted a settlement that would permit lengthy delays; he promoted a plan for "desegregating" Bakersfield, California, that he called a "blueprint for desegregation" but that *The New York Times* called a "blueprint for evasion."[12]

Reynolds summed up his position with the statement that "future enforcement policies will be aimed" not at eliminating segregation by all permissible means, but at remedying "substantial disparities in the tangible components of education" between minority and white children—a latter-day restatement of "separate but equal."[13]

The Administration was busy attacking school desegregation in other ways as well. When the Court began to insist on realistic desegregation, segregated white private "academies" were started. At first they received state financing, but the Supreme Court stopped that. When they tried to use their educational status to qualify for tax-exempt status, the Internal Revenue Service refused, and the courts upheld the IRS. The issue ultimately went to the Supreme Court, at just about the time the Reagan Administration took office. In October 1981, Congressman Trent Lott of Mississippi wrote the White House challenging the IRS position and urging the Administration to switch sides and argue against the IRS position. Reagan noted on Lott's letter, "I think we should," and a team led by Meese and aided by Reynolds and his assistants, prepared a brief from which the deputy solicitor general, who was a career official and not a political appointee, was excluded. All in vain. With only Rehnquist dissenting, in 1983 the Court decisively rebuffed the Administration.[14]

Reynolds also tried to persuade the Court to review desegregation cases that he hoped to use as vehicles to undermine prior rulings. This, too, failed. When black parents in Charleston, South Carolina, unhappy with his position in a case involving their school system, asked the NAACP Legal Defense Fund to enter the case on their behalf, Reynolds instructed his staff to oppose the intervention, saying, "Those bastards just want to bring in the busing issue. . . . They're probably entitled to intervene, but let's make them jump through every hoop."[15]

No matter how zealously pursued, the Reagan-Reynolds policies could not satisfy the conservatives, for not only did they fail, but also they could reach only a small number of situations. Full relief could come only from Congress, through either legislation stripping the courts of the power to order busing, or by a constitutional amendment. But those avenues also failed. In 1982, Helms and Democrat J. Bennett Johnston came close when the Senate passed their bills to virtually strip federal judges of the power to order busing and to allow the attorney general to reopen old busing cases. The bills died in the House, however, and efforts to promote a constitutional amendment did even worse. For the rest of the Reagan presidency, the school desegregation wars were relatively quiet.

But there were rumbles of new problems as school districts under court order tried to get out from under them and adopted policies that might resegregate. These will probably soon come to the Court, for its present and future members to determine.[16]

Affirmative Action

Affirmative action—preferences for minorities and women formerly victimized by discrimination in hiring, education, and other contexts—was high on the Administration's hit list. The issue had set Jews against blacks, driving a wedge between two of the important partners in the civil rights coalition; opinion polls also showed widespread hostility to racial or ethnic hiring or other preferences.

In the early days of the civil rights movement it was thought that it would be enough to eliminate discriminatory laws and practices and to compensate the victims. That soon proved too optimistic. Deeply ingrained practices, prejudices, and fears had lingering effects that could not be rooted out so easily. Simply telling the Alabama State Police, which had not had a black trooper in all its thirty-seven years, to stop discriminating, did not bring blacks onto the force. As Justice Harry Blackmun put it, "In order to get beyond racism, we must first take account of race. . . . And in order to treat some persons equally, we must treat them differently."[17]

By the late 1960s, both the federal government in its dealing with federal contractors, and many courts, had begun to insist on measures aimed at future hiring and other opportunities. This often took the form of setting goals and timetables for attaining a percentage of minorities or women that would be roughly proportionate to their representation in the pool of qualified applicants. In many cases, employers, schools, colleges, and government agencies took the initiative and voluntarily adopted such programs, though this often was encouraged by a not-too-gentle nudge from either a federal agency like the Office of Federal Contracts Compliance in the Labor Department, or by the threat of a class-action lawsuit. Companies set up special units to administer these programs and began to examine closely their admission or hiring and promotion requirements to see whether these criteria, which often ruled out minorities and women, were really necessary. By the end of the 1970s there were hundreds of thousands of such plans covering many millions of workers, students, and others; the federal contractor program alone came to cover over three hundred thousand firms.

These preferences obviously hurt whites, males, and other groups not entitled to the preferences, although it is not clear how much. The preferences often produced resentment and a belief that normal merit or seniority considerations were being pushed aside unfairly. This was accompanied by a developing white backlash in the country and a feeling that blacks in particular had gotten enough and didn't need any more special help. There was also a concern that race was being used as a criterion, when the goal was to achieve a color-blind society in which a person's individual qualities would be the only important considerations.

Some of the Jewish groups—though not all—were especially upset. In the past, Jewish students had suffered from quota and other systems designed to restrict their admission into elite schools and colleges, particularly medical schools, and many had been forced to go abroad for their training while non-Jews with lesser academic and other qualifications were admitted. Harvard president A. Lawrence Lowell, for example, proposed such an explicit quota in 1922, and though his proposal was never formally accepted, there is clear evidence that the number of Jewish students at Harvard was kept down; there were similar restrictions at Yale and other leading schools.

Nevertheless, affirmative action plans were uniformly upheld by all the courts that initially dealt with the issues in the 1960s and early 1970s. Congress seemed to agree with these rulings. When Title VII of the 1964 Civil Rights Act, which banned discrimination in employment, was expanded in 1972, the Senate by 2–1 margins rejected efforts by Senator Sam Ervin to block race-preferential hiring and other programs.

The Court finally got to the issue in 1978. The case involved the admission to the University of California at Davis medical school of a highly qualified white candidate named Alan Bakke, who had been turned down while minority group members with lower grades and lower test scores were admitted under a special program that set aside sixteen places for minorities. Many schools, universities, and civil rights groups felt that without such affirmative action programs it would be impossible to undo the effects of discrimination against minorities and women that still kept them out of jobs and the other good things in American life.

The ultimate outcome in the *Bakke* case was Solomonic. The Court splintered three different ways, with no opinion for a majority but with five votes for allowing race-conscious affirmative action plans as long as they did not operate rigidly; the decisive opinion was by Justice Lewis F. Powell. The result was to allow university affirmative action plans to continue pretty much as before. Decisions of 5–4 with no opinion for a majority, and with numerous opinions by both winning and losing justices, became the dominant pattern in affirmative action cases during the next ten years.[18]

The Court followed swiftly with two more decisions upholding affirmative action. In *Weber* v. *United Steel Workers* (1979) it approved a voluntary affirmative action craft training program at the Kaiser Aluminum plant in Gramercy, Louisiana. In 1980 it upheld a 10 percent minority business set-aside that Congress had mandated for federally financed public works programs undertaken by state and local governments.[19]

From its first days, the Reagan Administration targeted the Court's affirmative action decisions. Reagan had attacked quotas during the campaign, and it seemed to be at the top of Civil Rights Division chief Reynolds's agenda. Wrapping himself with out-of-context quotes from Thurgood Marshall, Martin Luther King, and other civil rights leaders, and proclaiming his zeal for a color-blind society, he attacked affirmative action as creating a "racial spoils system" and a reverse form of racism equivalent to that inflicted on blacks. He also opposed affirmative action for women.

In December 1981 Reynolds announced that he would try to get the Court to overrule the *Weber* case, in which it had upheld Kaiser's affirmative action program. Reynolds called the decision "wrongly decided."[20]

Reagan went after affirmative action in other ways. After what seemed like a compromise of a bitter battle with civil rights groups and their friends in Congress, Reagan double-crossed them and instead of appointing a balanced Civil Rights Commission, appointed a commission that promptly made the denigration of affirmative action its primary task. In an ironic note to what was supposed to be an attack on race-consciousness, Reagan appointed the black Clarence Pendleton to head the Civil Rights Commission, even though Pendleton had no civil rights background, and another black, Clarence Thomas, to head the Equal Employment Opportunities Commission.*

For his part, Reynolds was busy on other fronts besides litigation. He helped undermine the federal government's own affirmative action programs, and he urged the president to revoke the executive order that imposed affirmative action requirements on federal contractors. The latter effort was opposed by Secretary of Labor Bill Brock, a powerful figure in the Administration, and it failed dismally, one of Reynolds's worst setbacks.

At first, things started out well for him. After the 1980 minority business set-aside case, the Court did not decide an affirmative action case until 1984, when the Court decided a case from Memphis, Tennessee, *Firefighters* v. *Stotts.* The case involved one of the most difficult of all affirmative action problems: When an affirmative action plan is in operation under which some minorities or women have been hired, who is to be laid off when there are cutbacks? Normally, seniority would govern, but if so, the results of the affirmative action plan would be nullified, since those hired under the plan almost always have less seniority.[21]

Nevertheless, the Court refused to allow layoffs of more senior workers in order to preserve affirmative action gains. This surprised almost no one—seniority has been a special favorite of the Court, and many lower court judges who had had no problems with hiring preferences had been uneasy about laying off specific identified individuals, although all the lower courts that had actually dealt with *Stotts*-type cases had ruled in favor of affirmative action and keeping the minorities or women on the job.

The *Stotts* opinion seemed to go farther. The government had argued that all race-conscious relief was barred except for specific identified people who had themselves been victims of the discrimination. Future-oriented relief for people who could not prove that they themselves had wrongly been denied a job or promotion was illegal and unconstitutional. Although unnecessary to the decision, Justice Byron White, writing for the majority, seemed to buy the government's argument.[22]

---

*In preparation for the first meeting of the newly reconstituted Civil Rights Commission, Executive Director Linda Chavez proposed an agenda that included supporting a Supreme Court challenge to a Detroit affirmative action plan—a challenge that the Court promptly rejected—and suggested studies that would try to show a connection between "a general decline in academic standards" and "the advent of affirmative action in education," on "the adverse consequences of affirmative action programs on Americans of Eastern and Southern European descent" (meaning Jews and Italians primarily), and a quick end to studies of the impact of cuts in federal aid on minorities and women. Chavez's anti–affirmative action positions did her little good politically—in 1986 she lost badly to Barbara Mikulski in a Maryland U.S. Senate race.

The decision sent shock waves through the civil rights community. Although the decision itself was clearly limited to a special situation involving seniority and layoffs, White's language was ominous.

The White opinion, of course, had the opposite effect on Reynolds. Reading it as broadly as possible, he immediately fired off letters to fifty-one state and local governments telling them their affirmative action plans were illegal and should be scrapped. The Administration's much-touted allegiance to localism and states rights was forgotten.

All but one of the localities turned Reynolds down flat. Many senators and congressmen were angered by this indifference to local prerogatives, especially since there was no longer any substantial controversy about the plans. Whatever frictions there might originally have been had largely calmed down, but the Reynolds effort to reopen these issues had revived the tensions. Indianapolis mayor Richard Hudnut, a former Republican congressman, declared of his city's plan, "It is useful for the city, and we shall continue to work under it." Reynolds was so angered by the Indianapolis response that he sued the city and in the process provoked serious acrimony between black and white members of the policemen's union over what position the union should take in the suit.

Reynolds did no better in the courts. Every court that considered his broad reading of the *Stotts* opinion rejected it, and at the hearings on his unsuccessful nomination for promotion to associate attorney general, senators berated him for trying to stretch the *Stotts* ruling.[23]

In 1986 the Supreme Court again ruled on affirmative action. In three cases, a solid majority—one of the few such majorities in these cases—expressly declared that race-conscious preferences for those who were not themselves victims of prior discrimination are legal in hiring, apprenticeship, union membership, and other contexts as long as no layoffs are involved and as long as such programs are necessary, temporary, flexible, and not too harmful to majority employees. As usual, the Court was sharply splintered, though all the justices seemed to reject the Administration's demand that there be no future-oriented goals and timetables and that relief be restricted to those who could show that they had been the specific victims of the discrimination. What was left uncertain was how stringently such limits as flexibility and temporariness would be interpreted.[24]

Those questions were soon answered, however. Less than a year later, the Court came close to finishing off the Administration's efforts to kill affirmative action. In an opinion for a five-member majority, with an additional and separate statement from Justice O'Connor, six members of the Court gave the stamp of approval to almost all voluntary affirmative action plans that were designed to get some qualified women and minorities into jobs and senior positions from which they had traditionally been excluded, as long as the flexibility and other requirements were met. The case was *Johnson* v. *Transportation Agency of Santa Clara County.* Three justices dissented, with the newly appointed Antonin Scalia angrily arguing for himself and Rehnquist that the 1979 *Weber* case be overturned.[25]

The *Johnson* decision left some important issues undecided, and Reagan appointees on the lower courts have already used these uncertainties to invalidate some plans. Two replacements on the Supreme Court from among the five-member majority in the 1987 case could change things significantly, especially since Scalia's dissenting opinion makes it clear that he, Rehnquist, and White are willing to overrule the precedents allowing affirmative action. Even though such programs are now quite popular among many employers—the National Association of Manufacturers and the United States Chamber of Commerce both opposed the Administration's position—and recent polls show that the American people no longer have any great objection to them, a relatively small shift in the Court's membership could result in rulings striking down many if not most plans.[26]

Voting Rights

Among the conservatives' many civil rights defeats, none was greater than its failure to cripple the extension of the Voting Rights Act.

The Voting Rights Act of 1965, a direct consequence of the Selma march to Montgomery, Alabama, led by Dr. Martin Luther King, Jr., is probably the most successful of all the civil rights enactments. It enabled black voting in the areas covered by the act to rise from 29 percent before 1965 to about 50 percent in 1982. Key sections of the law had to be extended by August 6, 1982, however, or they would have expired.

Despite its successes, minority voting still is threatened by racism, bigotry, and just plain politics. In many areas covered by the act, minority voter registration still is far behind white registration, which is about 75 percent. For this reason, extension of the act in 1982 was crucial, and, given control of the White House and the Senate by those not normally friendly to blacks, it seemed far from certain. Most of the enforcement efforts involved the South, and powerful southerners, like Judiciary Committee chairman Strom Thurmond, argued that it was time to stop singling out that region.[27]

The strategy developed by Senator Orrin Hatch and taken up by Attorney General William French Smith was not to oppose an extension but to weaken enforcement of the act. To do this, they urged that plaintiffs be required to prove that those who adopted a challenged voting practice did so because they *intended* to discriminate against blacks or others. It was not enough that the practice had *resulted* in discrimination.

Had the intent provision been adopted, lawsuits under the act would have become very difficult to win. Evidence of intent is often impossible to find. Many voting practice procedures go back to Jim Crow days, and the records are spotty or nonexistent. Furthermore, motivation is difficult to prove in any context, and laws like the Voting Rights Act obviously have made officials more circumspect.

The civil rights community mobilized a massive grass-roots campaign and in an impressive display of political muscle and shrewd strategy simply overwhelmed the opposition—the final House and Senate votes were 389–24 and 85–8, respectively, including many southerners. Reynolds and Solicitor General Charles Fried attempted to salvage something from this defeat by trying to persuade the Supreme Court to read the 1982 amendment very narrowly, but that ploy was no more effective, especially after the principal authors of the bill, who included both leading Republicans and Democrats, filed a friend-of-the-court brief opposing the Reynolds-Fried reading. The solicitor general lost again, this time 9–0.[28]

The Administration's only recourse was to manipulate the vast enforcement and review powers given the Justice Department by the statute, and this Reynolds did. He filed almost no enforcement suits, and he repeatedly approved voting procedures that courts later found to be discriminatory. In some of these cases, there was evidence of political influence by white southern congressmen. In two cases from Louisiana and Montgomery, Alabama, Reynolds approved plans diluting black votes that his own staff had found discriminatory; the Louisiana plan had been put together at a meeting from which black legislators were excluded. Federal courts later upheld the staff.[29]

Discrimination Against the Handicapped

The Administration did just as badly with the Rehabilitation Act of 1973. Two cases before the Supreme Court involved two current public health problems: treatment of newborn infants with serious birth defects, and AIDS.

In response to the anti-abortion forces, the Administration overturned a 1977 HEW decision and reinterpreted the Rehabilitation Act to impose federal standards for treatment of seriously ill newborn infants, and generally to require heroic measures to keep such infants alive, regardless of parental consent.

In 1983, "Baby Jane Doe" was born with multiple congenital defects, including spina bifida and other serious problems. After consulting with doctors, religious advisers, and others, her parents decided to forgo surgery that might prolong her life but not eliminate the severe infirmities. All the courts and the New York State child protection agency agreed with that judgment.

The Administration has constantly painted itself as a states rights champion. During the 1980 campaign, for example, Reagan had often talked about returning government to the people and away from Washington bureaucrats, and in November 1986 the Administration issued a report deploring the centralization of governmental power in Washington. Also, in 1984 Congress passed legislation making it quite clear that it wanted treatment decisions about newborn children with birth defects to be made by the states, all of which had long-established methods and procedures for dealing with such agonizing problems.

Nevertheless, the Administration, through Solicitor General Fried, persisted in trying to override state procedures and impose federal standards, and urged this position on the Supreme Court.

The Administration lost again. "Nothing even remotely suggests" that Congress wanted to get the federal government involved in these kinds of "treatment decisions," said the Court, and it forbade the Administration to try to force the states to follow the federal regulations.[30]

The Administration also lost when it tried to twist the 1973 Rehabilitation Act to deny protection against discrimination to the victims of contagious diseases. In a bizarre reading of the act, the Justice Department construed it as not covering the discharge of an employee out of the employer's or other employees' fear of contagion, even if the fear was unwarranted. Somehow, such discharges were not "by reason of" the handicap. The department's reading would enable employers to fire anyone with AIDS because of the employer's or other employees' fear, revulsion, or just plain prejudice, regardless of how unlikely the contagion; if the employer defended by saying that it was motivated by its or its employees' fear of being infected, it would be impossible to refute that. State agencies and other groups repudiated the department's reading, and employers who had generally assumed the act applied to contagious diseases were confused.[31]

The issue came before the Supreme Court during the 1986–87 term, in a tuberculosis case. In 1979 a Florida teacher was dismissed because she had tuberculosis. She sued under the Rehabilitation Act, and the Administration opposed her, claiming that contagious diseases were not covered by the act, even if the individual was not herself contagious. Again, the Supreme Court ruled against the Reaganites—contagious diseases *are* covered by the act, the Court said, with only Rehnquist and Scalia dissenting.[32]

As in other civil rights contexts, court defeats did not affect Reynolds's enforcement powers, and he used them, or rather chose not to use them. He filed almost no enforcement suits under the Rehabilitation Act, construed pertinent federal decisions to grant as few rights as possible, and frequently switched the government's position to side against the plaintiffs in major lawsuits.[33]

Conservative Democratic senator Dennis DeConcini of Arizona summed up Reynolds's civil rights record when voting against his promotion to associate attorney general and, by implication, the Administration's record. Reynolds, said DeConcini, had a "tendency to uphold the laws and decisions he like[d] and ignoring or refusing to follow or enforce the ones he [didn't]; and altered the truth to suit his own purposes."[34]

ANTITRUST AND ECONOMIC REGULATION

The Reagan Administration may have disappointed its right-wing allies on the social agenda, but on economic issues no one could fault its zeal or its successes. In some areas like deregulation, it clearly did not get everything, though even in this area there were some very substantial achievements. In antitrust matters it accomplished virtually all it wanted.

Antitrust

The antitrust laws are now so central a part of American life that no one would seriously consider repealing them. Nevertheless, Americans have always been willing to tolerate lax or nonexistent enforcement. Whether because of a subconscious admiration of the robber barons and their current descendants, or because of a partiality for bigness for its own sake, or because of a recurrent but usually inaccurate belief that antitrust gets in the way of more important things—whatever the reason, during much of our history, antitrust enforcement has been quite feeble.

There are four major laws, each of which was passed with overwhelming public support and, until recently, without much dispute as to their purposes: the Sherman Act in 1890, with its broad ban on contracts and conspiracies in restraint of trade, and on attempts to achieve a monopoly; the Clayton Act of 1914, designed to make sure that small and new businesses are not excluded or taken advantage of in the distribution process; the Robinson-Patman Act of 1938, which prevents price discrimination against small retailers and other small-business people; and the 1950 Celler-Kefauver Act, which tries to block big mergers in order to slow down the concentration of economic power and the threat such concentration poses to political democracy, as well as harm to small competitors. It was hoped and expected that this legislation also would produce lower prices and better quality, but the social and political goals were central.

Usually there has been general agreement on these goals. Even Nixon's attorney general John N. Mitchell declared that "the danger that . . . superconcentration poses to our economic, political, and social structure cannot be overestimated."[35]

The Warren Court took these antitrust goals very seriously, and when the first cases under the 1950 Celler-Kefauver Act came before the Court in the 1960s, the act was interpreted to bar most mergers of any size. The Court tried to lay out some simple yardsticks of legality so that business people and others would readily know whether a proposed merger was legal.[36]

To some, these yardsticks seemed not just simple but simplistic. Also, from 1965 through the early 1970s, Congress and the Nixon Administration were putting together the modern regulatory state, passing many new regulatory statutes in environmental, safety, and health matters and creating some twenty-one new agencies. The proliferation of regulatory burdens from the new statutes, and a general disillusionment with government efforts to shape and improve things, produced a powerful and widespread campaign to cut back on government regulation and to overturn the Warren Court's antitrust jurisprudence.

The first significant antitrust blow was struck in a 1979 case from California in which the Supreme Court allowed the Sylvania Electric Company to deny one of its franchisees in San Francisco the right to also sell Sylvania products in Sacramento, which was another franchisee's territory. The Warren Court had made this kind of arrangement almost always illegal, regardless of why it was adopted. The Burger Court took a more "sophisticated" view, and drawing on current economic theory, declared that these kinds of agreements had to be looked at on a case-by-case basis to determine whether they were "reasonable." The result was uncertainty as to what was legal, with lengthy and expensive trials featuring armies of highly paid, competing economists and lawyers.[37]

Ronald Reagan probably knows little about economic theory and even less about antitrust law, but since going to work for General Electric, he has known he was against government regulation of business. He entered the national political scene with "The Speech" at the 1964 Republican Convention in which he lambasted government intervention into "health, housing, farming, industry, commerce, education," TVA, and welfare, as well as the progressive income tax and, of course, his favorite target, the federal bureaucracy.[38]

The Reagan Administration and its allies were thus committed to ending as much regulation as possible. Their greatest success was with the antitrust laws. By the time the first term had ended, little antitrust activity was being undertaken by the federal government, and not much more anywhere else.

The antitrust laws are enforced primarily in three ways: government suits by the Antitrust Division of the Department of Justice; administrative and ultimately court suits by the Federal Trade Commission; and private suits for triple damages by people injured by an alleged violation of the antitrust laws.

The Federal Trade Commission, which had come under heavy congressional fire under the Carter Administration for excessive zeal, was emasculated by putting it under the control of economist James Miller, whose mission was to make sure that the agency did not stand in the way of business unless things really got out of hand; during the Reagan years, things almost never did.

The Antitrust Division was turned over to a law professor from Stanford, William F. Baxter, a man whom many senators came to consider the most arrogant public official they had ever encountered. Baxter was a devotee of the University of Chicago school of economics, which analyzes all economic issues—and for some of its adherents, all other problems—by one economic yardstick: whether the practice or policy in question will produce more goods and services with fewer resources. Its basic assumption is that whatever businessmen do is "efficient," because they are always acting to increase their profits.

Baxter immediately set about undermining and overturning established antitrust law. He attacked Warren Court precedents at every opportunity, often calling them "rubbish," "wacko," "misguided," and "not very well informed." He tried to persuade the Supreme Court to overturn a seventy-year-old rule that a seller cannot tell a buyer what to charge when the buyer tries to resell the product, a practice euphemistically called "fair trade." When sellers in some states were allowed such a right, between 1938 and 1975, resale prices were much higher. Congress got so angry with Baxter about this that a bipartisan amendment was attached to an appropriations bill denying him the authority to argue his position in the Supreme Court. "It's perfectly true that I am disregarding some of the things that the Supreme Court and other courts have from time to time said about the antitrust laws," he admitted to *The Wall Street Journal*, "just as the courts themselves have frequently and inevitably disregarded what prior courts have said about the antitrust laws."[39]

More important, Baxter virtually ended all Antitrust Division enforcement except for cases involving bid-rigging among contractors on public highway and airport construction.

Despite the rather clear mandates of both the 1950 Celler-Kefauver Act and the Supreme Court, Baxter encouraged a merger boom. As he consistently made clear in his testimony, speeches, and articles, he had almost never met a merger he didn't like. Businesspeople began to put together giant combinations that they would not have even considered before Baxter took over, and the number of huge mergers broke records year after year, often with government help in designing and facilitating the combination. In 1980 there were 2,326 mergers. In 1986 the number had soared to 4,314 mergers. The overall value of the companies involved in the mergers rose sixfold to $204.4 billion.[40]

This merger explosion was occurring at the same time as it was becoming increasingly clear that many if not most of these combinations were wasteful and inefficient, intended primarily to increase the status, self-esteem, and stock portfolios of managers. As the Ivan Boesky and other abuses revealed, the merger epidemic also encouraged greed and illegality.

Baxter's policies operated directly only on government litigation, but he filed numerous friend-of-the-court briefs on behalf of antitrust defendants in private litigation. Perhaps most important, Reagan appointees on the Courts of Appeals like Richard A. Posner, Robert Bork, and Frank Easterbrook, all of whom had been antitrust specialists before going on the bench, systematically began to rewrite and weaken antitrust law without bothering to wait for the Supreme Court. Even a sympathetic antitrust defense lawyer was moved to comment that Posner displayed "almost religious zeal" and lacked "a judicial and restrained approach to finding the law."[41]

Government antitrust enforcement having been effectively halted by 1986, the Antitrust Division decided that the next goal was what it called "legislative reform." This turned out to be a six-bill package weakening the law on mergers, reducing the penalties for a violation, and in general trying to lock into permanent legislation the Administration's anti-antitrust policies. The bills went nowhere, for even the Republican-controlled Senate had little sympathy for most of the Administration's antitrust policies. On the appeals bench, however, there are many true believers in the Chicago gospel, and since antitrust is largely a judge-made product, their impact is likely to be long-lasting.

Regulation

Congress started the regulatory process in 1887 when it established the Interstate Commerce Commission to regulate railroads. Since then, and especially during the New Deal and the early years of the Nixon Administration, the number of regulatory agencies has multiplied many times. From 1970 to 1979, the number of federal agency employees multiplied from twenty-eight thousand to seventy-one thousand, as almost every facet of the economy came under some sort of governmental scrutiny.

The reasons for this regulatory expansion are obvious. Although it is now clear that the creation of the ICC was largely instigated by the railroad industry to end competition in transportation, most of the regulation of the first half of the century was designed to protect consumers from price gouging by public utilities, and the financial markets against abuse. Recent regulation has responded to the many safety, health, environmental, financial, and other problems created by the modern industrial state.

All efforts to control complex industrial or social reality are inevitably plagued by serious problems, and regulation has had more than its share. It is expensive, its results are often hard to see and sometimes contrary to what was intended, and the procedures are often cumbersome.

With all these faults, however, a modern industrial society cannot do without trying to control the enormous problems it creates, as current safety and other problems with the deregulated airline industry show. And even the best and most effective regulation will draw complaints from those who see their cash flow and bottom line affected by regulation.

The combination of business resistance to any meaningful regulation, and the very real faults of some regulatory systems combined to stimulate a powerful campaign against regulation that both liberals and conservatives joined. The early goal was to eliminate some of the faults. Senator Edward Kennedy and others had been urging some deregulation, and the Carter Administration had made substantial moves in that direction, deregulating the airline and trucking industries.

The Reagan Administration, however, intended to go farther—to free business from federal regulation as much as possible, to deregulate for the sake of deregulation. The ultraconservative Heritage Foundation had compiled a list of thousands of regulatory changes to dismantle environmental, safety, health care, and other forms of regulation, and these became a blueprint for the new Administration.[42]

Alas, after four years, Heritage was forced to issue a second set of fifteen hundred recommendations because the high hopes had been dashed. Complaining about a "disturbing loss of momentum and sense of direction," it lamented that "only two pieces of reform legislation" had passed and that Congress had refused to pass other "reform laws"—there had actually been "regulatory increases," particularly in foreign trade. Overall, the Administration had failed to "remain true to stated goals, such as replacing engineering standards with performance goals." Ultimately the Heritage group blamed it all on a failure in "educating the public"—a failure to persuade the American people that they should want dirtier air and water, unsafe and unhealthy working conditions, and high-profit price gouging by market-dominant companies.[43]

Of equal importance was the Administration's failure in court. The air bag case was the biggest setback.

For years it had been clear that while seat belts substantially reduce injuries, too many people refused to buckle up. In 1977 the Carter Department of Transportation ordered manufacturers to install "passive restraints," such as air bags, beginning in 1982 and on all cars by 1984. The department estimated the air bags could prevent approximately twelve thousand deaths and a hundred thousand serious injuries each year.

The automobile companies, which had managed to stave off the air bag regulation in 1976, lobbied furiously to overturn the rule, and as soon as Reagan took office, they succeeded.

But not for long. The courts overwhelmingly reversed the Transportation Department's rescission of the air bag rule as "arbitrary and capricious." A unanimous Supreme Court ruled that the department had given no reason for killing the air bag rule, even though the agency acknowledged that "it had no basis . . . for changing its earlier conclusions in 1976 and 1977" about the "life-saving potential of the air bag." The effect of the ruling, as a *Wall Street Journal* report observed, was to tell federal officials that "they can't scrap regulations simply because the Reagan Administration, for example, prefers a climate of deregulation."[44]

Not surprisingly, a weakened and distracted Reagan Administration was able to do even less in its second term. In November 1986, one Administra-

rter grumbled that "the bureaucracy under Reagan spews out
.1s only slightly more slowly than it did before."[45]

CRIMINAL PROCEDURE

It is not surprising that the Reagan Administration should come out
strongly against judges who are "coddling criminals." Crime has been a
powerful political issue in national and local politics since Barry Goldwater
attacked the courts during his 1964 campaign.

What *was* surprising (except perhaps to the politically cynical) was the
renewal of the assault on a Court that with fifteen years of 7–2 and 6–3
decisions had whittled down most of its predecessor's rulings favoring
defendants. As late as 1986, President Reagan was blaming "liberal judges
who are unwilling to get tough with the criminal element in this society"
for the "crime epidemic," even though by then most federal judges were
Nixon, Ford, and Reagan appointees, and most of the state courts have
little sympathy for the criminal defendant.[46]

The Warren Court had indeed revolutionized state and federal criminal
procedure. The process had actually begun in the 1930s, when the Court
began to look at some of the more egregious horrors in the way criminal
defendants were being treated by state and local officials and judges, particularly in the South. In 1933 it overturned the rape convictions and death
penalties that Alabama had imposed on the Scottsboro boys, because for
all practical purposes the boys did not have counsel—the judge had appointed the entire bar to represent the defendants on the day of the trial.
Three years later it set aside a Mississippi murder conviction in which a
black defendant was hanged twice by the neck and whipped until he
confessed; the deputy sheriff in charge conceded that one prisoner
had been beaten but "not too much for a Negro; not as much as I would
have done if it were left to me." Apart from these cases, the Court did relatively little to protect the rights of defendants during the 1940s and
1950s.[47]

Things changed with a rush in the 1960s. Between 1961 and 1967 the
Court:

- Required state criminal courts to adhere to the long-standing federal rule excluding evidence obtained in violation of the Fourth Amendment's prohibition
against unreasonable searches and seizures. This was probably the single most
important decision, partly because it was the first, and partly because it affected

so much police activity. Many states had simply ignored the constitutional provision and had to make a massive adjustment in their investigative procedures and training.[48]

- Required states to provide free counsel to all people charged with a serious crime.[49]
- Recognized a right to counsel in the police station or after indictment, when police interrogate a suspect.[50]
- Required states to honor a defendant's right to be free from self-incrimination.[51]
- Required police who interrogate suspects in custody to warn them of their right not to incriminate themselves and of the availability of a free lawyer.[52]
- Insisted that the procedures by which witnesses identify suspects meet minimal standards of fairness to reduce the risk of faulty identification.[53]
- Insisted on certain minimal constitutional standards for any police wiretapping.[54]
- Made it easier for state prisoners to go to federal court to challenge the constitutionality of their convictions.[55]

By the end of 1967 the reform impulse was spent as riots, politics, and continual attacks from the law-enforcement establishment, often supported by academic criticism of some of the Court's work, took over. The election of Richard Nixon in 1968 sealed the end, even though much still remained to be done.

Nixon made four appointments to the Court, and the litmus test was their views on criminal procedure. As one Washington lawyer put it, "You have to regard all the criminal decisions of the Warren Court as wrong." Burger had campaigned for the chief justiceship by attacking *Miranda*; Powell had written a defense of some of the Administration's more dubious constitutional positions; Rehnquist had established his reactionary credentials in many ways; and Blackmun had been a tough judge. All turned out to be hard-liners on criminal law and usually voted that way.[56]

Within a few years, most of the Warren Court's decisions were drastically cut back. Both *Miranda* and *Mapp* were riddled with exceptions and restrictions. The identification procedure ruling was drastically limited. It was made very difficult for state prisoners to get into federal court to challenge a federal constitutional violation. It also became obvious that the Court wasn't interested in reviewing cases where the lower court had upheld the conviction, but any case in which a defendant won a constitutional point was a good candidate for being heard and reversed by the Court, especially if it involved illegal drugs.[57]

Despite this substantial shrinkage of defendants' rights, the Court did establish or reinforce certain rights and governmental limits, in both the interrogation and search contexts, and especially in national security surveillance on dissenters. And it did not go all the way and overrule the *Mapp* exclusionary rule and *Miranda* warning cases, though it severely limited their impact. It is this refusal on which the attorney general jumped.

Meese announced his views on defendants' rights soon after he came to Washington. In May 1981 he called the American Civil Liberties Union a "criminals' lobby." Shortly after he became attorney general, he attacked the Supreme Court for the *Mapp* and *Miranda* decisions, which he called "infamous" decisions that "only help criminal defendants." "If a person is innocent of a crime," he declared, "then he is not a suspect."[58]

Shortly after the outcry that usually follows the attorney general's more outrageous utterances, he—also as usual—backed off, saying, "I do not believe that simply because a suspect is being questioned or even arrested he or she is necessarily guilty."[59]

He did not back off his views on the desirability of overruling *Mapp* and *Miranda*, however, and in early 1987 his Office of Legal Policy issued a study calling for the overruling of *Miranda* because it had seriously interfered with law enforcement. The paper was assailed by experts as filled with distortions and misrepresentations; one of the experts quoted in the report disputed the use made of his studies, saying they offered "absolutely" no support for the Administration's claims that *Miranda* had resulted in fewer convictions. The executive director of the National District Attorneys' Association commented that "to totally do away with *Miranda*, I don't think a majority of prosecutors would agree with that." Andrew Frey, the chief advocate for the government in the Supreme Court on criminal cases for over twelve years and the winner of many of the key law-enforcement precedents, explained that "the Court is in no mood to overrule *Miranda.*" And New York City United States Attorney Rudolph W. Giuliani, a former assistant attorney general under Reagan's first attorney general, William French Smith, said, "The *Miranda* warnings are simple and easy to give and are known by everyone. As a matter of reality and practicality, it doesn't prevent anyone from confessing who wants to confess."[60]

The timing of the report was particularly suspicious. The Court had recently reaffirmed in an opinion by hard-liner O'Connor that it thought *Miranda* marked a good compromise between the rights of the citizen and the needs of law enforcement, and it was clear that an effort to have the Court overrule the decision was futile.

The only plausible purposes to issuing the study were politics and publicity—an effort to placate the diehard conservatives with empty gestures, when the Administration was disappointing them on so many other matters.

APPENDIX II

Questions by the Honorable John P. East, the Honorable Jeremiah Denton, and the Honorable Orrin G. Hatch for Joseph H. Rodriguez, Nominee for the United States District Court for the District of New Jersey

1. Do you believe that the Constitution guarantees a "right to privacy"? If so, please indicate the constitutional sources of that right, its precise nature and its limitations.

2. (a) In his dissent to the majority opinion of the Supreme Court in *Roe* v. *Wade,* 410 U.S. 113 (1973), Justice Byron R. White made the following statement: "As an exercise of raw judicial power the Court perhaps has authority to do what it does today, but in my view its judgment is an improvident and extravagant exercise of the power of judicial review which the Constitution extends to this Court." Do you agree or disagree with Justice White's statement? Why or why not?

(b) In his dissent to the same *Roe* opinion, Justice William H. Rehnquist made the following statement: "The decision here to break the term of pregnancy into three distinct terms and to outline the permissible restrictions the state may impose upon each one partakes more of judicial legislation than it does of the determination of the intent of the drafters of the Fourteenth Amendment." Do you agree or disagree with this statement? Why or why not?

3. (a) In *Roe* v. *Wade,* the Supreme Court determined that even the "viable" unborn human fetus is not a "person" as that term is used in the Fifth and Fourteenth Amendments to the Constitution. Do you believe that a "viable" fetus is a human being? If so, do you agree with the Court's finding that the "viable" fetus is not a "person"? If so, on what basis can a valid constitutional distinction be drawn between a "human being" and a "person"?

(b) Is a child who is born alive after an abortion a "person" under the Fifth and Fourteenth Amendments? Does the "right to an abortion" that the Court created with its *Roe* decision have any application after a child is born alive as the result of an abortion?

(c) Is a handicapped, or severely handicapped, child born alive a "person" under the Fifth and Fourteenth Amendments to the Constitution?

4. (a) Does the "right to privacy" from which the *Roe* v. *Wade* abortion privacy doctrine of the Supreme Court is derived have any application to any right of the parent of a handicapped newborn child to decide whether to provide him or her with life-saving medical care, and/or ordinary care in the form of nutritional sustenance and liquids (whether by natural or intravenous means)? If so, why? If not, why not?

(b) Do you believe that legislation ever can be held to be invalid because those who enacted it did so based on the belief that the conduct proscribed is morally wrong, or that an activity or institution encouraged or helped by the legislation is morally right? What difference to the Administration's case, if any, does it make whether such moral beliefs are based on a belief in the existence of a Supreme Being?

5. In 1972 the Supreme Court in *Furman* v. *Georgia,* 408 U.S. 238, struck down Federal and state death penalty statutes that allowed for unguided discretion by the trier of fact to determine whether or not the death penalty should be imposed. On February 22, 1984, through the able leadership of the distinguished Chairman of this Committee, the Senate passed by a vote of 63–32, S. 1765, a bill to establish constitutional procedures for the imposition of the sentence of death for certain federal offenses. What is your view on the death penalty?

6. The Department of Justice recently noted that the number of prisoners challenging the validity of their state convictions through Federal habeas corpus petitions rose nearly 700 percent from 1961 through 1982, but only a small number of inmates were successful in gaining any type of release. In an attempt to control the flow of frivolous collateral attacks on a criminal defendant's convictions, the Senate, again through the able leadership of Chairman Thurmond, passed on February 6, 1984, S. 1763, a bill to reform current habeas corpus procedures.

In your view, should any limits be placed on criminal defendants' ability to collaterally attack this conviction? If so, what are the limits?

7. On February 7, 1984, the Senate passed S. 1764, a bill which limits the use of the Exclusionary Rule by providing that evidence obtained in a search or seizure and which is otherwise admissible as evidence will not be excluded in a Federal trial if the search or seizure was undertaken in a reasonable, good faith belief that it conformed to the Fourth Amendment.

Do you believe that there should be any limits placed on the use of the Exclusionary Rule? If so, do you believe that S. 1764 or this type of limitation is appropriate?

8. The First Amendment forbids the establishment of a State religion. The First Amendment also prohibits interference with the free exercise of religion. This second prohibition apparently is often overlooked. Please share with the Committee your views on the free exercise clause as it relates to prayer in public schools.

9. Is it unconstitutional for state or local governments to give tuition vouchers to parents of all children who attend nonpublic schools? Does it make any difference whether most of these children attend religious schools, provided that the law makes no distinction between religious and nonreligious schools?

10. The Second Amendment to the Constitution states that "a well-regulated militia being necessary to the security of a free State, the right of the people to keep and bear arms shall not be infringed." In light of that constitutional prohibition, to what extent, if any, do you feel that Congress could curtail the right of the people to keep and bear weapons that are of value to common defense?

11. Would you give your present personal position with regards to the Equal Rights Amendment?

12. (a) What did the Supreme Court hold in *Regents of the University of California* v. *Bakke,* 438 U.S. 256 (1978)? Do you believe that this holding was correct? Why or why not?

(b) In his dissent to the majority opinion on the Supreme Court in *Fullilove* v. *Klutznick,* 448 U.S. 448 (1980), Justice John Paul Stevens noted that the compelling government interest of curing the effects of past racial discrimination will justify a classbased infringement of the legitimate interests and expectations of innocent third parties only to the extent necessary to restore proven discriminatees to the position they would have occupied in the absence of the discrimination. What role should affirmative action type remedies take in dealing with individuals who have not been victims of discriminatory practices?

13. (a) Do you believe that *Brown* v. *Board of Education,* 347 U.S. 483 (1954), was correctly decided? What disagreements, if any, do you have with the language or reasoning of the Court's decision in that case?

(b) Do you believe that *Swann* v. *Charlotte-Mecklenburg Board of Education,* 402 U.S. 1 (1971), was decided correctly? If so, do you believe that there is a conflict or tension between the constitutional right to color-blind treatment that was announced in *Brown* and the right (or, if it makes a difference, the remedy) of race-conscious school assignment that was announced in *Swann*? If so, how do you reconcile this tension or conflict?

14. (a) What limitations, if any, do you believe there are on the constitutional power of Congress to enact exceptions to the jurisdiction of the Federal courts and regulations of this jurisdiction?

(b) What are the sources of these limitations?

15. Section 9(a) of the National Labor Relations Act states:

> Representatives designated or selected for the purposes of collective bargaining by the majority of the employees in a union appropriate for such purposes, shall be the exclusive representatives of all the employees in such a unit for the purposes of collective bargaining in respect to rates of pay, wages, hours of employment or other conditions of employment . . .

Keeping in mind that unions are private associations rather than governments, do you think that the granting of exclusive representation powers to unions by the National Labor Relations Act is unconstitutional?

16. Do you concur with the Supreme Court's decision in *Abood* v. *Detroit Board of Education* and *Ellis/Fails* that mandatory service fees collected from non-union members under the jurisdiction of an exclusive bargaining agent can only be used to pay direct collective bargaining and grievance administration costs?

17. In *United States* v. *Enmons,* the Supreme Court affirmed a District Court ruling that the Hobbs Act did not prohibit the use of violence in obtaining legitimate union objectives. What is your analysis of the *Enmons* decision?

18. List any advisory, consultative, honorary or other part-time service or positions with Federal, State, or local governments.

19. List all positions held as an officer, director, trustee, partner, proprietor, agent, representative, or consultant of any corporation, company, firm, partnership, or other business enterprise, educational or other institution.

20. List all memberships and offices held in professional, fraternal, scholarly, civic, business, charitable and other organizations.

21. List all offices with a political party which you have held or any public office for which you have been a candidate.

22. List all memberships and offices held in and services rendered to all political parties or election committees during the last 10 years.

23. Itemize all political contributions to any individual, campaign organization, political party, political action committee, or similar entity of $15 or more for the past 10 years.

Notes

Introduction

1. Hand, *The Bill of Rights* (New York: Atheneum, 1964), p. 34.
2. *Dred Scott* v. *Sandford,* 60 U.S. (19 How.) 393 (1857); *Plessy* v. *Ferguson,* 163 U.S. 537 (1896).
3. *Brown* v. *Board of Education,* 347 U.S. 483 (1954); *Brown* v. *Board of Education,* 349 U.S. 294 (1955).
4. Chayes, "Public Law Litigation and the Burger Court," 96 *Harv. L. Rev.* 4, 6 (1982).
5. The most comprehensive study of this new political force is by Crawford, *Thunder on the Right* (New York: Pantheon, 1980); see also Judis, "The Right—Is There Life After Reagan?," *The Progressive* (October 1986), p. 20.
6. Paul Weyrich is quoted in *The New York Times* (November 30, 1987).

Chapter 1

1. Richard Viguerie is quoted in "Right-Wing Support for Bork," *People for the American Way Newsletter* (August 1987).
2. McClellan, "The Judicalization of the American Republic" in McGuigan and O'Connell (eds.), *The Judges War* (Washington, D.C.: Free Congress Research and Education Foundation, 1987), pp. 61, 95.
3. Major actors in this movement are listed in Crawford, *Thunder on the Right* (New York: Pantheon, 1980) and in Blumenthal, *The Rise of the Counter-Establishment* (New York: Times Books, 1986).
4. McClellan, "A Lawyer Looks at Rex Lee," 1 *Benchmark* 1 (March–April 1984).

5. *Legal Times* (September 15, 1980).

6. The judiciary plank of the 1980 Republican Party platform is reprinted in 38 *Cong. Q. Weekly Rep.* 2046 (1980).

7. Nina Totenberg interviews with Bruce Fein, National Public Radio (October 2 and 9, 1984); see also Fein, "A 'Reagan' Court Would Overturn Past Errors," *Human Events* (July 6, 1983).

8. Stern, "Judging the Judges: The First Two Years of the Reagan Bench," 1 *Benchmark* 3 (July–October 1984).

9. Epstein, *Takings—Private Property and the Power of Eminent Domain,* p. 281 (Cambridge, Mass.: Harvard University Press, 1985) (New Deal is unconstitutional).

10. Statistics on the number of appellate cases can be found in the annual reports of the Administrative Office of the U.S. courts. The 18,199 cases include only decisions on the substance of the claim, not on procedural points. The *Abscam* cases included *United States* v. *Kelly,* 707 F. 2d 1460 (D.C. Cir. 1983) and *United States* v. *Myers,* 692 F. 2d 823 (2d Cir. 1982).

11. *MCI Telecommunications Corp.* v. *FCC (Execunet I),* 561 F. 2d 365 (D.C. Cir. 1977); *MCI Telecommunications Corp.* v. *FCC (Execunet II),* 580 F. 2d 590 (D.C. Cir. 1978).

12. *United States* v. *American Telephone & Telegraph Company,* 552 F. Supp. 131 (D.D.C. 1984) (approving AT&T consent decree).

Chapter 2

1. Congressman Lott is quoted in *The Washington Post,* (November 24, 1987).

2. For a summary of the Warren Court's activities in these and other areas see "Symposium: The Warren Court," 67 *Mich. L. Rev.* 219 (1968).

3. *Mapp* v. *Ohio,* 367 U.S. 643 (1961); *Miranda* v. *Arizona,* 384 U.S. 436 (1966).

4. *Chisholm* v. *Georgia,* 24 Dall. 419 (1793).

5. *Roe* v. *Wade,* 410 U.S. 113 (1973). The paragraphs on the history of abortion in America are drawn largely from Luker, *Abortion and the Politics of Motherhood* (Berkeley: University of California Press, 1984); Mohr, *Abortion in America: The Origins of Evolution and National Policy, 1800–1900* (New York: Oxford University Press, 1978).

6. *Buck* v. *Bell,* 274 U.S. 200, 207 (1927).

7. *Skinner* v. *Oklahoma,* 316 U.S. 535, 536 (1942).

8. *Griswold* v. *Connecticut,* 381 U.S. 479, 486 (1965). The extension to

unmarried couples referred to in the next paragraph was in *Eisenstadt* v. *Baird,* 405 U.S. 438, 453 (1972).

9. Mohr, n. 5, p. 256; Luker, id., p. 272, n. 3 (legislation modeled on ALI proposal).

10. The cases are collected in appellant Roe's jurisdictional statement in *Roe* v. *Wade,* pp. 19–22.

11. For a portrait of Chief Justice Earl Warren, see White, *Earl Warren: A Public Life* (New York: Oxford University Press, 1982).

12. The Swaggart suspension was reported in *The New York Times* (February 22, 1988) and dominated the press and comedians' monologues after it was revealed.

13. The Burger interview is in *The New York Times* (July 4, 1971).

14. The Cooke quote is in Woodward and Armstrong, *The Brethren* (New York: Simon & Schuster, 1979), p. 238; the prayer for Justice Brennan's death is reported in Caplan, *The Tenth Justice* (New York: Alfred A. Knopf, 1987), p. 271.

15. Ely, "The Wages of Crying Wolf: A Comment on *Roe* v. *Wade,*" 82 *Yale L. J.* 920, 947 (1973); Cox, *The Role of the Supreme Court in American Government* (New York: Oxford University Press, 1976), pp. 113–14. Supporters' comments include Karst, "The Freedom of Intimate Association," 89 *Yale L. J.* 624 (1980); Heymann and Barzelay, "The Forest and the Trees: *Roe* v. *Wade* and Its Critics," 53 *B.U. L. Rev.* 765 (1973). Poll results are reported in Luker, n. 5, pp. 225–26; the poll taken during the Bork confirmation controversy that shows substantial support for the Supreme Court's abortion decision is reported in Martilla and Kiley, *A National Survey of Attitudes Toward the Supreme Court and the Bork Nomination* (Boston: 1987), p. 2. A January 1988 Gallup poll showed a 5:4 ratio against "making it more difficult for a woman to get an abortion." *The Washington Post,* January 23, 1988.

16. The activities of the anti-abortionists are discussed in Luker, n. 5, pp. 127–215.

17. Robertson and Baker are quoted in Reichley, *Religion in American Public Life* (Washington, D.C.: The Brookings Institution, 1985), p. 320.

18. President Reagan is quoted in Caplan, n. 14, p. 270.

19. See Rex Lee draft of *History of the Office of the Solicitor General* quoted in Caplan, n. 14, pp. 144–46.

20. *Akron* v. *Akron Center for Reproductive Health, Inc.,* 462 U.S. 416 (1983).

21. 462 U.S. at 452.

22. Caplan, n. 14, p. 146.

23. *Thornburgh* v. *American College of Obstetricians and Gynecologists,* 106 S. Ct.

2169 (1986). For a critical examination of Charles Fried's aggressiveness as solicitor general, see Caplan, n. 14, especially pp. 135–50 on the Thornburgh case.

24. *United States* v. *Macintosh,* 283 U.S. 605 (1931); *Zorach* v. *Clauson,* 343 U.S. 306, 313 (1952). The historical paragraphs are drawn from Handy, *A Christian America: Protestant Hopes and Historical Realities,* 2nd ed. (New York: Oxford University Press, 1984); Murphy, *The Constitution in Crisis Times— 1918–1969* (New York: Harper & Row, 1971); Reichley, n. 17.

25. *Permoli* v. *First Municipality of New Orleans,* 3 How. 589, 609 (1844).

26. *Church of Holy Trinity* v. *United States,* 143 U.S. 457, 471 (1892).

27. The geography book is quoted in Handy, n. 24, p. 88.

28. *Cantwell* v. *Connecticut,* 310 U.S. 296 (1940); *Everson* v. *Board of Education,* 330 U.S. 1 (1947).

29. *Everson* v. *Board of Education,* 330 U.S. 1, 15–16 (1947); id., 31 (dissent).

30. *Engel* v. *Vitale,* 370 U.S. 421 (1962); *Abington School District* v. *Schempp,* 374 U.S. 203 (1963).

31. Handy, n. 24, pp. 193–94.

32. The Alabama congressman is quoted in Murphy, n. 24, p. 392; Congressman Rivers and a similar comment by Senator Sam Ervin are quoted in Pfeffer, *Church State and Freedom,* rev. ed. (Boston: Beacon Press, 1967), p. 466.

33. The boast was related to me in a confidential interview with the judgeship candidate.

34. *Edwards* v. *Aguillard,* 107 S. Ct. 2573 (1987).

35. The Reagan speech to the Catholics was made on October 19, 1980; his faith in the Bible is reported in *Washington Star* (August 23, 1980) and in *The New York Times* (November 22, 1987).

36. *Mueller* v. *Allen,* 463 U.S. 388 (1983) (tax deduction); *Marsh* v. *Chambers,* 463 U.S. 783 (1983) (chaplain); *Lynch* v. *Donnelly,* 465 U.S. 668 (1984) (creche).

37. The moment of silence case is *Wallace* v. *Jaffree,* 472 U.S. 38 (1985). The school aid cases are *Aguilar* v. *Felton,* 473 U.S. 402 (1985), and *Grand Rapids School District* v. *Ball,* 473 U.S. 373 (1985).

38. Testimony of Robert Kapp, Lawyers' Committee for Civil Rights Under Law at *Hearings Before the U.S. Senate Judiciary Committee on the Nomination of William Bradford Reynolds to Be Associate Attorney General,* 99th Cong., 1st sess., p. 234 (1985).

39. The Baxter testimony is quoted in *The Wall Street Journal* (July 8, 1981). The congressional refusal to let him argue the legality of resale price maintenance is noted in *Monsanto Company* v. *Spray-Rite Service Corporation,* 465 U.S. 752, 761, n. 7 (1984).

40. Quoted in *The Wall Street Journal* (July 1, 1981).

41. "Justice Under Reagan," *U.S. News & World Report* (October 14, 1985), p. 67.

Chapter 3

1. The Meese comments were in an interview with *The Washington Post* (August 25, 1985) and in a speech to the District of Columbia chapter of the Federalist Society (November 15, 1985), pp. 12–13; the Fried comment was in a private conversation with the author (November 1987).

2. *The New York Times* (January 28, 1983).

3. Smith, "Urging Judicial Restraint," 68 *ABA Journal* 59 (January 1982).

4. Address of Edwin Meese before the American Bar Association (July 9, 1985), pp. 13–14. Meese's overall performance as attorney general is critically discussed in Caplan, *The Tenth Justice* (New York: Alfred A. Knopf, 1987), especially pp. 115–34.

5. Meese's and Eastland's comments are reported in Taylor, "Meese and His Candor," *The New York Times* (August 3, 1985). Meese's pullback tactics are described in Taylor, "Meese and the Supreme Court; He Deals with Critics by Softening His Remarks," *The New York Times* (November 19, 1986).

6. Address of Edwin Meese to the District of Columbia chapter of the Federalist Society (November 15, 1985), pp. 8–9, 14.

7. Address of Edwin Meese at Tulane University, "The Law of the Constitution" (October 21, 1986).

8. Meese, "The Tulane Speech: What I Meant," *The Washington Post* (November 13, 1986). See also Taylor, n. 5 (November 19, 1986).

9. The 1925 case that first applied the Bill of Rights to the states was *Gitlow* v. *New York,* 268 U.S. 652. The 1931 case that extended freedom of the press to the states was *Near* v. *Minnesota,* 283 U.S. 697.

10. Comment of Professor Charles E. Rice in *The Wall Street Journal,* quoted in Schwartz, "Mr. Meese and the Bill of Rights," 6 *Calif. Lawyer* 35 (April 1986).

11. The Bork statement appears in Bork, *Tradition and Morality in Constitutional Law* (Washington, D.C.: American Enterprise Institute, 1984), p. 10.

12. Bork, "Neutral Principles and Some First Amendment Problems," 47 *Ind. L. J.* 1 (1971). The footnote reference is to Bork, "The Supreme Court

Needs New Philosophy," *Fortune* (December 1968), pp. 138, 141.

13. Farrand (ed.), *The Records of the Federal Convention of 1787* (New Haven, Conn.: Yale University Press, 1966), p. xiii.

14. Kelly, "Clio and the Supreme Court: An Illicit Love Affair," 1965 *S. Ct. Rev.* 119, 134.

15. The change is discussed by Levy in "The Legacy Reexamined," 37 *Stan. L. Rev.* 767 (1985).

16. See, e.g., Wood, "The Fundamentalists and the Constitution," *The New York Review* (February 18, 1988), p. 33; Botein, "Religious Dimensions of the Early American State" in Beeman, Botein, and Carter (eds.), *Beyond Confederation* (Chapel Hill: University of North Carolina Press, 1987), pp. 315, 317; James Hutson, quoted in *The New York Times* (July 29, 1987); Schlesinger, "On Original Intent," *The Wall Street Journal* (January 17, 1986).

17. Quoted in Bickel, "The Original Understanding and the Segregation Decision," 69 *Harv. L. Rev.* 1, 59 (1955).

18. *Regents of University of California* v. *Bakke,* 438 U.S. 265, 397 (1978) (Marshall, J.) (concurring in judgment and dissenting in part).

19. Bruce Fein interview with Nina Totenberg, National Public Radio (October 1, 1984).

20. *West Virginia State Board of Education* v. *Barnette,* 319 U.S. 624 (1943) (Jackson, J.); "The Federalist No. 78" in *The Federalist Papers,* Fairfield ed. (Baltimore, Md.: Johns Hopkins University Press, 1981), p. 231.

21. *National League of Cities* v. *Usery,* 426 U.S. 833 (1976).

22. *Garcia* v. *San Antonio Metropolitan Transit Authority,* 469 U.S. 420 (1985).

23. Ibid. at 567 (Powell, J., dissenting). The soundness of the Blackmun-Marshall advice was demonstrated within months when Congress, in response to state and local pressure, quickly revised the Fair Labor Standards Act to ease the financial burden on state and local governments. 99 Stat. 787 (1985).

24. *The Wall Street Journal* suggestions are in editorial, "Economic Civil Rights" (July 5, 1985). The federalism report is discussed in Schwartz, "Federalism—Then and Now," 7 *Calif. Lawyer* 52 (August 1987). Meese's efforts to enhance executive power are discussed in Caplan, n. 4, pp. 131–32, and *The New York Times* (November 6, 1985).

25. *Hearings Before U.S. Senate Judiciary Committee on the Nomination of William Bradford Reynolds to Be Associate Attorney General,* 99th Cong., 1st sess., pp. 971–78 (1985). For a discussion of the efforts to bar affirmative action, see Caplan, n. 4, pp. 85–92.

26. Solicitor general Charles Fried's call for "a dose" is reported in "Symposium on Crisis in the Courts," 5 *Manhattan Report* 3 (1985). Fried's activities as solicitor general are discussed in Caplan, n. 4.

27. Bork comment, Milton Handler Symposium (November 15, 1986), reported in *Hearings Before the U.S. Senate Judiciary Committee on the Nomination of Robert H. Bork to Be Associate Justice of the Supreme Court of the United States,* 100th Cong., 1st sess., p. 2057 (1987) (unofficial committee print).

Chapter 4

1. The anonymous Republican is quoted in Cohen, "The Post-Reagan Right," *Nat. J.* 488 (February 28, 1987).
2. D. Bandow, "A Do-It-Yourself Agenda for President Reagan," 8 *Cato Policy Report* 1, 10 (November–December 1986).
3. Cohen, "Conservatives Step Up Efforts to Promote Reagan-Minded Judges to U.S. Bench," *Nat. J.* 1560 (July 6, 1985).
4. Epstein, *Takings—Private Property and the Power of Eminent Domain* (Cambridge, Mass.: Harvard University Press, 1985), p. 281.
5. The comments of Wilson and Rutledge are reported in Farrand (ed.), *The Records of the Federal Convention of 1787* (New Haven, Conn.: Yale University Press, 1966), p. 119. Morris's views are from Hunt and Brown (eds.), *The Debates of the Federal Convention of 1787, Reported by James Madison* (New York: Oxford University Press, 1920), p. 529.
6. The most complete survey of Supreme Court nominations is in Abraham, *Justices and Presidents: A Political History of Appointments to the Supreme Court,* 2nd ed. (New York: Oxford University Press, 1985). See id. at pp. 73 and 81 for Jay and Rutledge. See also Tribe, *God Save This Honorable Court* (New York: Random House, 1985), which contains a valuable chart detailing Senate treatment of all Supreme Court nominees prior to 1986, pp. 142–51.
7. Abraham, n. 6, pp. 125–31.
8. Ibid., pp. 178–81. The most complete narrative of the Brandeis nomination is in Todd, *Justice on Trial: The Case of Louis D. Brandeis* (New York: McGraw-Hill, 1964).
9. Abraham, n. 6, p. 43.
10. Ibid., pp. 281–88.
11. The Hruska statement is quoted in *1970 Congressional Quarterly Almanac,* p. 159.
12. For Grover Rees, see *Hearings Before the U.S. Senate Judiciary Committee on the Nomination of Sandra Day O'Connor to Be Associate Justice of the Supreme Court,* 97th Cong., 1st sess., p. 174 (1981). Senator Sam Ervin's views are in "Individual Views of Mr. Ervin" in *Report of the Senate Judiciary Committee on the Nomination of Abe Fortas . . . ,* 90th Cong., 2nd sess., p. 32 (1969). Professor

Black's views are in "A Note on Senatorial Consideration of Supreme Court Nominees," 79 *Yale L. J.* 657, 663 (1970). See also 133 *Cong. Rec.* S10522 (July 23, 1987) (daily ed.) (remarks of Senator Joseph Biden).

13. Address at the University of Minnesota, "On the Appointment of Supreme Court Justices" (October 19, 1984). See *The New York Times* (October 20, 1984). For Rehnquist's more explicit views that the Senate should look closely at a nominee's philosophy, see Rehnquist, "The Making of a Supreme Court Justice," 29 *Harvard Law Record* 7 (October 8, 1959).

14. Rehnquist, n. 13, quoted in *The New York Times* (October 20, 1984).

15. Ambrose, *Eisenhower: The President* (New York: Simon and Schuster, 1984), pp. 128, 129.

16. See Holmes's dissent from the decision in *Lochner* v. *New York,* 198 U.S. 45, 64 (1905), a decision that was also condemned by Theodore Roosevelt.

17. The Lee remark is in *The Washington Post* (June 29, 1986).

18. For the Fishbourne incident, see Harris, *The Advice and Consent of the Senate* (Berkeley: University of California Press, 1953), pp. 27–28. A few of the many more recent examples are in 1977 *Cong. Q. Almanac* 48-A (Theodore Sorensen); *The Wall Street Journal* (May 21, 1986) (Equal Employment Opportunity Commission general counsel nominee).

19. Harris, n. 18, pp. 215–16, 220, 221, 231, 232, 321–23. The Virginia incident is discussed at length in Koeniger, "The New Deal and the States: Roosevelt versus the Byrd Organization in Virginia," 68 *J. Amer. Hist.* 876 (1982). Other studies of lower court appointments include O'Brien, *The Politics of Appointing Judges* (New York: Twentieth Century Fund, forthcoming); Hall, *The Politics of Justice: Lower Federal Judicial Selection and the Second Party System, 1829–61* (Lincoln: University of Nebraska Press, 1979); Howard, *Courts of Appeals in the Federal Judicial System: A Study of the Second, Fifth, and District of Columbia Circuits* (Princeton, N.J.: Princeton University Press, 1981); and Schmidhauser, *Judges and Justices: The Federal Appellate Judiciary* (Boston: Little, Brown, 1979).

20. Wald, "Some Thoughts on Judging as Gleaned from One Hundred Years of the *Harvard Law Review* and Other Great Books," 100 *Harv. L. Rev.* 887, 888 (1987).

21. Burke, "The Path to the Court" (unpublished doctoral dissertation, 1958), p. 200.

22. Beveridge, *The Life of John Marshall* (Cambridge, Mass.: Houghton Mifflin, 1916), vol. 3, p. 37.

23. Ibid., pp. 37, 34.

24. Turner, "The Midnight Judges," 109 *U. Pa. L. Rev.* 494, 521 (1961).

25. Beveridge, n. 22, p. 82.

26. Freund, "Supreme Court (History)" in Levy, Karst, and Mahoney (eds.), *Encyclopedia of the American Constitution* (New York: Macmillan, 1986), vol. 4, pp. 1813–14.

Chapter 5

1. The 1981 division is set forth in *Cong. Q.* 1760 (November 17, 1985). The December 31, 1987, figures are based on information provided the author by the Justice Department.

2. O'Brien, *The Politics of Appointing Judges* (New York: Twentieth Century Fund mimeo; 1988 publication forthcoming), p. 37.

3. ABA ratings are summarized in Goldman, "Reaganizing the Judiciary: The First Term Appointments," 68 *Judicature* 313, 319, 325 (1985); O'Brien, n. 2, p. 97.

4. See Goldman, n. 3. Dunham, "Courting Youth," *Dallas Times Herald* (March 9, 1985). In a paper issued on December 14, 1987, *Myths and Realities—Reagan Administration Judicial Selection,* the Justice Department tried to refute this, but its data were based on averages, and the paper ignores the youth focus during the second term. The paper also glosses over the fact that the emphasis on youth was particularly strong among the ideologically extreme choices, such as Posner, Easterbrook, Kozinski, and Scalia. In addition, the paper tried to explain away the disproportionately large number of split "qualified" decisions by the ABA, by challenging ABA standards and focusing on the first term.

5. O'Brien, n. 2, pp. 62–63 (mimeo).

6. Harris, *The Advice and Consent of the Senate* (Berkeley: University of California Press, 1953), p. 100.

7. Kurtz, "GOP Senators Foiled on Judicial Nominees," *The Washington Post* (February 20, 1987). The veto of Carol Welch is reported in *The Washington Post* (January 11, 1988).

8. Justice O'Connor's record and reputation in Arizona are reported in *The New York Times* (July 8, 1981).

9. The statistics are collected annually in the November issues of the *Harvard Law Review.*

10. See Mann, "Smeared," *The Washington Post* (January 13, 1982).

11. Barbash, "Protesters Deny Women Judgeship," *The Washington Post* (December 23, 1981).

12. Ibid.

13. Mann, n. 10.

14. Fielding is quoted in Barbash, n. 11.

15. Posner, *The Economics of Justice* (Cambridge, Mass.: Harvard University Press, 1981).

16. Posner, *Economic Analysis of Law,* 2nd ed. (Boston: Little, Brown, 1977), p. 25.

17. The baby sales figures and analysis are from Posner and Landes, "The Economics of the Baby Shortage," 7 *J. Legal Studies* 323 (1978). See also Press and McDaniel, "Free-Market Jurist," *Newsweek* (June 10, 1985), p. 93. Discrimination is discussed in Posner, n. 15, pp. 351–407, and n. 16, pp. 525–34.

18. Both the *Journal* comment and the Ackerman remarks are from Barrett, "Influential Ideas: A Movement Called 'Law and Economics' Sways Legal Circles," *The Wall Street Journal* (August 4, 1986).

19. *Hearings Before the U.S. Senate Judiciary Committee on the Selection and Confirmation of Federal Judges,* 97th Cong., 1st sess., p. 70 (1981) (Percy sponsoring Posner).

20. Posner's comment, ibid., p. 71. Siegan's views are in *The Supreme Court's Constitution* (New Brunswick, N.J.: Transaction, 1987), passim. The antitrust comments are discussed in Appendix I.

21. The ABA's rating of Wilkinson is explored in *Hearings Before the U.S. Senate Judiciary Committee on Federal Appointments,* 98th Cong., 2nd sess., pp. 229, 245, 318–23, 376–77 (1984).

22. Quoted in 130 *Cong. Rec.* S9276 (July 26, 1984).

23. The *Virginian-Pilot* is quoted in Margolick, "Critics Question Experience of Reagan's Choice for Judgeship," *The New York Times* (April 1, 1984).

24. *Hearings,* n. 21, p. 51.

25. *Hearings,* n. 21. The Powell calls are discussed in *Hearings,* p. 290, and the calls by two high-ranking Justice Department officials, Deputy Attorney General Edward Schmults and Assistant Attorney General Jonathan Rose, are discussed on pp. 272–92.

26. *Hearings,* n. 21, p. 376, and 130 *Cong. Rec.* S9274 (July 26, 1984).

27. *Hearings,* n. 21, p. 368.

28. Goldman, n. 3.

Chapter 6

1. *NLRB* v. *Bildisco & Bildisco,* 465 U.S. 513 (1984). The legislation creating new judgeships is the Federal Judgeship Act of 1984, P.L. 98-353, which created twenty-four appellate and sixty-one district court judgeships.

2. See generally Nina Totenberg interviews with Bruce Fein, National Public Radio (October 2 and 9, 1984).

3. The Jonathan Rose remark is in *Legal Times* (October 22, 1984).

4. Fred Fielding is quoted in Brownstein, "With or Without Supreme Court Changes, Reagan Will Reshape the Federal Bench," *Nat. J.,* p. 2340 (December 8, 1984). The quoted skepticism is from a private conversation with a liberal law school professor.

5. The letter from the thirteen senators is reported in *The Washington Post* (March 23, 1985).

6. Abramson quoted ibid.; *Economist* (April 13, 1985), p. 28.

7. Senator Moynihan is quoted in *The New York Times* (April 2, 1985).

8. Senator D'Amato is quoted in *The Washington Post* (March 31, 1985).

9. Daniel Popeo is quoted in *The New York Times* (April 2, 1985). See also editorial, "Wrong Way to Reject a Judge," *The New York Times* (April 6, 1985).

10. *The New York Times* (April 2, 1985).

11. Interview by author with William E. Hellerstein (June 1985).

12. The White House comment is reported in *The New York Times* (April 1, 1985). The Fielding statement is from an interview with Nina Totenberg, National Public Radio (August 28, 1985). The Strauss incident in the footnote is reported in *Nat. L. J.* (October 26, 1987).

13. Editorial, "Who Clears Judges?," *The Washington Post* (April 8, 1985).

14. *The New York Times* (April 18, 1985).

15. Senator Biden is quoted in *The Washington Post* (April 5, 1985).

16. Senator Hatch is quoted in *The New York Times* (April 16, 1985).

17. Fred Fielding is quoted in "Justice Under Reagan," *U.S. News & World Report* (October 14, 1985), p. 61. Meese is quoted in O'Brien, *The Politics of Appointing Judges* (New York: Twentieth Century Fund, 1987) (mimeo), p. 64.

18. Herbert Ellingwood is quoted in *Nat. L. J.* (September 15, 1980).

19. *The Wall Street Journal* (March 20, 1987).

20. Telephone interview by the author with Lizabeth Moody (July 9, 1987).

21. Totenberg, n. 12.

22. Each of these reports is based on confidential telephone interviews with the author in the summer and fall of 1987.

23. Sheldon Goldman is quoted in *The New York Times* (December 18, 1984); editorial, *Los Angeles Times* (October, 1985).

24. Phillip Kurland is quoted in *U.S. News & World Report* (October 14, 1985), p. 65.

25. The Silberman-Crocker Bank story is in *The Wall Street Journal* (October 21, 1985).

26. O'Brien, n. 18, p. 97; Simon, "Judging Judges: The Senate's Role in Judicial Appointments," address to National Press Club (March 10, 1986), p. 2.

27. Cohen, "Conservatives Step Up Efforts to Promote Reagan-Minded Judges to U.S. Bench," *Nat. J.* 156 (July 6, 1985). See also *Cong. Q. Weekly Report* (September 7, 1985), p. 1759.

28. Schwartz, *The New Right's Court Packing Campaign* (Washington, D.C.: People for the American Way, 1985).

29. *The Washington Post* (November 12, 1985).

30. Ibid.

31. Ibid.

32. Jesse James, Jr., is quoted in Wertheimer and Freedman, "A Senate Panel's Lax Review," *Chicago Tribune* (November 1, 1985).

33. The manual is discussed in *Hearings Before the U.S. Senate Judiciary Committee on Federal Appointments,* 99th Cong., 1st sess., part 2, pp. 103, 122–23 (July 17, 1985) (testimony of Government Accountability Project).

34. *Special Counsel* v. *Guadalupe Saldana,* Dkt. No. H012068210023 (December 21, 1983), reported in *Hearings,* n. 33, p. 126.

35. *Hearings Before the U.S. Senate Judiciary Committee on Federal Appointments,* 99th Cong., 2nd sess., p. 53 (February 5, 1985).

36. Ibid., p. 28. The Reynolds letter is excerpted at p. 31, and in Americans for Democratic Action fact sheet, in author's files.

37. The appellate decision is described in *The Washington Post* (July 4, 1987). The cases are discussed throughout *Hearings Before the U.S. Senate Judiciary Committee on the Nomination of Jefferson B. Sessions III,* 99th Cong., 2nd sess. (1986), especially pp. 181–299.

38. Ibid., pp. 3, 28–30.

39. Senator Heflin's comments are in *Cong. Q.* 1297 (June 7, 1986). Meese's comments are in *The Washington Post* (June 6, 1986).

40. *Indianapolis Star* (June 20, 1986); *The Wall Street Journal* (October 21, 1985).

41. Judicial Selection Project letter to American Bar Association, Standing Committee on the Federal Judiciary (January 10, 1986), in author's files.

42. *Legal Times* (June 15, 1987).

43. Lino Graglia's record is summarized in editorial, "Strict Constructionist," *Los Angeles Times* (November 8, 1985); the ad signed by Graglia appears in *Austin American Statesman* (December 7, 1979); the Louisiana incident is reported in *U.S. News & World Report* (January 19, 1981), p. 8.

44. Slotnick, "The ABA Standing Committee on Federal Judiciary: A Contemporary Assessment—Parts 1, 2," 66 *Judicature* 349, 385 (April–May 1983).

45. Popeo and Kamenar, "The Questionable Role of the American Bar Association in the Judicial Selection Process" in McGuigan and O'Connell (eds.), *The Judges War* (Washington, D.C.: Free Congress Research and Education Foundation, 1987), pp. 177–91.

46. Kurland is quoted in McFeeley, *Appointment of Judges—The Johnson Presidency* (Austin: University of Texas Press, 1987), pp. 23–24; Senator Simon and Nan Aron are quoted in *The Washington Post* (December 24, 1985).

47. Lacovara, "The Wrong Way to Pick Judges," *The New York Times* (October 3, 1986).

48. Ibid.

49. Nina Totenberg, National Public Radio (December 5, 1985).

50. *The New York Times* (July 5, 1986).

Chapter 7

1. The Chicago Council of Lawyers' letter appears in *Hearings Before the U.S. Senate Judiciary Committee on Federal Appointments,* 99th Cong., 2nd sess., pp. 205–6 (1986).

2. See generally ibid., pp. 183–236; Senate Judiciary Committee Report, *Minority Views, Nomination of Daniel A. Manion,* 99th Cong., 2d sess., p. 14 (June 19, 1986).

3. Ibid.

4. The letter is reprinted in 132 *Cong. Rec.* S8484 (June 25, 1986).

5. Editorial, "Senatorial Tempriment," *The Wall Street Journal* (June 2, 1986).

6. Editorial, "Strict Judging for the Bench," *Orlando Sentinel* (May 13, 1986); editorial, "Unqualified Nominee," *Arizona Daily Star* (May 7, 1986).

7. *Economist* (May 17, 1986), pp. 24–25.

8. Senator Thurmond is quoted in *Minneapolis Star & Tribune* (June 25, 1986).

9. The events of June 26, 1986, are described by Nina Totenberg, National Public Radio (June 27, 1986); see also *Cong. Q.* 1541–42 (July 5, 1986).

10. *The New York Times* (July 5, 1986); editorial, "Manion 'Trade,' " *Seattle Post-Intelligencer* (June 30, 1986).

11. A year after Manion went on the bench, a sympathetic journalist reviewed his work and concluded that "Manion's work is average at best." He was "conscientious, serious, fair-minded and eager to learn" but "a weak writer with just an average capacity for legal reasoning and only spotty knowledge of the issues that come before the court," often missing the point. Adler, "Not That Dumb," *The American Lawyer* (January/February 1988), p. 32.

12. For critical evaluations of Burger, see Totenberg and Barbash, *The Washington Post,* Outlook Section (June 22, 1986). Woodward and Armstrong, *The Brethren* (New York: Simon and Schuster, 1979).

13. "Reagan's Mr. Right," *Time* (June 30, 1986), p. 24.

14. *Bob Jones University* v. *United States,* 461 U.S. 574 (1983) (segregated private schools); *Cleveland Board of Education* v. *LaFleur,* 414 U.S. 632 (1974) (pregnancy leave); *Frontiero* v. *Richardson,* 411 U.S. 677 (1973) (servicewomen); *Memorial Hospital* v. *Maricopa County,* 415 U.S. 250 (1974) (medical care and residency); *U.S. Department of Agriculture* v. *Murry,* 413 U.S. 508 (1974) (food stamps); *Hutto* v. *Finney,* 437 U.S. 678 (1978) (prison conditions); *Cruz* v. *Beto,* 405 U.S. 319 (1972) (Buddhist prisoner); *Thomas* v. *Review Board,* 450 U.S. 707 (1981) (Jehovah's Witness); *Keyes* v. *School Dist. No. 1, Denver, Colo.,* 413 U.S. 189 (1973) (school desegregation).

15. *Sugarman* v. *Dougall,,* 413 U.S. 634 (1973) (aliens); *Trimble* v. *Gordon,* 430 U.S. 762 (1977) (illegitimate children); *Frontiero* v. *Richardson,* 411 U.S. 677 (1973) (women); but see *Meritor Savings Bank* v. *Vinson,* 106 S. Ct. 2399 (1986) (sexual harassment under Title VII).

16. *Wallace* v. *Jaffree,* 472 U.S. 38 (1987) (moment of silence); *Mueller* v. *Allen* 463 U.S. 388 (1983) (tuition tax credits); *Stone* v. *Graham,* 449 U.S. 39 (1980) (Ten Commandments).

17. *Memorandum of the AFL-CIO with Respect to the Nomination of Justice William Rehnquist to Be Chief Justice of the United States* (September 9, 1986), pp. 3–4, in author's files.

18. *First National Bank* v. *Bellotti,* 435 U.S. 765, 823 (1978) (Rehnquist, J., dissenting); *Buckley* v. *Valeo,* 424 U.S. 1, 291 (1976) (Rehnquist, J., concurring and dissenting).

19. *The Washington Post* (July 6, 1986).

20. The memorandum appears in testimony of Julius L. Chambers, Legal Defense Fund, at *Hearings Before the U.S. Senate Committee on the Judiciary on the Confirmation of William Hubbs Rehnquist to be Chief Justice of the United States,* 99th Cong., 2nd sess., p. 896 (1986). The case was *Terry* v. *Adams,* 345 U.S. 461 (1953).

21. Kluger, *Simple Justice* (New York: Vintage Books, 1977), pp. 605–6.

22. Rehnquist's change of heart is in *Hearings Before the U.S. Senate Judiciary Committee on the Judiciary on the Nominations of William H. Rehnquist and Lewis F. Powell, Jr.,* 92nd Cong., 1st sess., p. 70 (1971).

23. *Hearings,* n. 20, pp. 145–47.

24. *Laird* v. *Tatum,* 408 U.S. 1 (1972).

25. 93 S. Ct. 7 (1972).

26. The Hazard letter is reported in *The New York Times* (September 10, 1986).

27. Senator Biden's question is in *Hearings,* n. 20, p. 601.

28. The Powell statement is in *United States* v. *Richardson,* 418 U.S. 166, 192 (1974) (Powell, J., concurring).

29. Morrison and Stenhouse, "The Chief Justice of the United States: More Than Just the Highest-Ranking Judge," 1 *Const. Comm.* 57 (1984).

30. The comment was made by Stephen Wermiel of *The Wall Street Journal* on *Washington Week in Review,* National Public Radio (August 1, 1986).

31. *Community for Creative Non-Violence* v. *Watt,* 703 F. 2d 586, 622 (1983) (Scalia, J., dissenting).

32. O'Connell and McGuigan, "Rehnquisition: Rite of Passage for a Chief Justice" in McGuigan and O'Connell (eds.), *The Judges War* (Washington, D.C.: Free Congress Research and Education Foundation, 1987), p. 56.

Chapter 8

1. The Reagan speech was quoted in a floor speech by Senator Joseph Biden that was excerpted in *The New York Times* (October 22, 1987).

2. Siegan, *The Supreme Court's Constitution* (New Brunswick, N.J.: Transaction, 1987). Siegan's views are excerpted and summarized in *The Washington Post* (January 13, 1988) and discussed in Schwartz, "Rolling Back the Constitution: The Siegan Nomination," *The Nation,* p. 13 (July 4–11, 1987).

3. The two retiring justices were Potter Stewart and Warren E. Burger, each of whom had become increasingly conservative, especially Burger.

4. See, e.g., *United States* v. *Calandra,* 414 U.S. 338 (1974); *Continental TV, Inc.* v. *GTE Sylvania, Inc.,* 433 U.S. 36 (1977). The 1986 Supreme Court voting statistics are reported in note, "The Supreme Court, 1986 Term," 101 *Harv. L. Rev.* 363 (1987).

5. *Branzburg* v. *Hayes,* 408 U.S. 665 (1972); *Pell* v. *Procunier,* 417 U.S. 817 (1974).

6. *United States* v. *U.S. District Court,* 407 U.S. 297 (1972).

7. The Powell article written prior to his appointment to the Supreme Court is "Civil Liberties Repression: Fact or Fiction?," *Richmond Times-Dispatch* (August 1, 1971), and is reprinted in *Hearings Before the U.S. Senate Judiciary Committee on the Nominations of William H. Rehnquist and Lewis F. Powell, Jr.,* 92nd Cong., 1st sess., p. 213 (1971).

8. *United States* v. *U.S. District Court,* 407 U.S. at 322.

9. *Warth* v. *Seldin,* 422 U.S. 490 (1975) (no standing under Constitution); *Havens Realty Corp.* v. *Coleman,* 455 U.S. 363 (1982) (standing allowed under Fair Housing Act).

10. *Regents of University of California* v. *Bakke,* 438 U.S. 265 (1978); *Fullilove* v. *Klutznick,* 488 U.S. 448 (1980).

11. The 5–4 statistics for 1986–87 are in note, n. 4, p. 365. The free speech cases are discussed in Barnett, "Free Speech in the New Court," 73 *ABA Journal* 48 (December 1987). I surveyed Powell's record the year before he retired in "Justice Lewis F. Powell, Jr.: A Pragmatic Independent," 72 *ABA Journal* 42 (June 15, 1986) (special issue). A more systematic and comprehensive survey is in Kahn, "The Court, the Community and the Judicial Balance: The Jurisprudence of Justice Powell," 97 *Yale L. J.* 1 (1987).

12. The Bruce Fein comments were in a Voice of America broadcast (July 31, 1987) and in *Newsweek* (September 14, 1987), p. 24. The Christian Voice spokesman was quoted in *Los Angeles Times* (October 4, 1987).

13. Cutler, "Saving Bork from Both Friends and Enemies," *The New York Times* (July 16, 1987).

14. *The Wall Street Journal* (October 7, 1987).

15. The Reagan statement appears in *The Washington Times* (October 15, 1987); Irvine, "The Big Media Taboo," *The Washington Times* (October 15, 1987).

16. See, e.g., Bork, "The Crisis in Antitrust," 65 *Colum. L. Rev.* 363 (1965); "The Rule of Reason and the Per Se Concept: Price Fixing and Market Division I, II," 74 *Yale L. J.* 775 (1965); 75 *Yale L. J.* 373 (1966). These views were later collected in Bork, *The Antitrust Paradox* (New York: Basic Books, 1978).

17. "Neutral Principles and Some First Amendment Problems," 47 *Ind. L. J.* 1 (1971).

18. Ibid., p. 8.

19. The criticism of the abortion decision is reported in *The New York Times* (September 13, 1987). The limited view of the Ninth Amendment is from a speech given by Bork in 1984 and cited in *Report of the Senate*

Committee on the Judiciary on the Nomination of Robert H. Bork, 100th Cong., 1st sess., p. 10 (1987).

20. The limited judicial role in enforcing equality is set forth in 41 *Ind. L. J.* 12; the June 1987 comment is in *Hearings,* n. 19, p. 46; the discussion of *Brown* v. *Board of Education* is in 41 *Ind. L. J.* 14–15.

21. The 1963 criticism of the Public Accommodations Act is in Bork, "Civil Rights—A Challenge," *New Republic* (August 31, 1963), p. 21; the Supreme Court's decision outlawing literacy tests is *Katzenbach* v. *Morgan,* 384 U.S. 641 (1966), and Bork's criticism of it is reported in *Report,* n. 19, pp. 42–43. The Coleman comment is in id., p. 43.

22. The 1971 discussion of free speech is in 41 *Ind. L. J.* 20; the 1987 comment was made in a United States Information Agency program (June 10, 1987), quoted in *Report,* n. 19, p. 56.

23. Caplan, *The Tenth Justice* (New York: Alfred A. Knopf, 1987), pp. 38–39.

24. *The Antitrust Paradox,* n. 16, pp. 409–13.

25. See *Barnes* v. *Kline,* 759 F. 2d 21 (D.C. Cir. 1985) (pocket veto); *Haitian Refugee Center* v. *Gracey,* 809 F. 2d 794 (D.C. Cir. 1988) (Haitian refugees); *Bartlett* v. *Bowen,* 816 F. 2d 695 (D.C. Cir. 1987) (Medicare patients); *Persinger* v. *Islamic Republic of Iran,* 729 F. 2d 835 (D.C. Cir. 1984) (American hostages); *Tel-Oren* v. *Libyan Arab Republic,* 726 F. 2d 744 (D.C. Cir. 1984) (suit against Libya); *Telecommunications Research and Action Center* v. *Allnet Communications Services, Inc.,* 806 F. 2d 1093 (D.C. Cir. 1986) (organizational standing).

26. *Rothery Storage & Van Co.* v. *Atlas,* 792 F. 2d 210 (D.C. Cir. 1986).

27. Compare Cutler, n. 13, with Cutler, *Hearings Before the U.S. Senate Judiciary Committee on the Nomination of Judge Antonin Scalia,* 99th Cong., 2nd sess., p. 153 (1986). The libel case is *Ollman* v. *Evans,* 750 F. 2d 970 (D.C. Cir. 1984).

28. *The Washington Post* (August 26, 1987) (poll results).

29. The planned and actual receipts are reported in *The Wall Street Journal* (September 30, 1987).

30. The Viguerie complaint is quoted in *Dallas Morning News* (October 4, 1987); the Popeo lament is in *Boston Globe* (August 4, 1987).

31. The comment about not "enough conservatives" is by Tom Korologos, Bork's congressional lobbyist, and appears in *The Washington Post* (October 24, 1987).

32. The law professors' and deans' opposition is in vol. 3, p. 1899, and vol. 2, pp. 80–97, of *Hearings Before the U.S. Senate Judiciary Committee on the Nomination of Robert H. Bork to Be Associate Justice,* 100th Cong., 2nd sess.

(unofficial committee print). The New York City Bar Association opposition is reported in id., vol. 2, p. 840. The important Kurland article is "Bork: The Transformation of a Conservative Constitutionalist," *Chicago Tribune* (August 18, 1987).

33. The survey was reported in *Nat. J.* 2612 (October 17, 1987).

34. Poll results were reported in *The New York Times* (July 24, 1987).

35. Will, "Biden and Bork," *The Washington Post* (July 2, 1987).

36. *The Washington Post* (October 4, 1987).

37. Cutler, Voice of America broadcast transcript (July 31, 1987), p. 8.

38. The "confirmation conversions" are discussed in *Report,* n. 19, pp. 93–95.

39. Poll results were in *The New York Times* (September 24, 1987). The *Atlanta Journal* poll was reported in *The Atlanta Journal and Constitution* (October 1, 1987).

40. Senator Sanford is quoted in *Los Angeles Times* (October 15, 1987).

41. Bork's comments were reported in *The Washington Post* (December 15, 1987).

42. Justice Frankfurter is quoted in Reske, "Did Bork Say Too Much?," 73 *ABA Journal* 74 (December 1987).

43. *The Wall Street Journal* (December 16, 1987); *The New York Times* (December 17, 1987).

44. Bork's statement was reported in *The New York Times* (September 2, 1987).

45. Schneider, "Americans Satisfied with the Judicial Status Quo," *Nat. J.* 2612 (October 17, 1987).

46. *The Washington Post* (October 24, 1987).

47. *Newsweek* (November 9, 1987), p. 42.

48. The "they'll object" challenge is reported in *Newsweek* (November 9, 1987), p. 42; the "facetious remark" explanation appears in *The New York Times* (November 12, 1987).

49. Mitchell Daniels is quoted in *The New York Times* (October 28, 1987).

50. The (anonymous) judge is quoted in *Legal Times* (November 2, 1987), p. 14.

51. *The Wall Street Journal* (November 2, 1987).

52. *Beller* v. *Middendorf,* 632 F. 2d 788, 810 (9th Cir. 1980).

53. Senator Helms is quoted in *Cong. Q.* 2671 (October 31, 1987).

54. For a discussion of the Ginsburg nomination and his questionnaire, see Schwartz, "Ginsburg Looks Like Another Bork in the Making," *Newsday* (November 4, 1987), p. 73. The questionnaire is reprinted in *The New York Times* (November 5, 1987).

55. Ibid.

56. Ginsburg's interest in cable TV is reported in *The Washington Post* (November 2, 1987), p. A1. The judge/administrator conflict is reported in *The New York Times* (November 9, 1987).

57. *Environmental Defense Fund* v. *Thomas, 627* F. Supp. 566, 567 (D.D.C. 1986).

58. Wohl, "Jewish Leaders on Supreme Court Nominee: Judicial View Vital, Religion Not a Factor," *Washington Jewish Week* (November 5, 1987).

59. *Legal Times* (November 9, 1987), p. 6.

60. The Reagan remark appears in *Miami Herald* (November 7, 1987). Apple, "For Reagan, an Old Trap—Rhetoric vs. Reality," *The New York Times* (November 7, 1987).

61. McDonald's lament is in *The New York Times* (November 15, 1987), sect. 4.

62. *The Wall Street Journal* (November 9, 1987). The inquiry mentioned in the footnote is reported in *The Washington Post* (December 24, 1987).

63. *The New York Times* (November 12, 1987), p. 1.

64. *TOPIC* v. *Circle Realty, 532* F. 2d 1273 (9th Cir. 1976) (housing); *AFSCME* v. *Washington, 770* F. 2d 1401 (9th Cir. 1985) (comparable worth). The NOW Legal Defense and Education Fund filed a statement with the Senate Judiciary Committee detailing Kennedy's rulings against women in employment discrimination cases. He had also made some speeches that expressed a very narrow view of the judicial role in protecting individual rights. See Taylor, "Judge Kennedy: Tilting Right but Not Far," *The New York Times* (November 15, 1987), p. 1; *Legal Times* (November 16, 1987); Kennedy, "Unenumerated Rights and the Dictates of Judicial Restraint," address at Stanford University (July 1986).

65. Joseph Rauh's comments appear in *Hearings Before the U.S. Senate Judiciary Committee on the Nomination of Anthony M. Kennedy to Be an Associate Justice of the Supreme Court,* 100th Cong., 1st sess., pp. 145–46 (December 16, 1987) (daily ed.).

66. On March 25, 1988, *The Washington Post* reported that the nomination was dead. Siegan's views apparently were too extreme for the Senate Judiciary Committee.

Chapter 9

1. The figures for the number of appointments were provided the author by the Justice Department.

2. *U.S. News & World Report* (February 2, 1987), p. 27. The two studies are Gottschall, "Reagan's Appointments to the U.S. Courts of Appeals: The

Continuation of a Judicial Revolution," 70 *Judicature* 48 (1986); Note, "All the President's Men? A Study of Ronald Reagan's Appointments to the U.S. Courts of Appeals," 87 *Colum. L. Rev.* 766 (1987). For a view more in accord with mine, see Wermiel, "Reagan Choices Alter the Makeup and Views of the Federal Courts," *The Wall Street Journal* (February 1, 1988).

3. Ibid., pp. 779, 781.

4. Ibid., n. 66.

5. Stern, "Judging the Judges," 1 *Benchmark* 2, 6 (July–October 1984).

6. Brett, "Monsanto: Great Expectations Unfulfilled," 30 *Antitrust Bulletin* 39, 55–56 (1985).

7. Kalinowski, "Antitrust Report," monthly supp. to *Anti. Law Tr. Reg.* (September 1986), p. 1. The state attorneys' views were filed in a petition for certiorari in *Olympia Equipment Leasing Co.* v. *Western Union Telegraph Co.,* 797 F. 2d 370, Sup. Ct. no. 86-1255, pp. 5–9, and summarized in Middleton, "Shaping a Circuit in the Chicago School Image," 34 *Nat. L. J.* (July 20, 1987).

8. *Marriott* v. *Faulkner,* 697 F. 2d 761 (7th Cir. 1983) (prisoner medical injury suits); *Phelps* v. *Duckworth,* 772 F. 2d 1410 (7th Cir. 1985) (Posner, J., concurring) (habeas corpus); *Menora* v. *Illinois High School Association,* 683 F. 2d 1030 (7th Cir. 1982) (yarmulkes). Posner's overall record is critically discussed in Wilson, "Constraints of Power," 40 *U. Miami L. Rev.* 1171, 1217 (1986).

9. *Edwards* v. *Aguillard,* 107 S. Ct. 2573 (1987) (creationism); *Johnson* v. *Transportation Agency of Santa Clara County,* 107 S. Ct. 1442 (1987) (affirmative action).

10. *Tavoulareas* v. *Piro,* 759 F. 2d 90 (D.C. Cir. 1985) (Mobil Oil); *In re Reporters Committee for Freedom of the Press,* 773 F. 2d 1325 (D.C. Cir. 1985) (access to documents).

11. *Synar* v. *United States,* 626 F. Supp. 1374 (D.C. Cir. 1986) (Gramm-Rudman-Hollings), *aff'd, Bowsher* v. *Synar,* 106 S. Ct. 3181 (1986); discrimination cases include *Trakas* v. *Quality Brands, Inc.,* 759 F. 2d 185 (D.C. Cir. 1985) (Scalia, J., dissenting) (sex-based discrimination); *Poindexter* v. *FBI,* 737 F.2d 1173 (D.C. Cir. 1984) (Scalia, J., concurring and dissenting) (race discrimination); *Carter* v. *Duncan-Huggins, Ltd.,* 727 F. 2d 1225 (D.C. Cir. 1984) (Scalia, J., dissenting) (race discrimination). Scalia's Court of Appeals record is discussed in Wilson, n. 8, p. 1181.

12. *Croson* v. *City of Richmond,* 822 F. 2d 1355 (4th Cir. 1987), probable jurisdiction noted (February 22, 1988). The *Wall Street Journal* article, which also contains the Reynolds quotation, is Wermiel, "U.S. Appeals Judge Draws Fire for Stance on Civil Rights, Praise for Intellect and Manner" (February 18, 1988).

13. *Flynt* v. *Falwell,* 797 F. 2d 1270 (4th Cir. 1986), *reversed,* 107 S.Ct. (February 24, 1988).

14. *Chapman* v. *Pickett,* 801 F. 2d 912 (7th Cir. 1986) (Easterbrook, J., dissenting).

15. *Stephens* v. *Heckler,* 766 F. 2d 284 (7th Cir. 1985).

16. Easterbrook's first year on the court is discussed in Wilson, n. 8, p. 1247.

17. *Associated General Contractors* v. *San Francisco,* 813 F. 2d 922 (9th Cir. 1987).

18. *Hall* v. *Santa Barbara,* 813 F. 2d 198 (9th Cir. 1986). In a February 1988 decision, the Supreme Court upheld rent controls in a case similar to Kozinski's, over another Rehnquist dissent, this time joined by Scalia. See *The New York Times* (February 25, 1988).

19. *Hammon* v. *Barry,* 826 F. 2d 73 (D.C. Cir. 1987).

20. *Allen* v. *Scribner,* 812 F. 2d 426 (9th Cir. 1987) (Noonan, J., dissenting).

21. *Farmworker Justice Fund, Inc.* v. *Brock,* 811 F. 2d 613 (D.C. Cir. 1987).

22. The Markman remark was in a private conversation with the author.

23. Carp and Rowland, *Policymaking and Politics in the Federal District Courts* (Knoxville: University of Tennessee Press, 1983), p. 63 (emphasis in original).

24. Middleton, n. 7, p. 1.

25. Karpay, "The D.C. Circuit's New Face," *Legal Times* (May 4, 1987), pp. 1, 12–13. The environmentalist problems are reported in Stanfield, "Out-Standing in Court," *Nat J.* (February 13, 1988), p. 388. The shift to the right is also exemplified by the decision in January 1988 striking down the Special Prosecutor law. Two staunch Reaganite judges—Laurence Silberman and Stephen Williams—ruled that the Ethics in Government Act of 1978, enacted in the wake of President Nixon's firing of Special Prosecutor Archibald Cox, was too great an encroachment on the President's powers. Judge Ruth Bader Ginsburg, a middle-of-the-road Carter appointee, dissented. *In re: Sealed Case,* Nos. 87-5261, 5264, 5265 (D.C. Cir. January 22, 1988). The Supreme Court has agreed to review the decision.

26. Corbin and Dickinson, "1985 Eleventh Circuit Survey: Employment Discrimination," 37 *Mercer L. Rev.* 1315 (1986).

27. *Hernandez-Cordero* v. *USINS,* 819 F. 2d 558, 564 (5th Cir. 1987) (Rubin, J., dissenting).

28. Senator Leahy's comment is in a speech before the Alliance for Justice Conference (February 12, 1987).

Chapter 10

1. The Powell language is from *United States* v. *Richardson*, 418 U.S. 166, 192 (1974).

2. Response to Judiciary Committee questionnaire on file with Senate Judiciary Committee.

3. Judge Ginsburg's response is excerpted in *The New York Times* (November 5, 1987).

4. Senator Heflin is quoted in *Hearings Before the U.S. Senate Judiciary Committee on the Nomination of Sandra Day O'Connor*, 97th Cong., 1st sess., pp. 26–27 (1981).

5. Bishop Hoadley is quoted in Lockhart, Kamisar, Choper, and Shiffrin, *Constitutional Law* (St. Paul, Minn.: West, 1986), p. 1. Hand, "The Contribution of an Independent Judiciary to Civilization," in *The Spirit of Liberty* (New York: Alfred A. Knopf, 1953), p. 155.

6. *Legal Times* (November 16, 1987), p. 16.

7. Freedman, "Assembly-Line Approval: A Common Cause Study of Senate Confirmation of Federal Judges" (Washington, D.C.: Common Cause, Jan. 1986).

8. *Legal Times*, n. 6.

9. The Mainstream Committee incident is reported in *The New York Times* (April 28, 1986).

10. The Phillips criticism was reported in *The Washington Post* (December 15, 1987); the McClellan criticism of Charles Fried is in "The Judicialization of the American Republic," in McGuigan and O'Connell (eds.), *The Judges War* 61, 95 (Washington, D.C.: Free Congress Research and Education Foundation, 1987); the Popeo comment is reported in *Boston Globe* (August 4, 1987), p. 16.

11. Rev. Jerry Falwell is quoted in *The Washington Post* (July 2, 1987).

12. For constitutional developments elsewhere in the world, see Capeletti, "The 'Mighty Problem' of Judicial Review and the Contribution of Comparative Analysis," 53 *S. Cal. L. Rev.* 409 (1980).

13. Hand, *The Spirit of Liberty*, n. 5, p. 189.

Appendix I

1. The classic history of school desegregation is Kluger, *Simple Justice* (New York: Vintage Books, 1977).

2. *Time* (October 18, 1981), p. 18.

3. *Greene* v. *County School Board of New Kent County,* 391 U.S. 430, 438–39 (1968).

4. *Swann* v. *Charlotte-Mecklenburg Board of Education,* 402 U.S. 1 (1971). The *Swann* case is the subject of B. Schwartz, *Swann's Way* (New York: Oxford University Press, 1986).

5. *Keyes* v. *School District No. 1, Denver, Colo.,* 413 U.S. 189 (1973).

6. *Milliken* v. *Bradley,* 418 U.S. 717 (1974) (suburbs); *Washington* v. *Davis,* 426 U.S. 229 (1976) (intent).

7. For Griffin Bell's background, see *Hearings Before the U.S. Senate Judiciary Committee on the Nomination of Griffin Bell to Be Attorney General,* 95th Cong., 1st sess., pp. 59, 74, 75 (1977).

8. *Dayton Board of Education* v. *Brinkman (Dayton I),* 433 U.S. 406 (1977).

9. *Dayton Board of Education* v. *Brinkman (Dayton II),* 443 U.S. 526 (1979); *Columbus Board of Education* v. *Penick,* 443 U.S. 449 (1979).

10. President Reagan was quoted in *Los Angeles Times* (March 6, 1980).

11. Testimony of William Bradford Reynolds before the House Subcommittee on Civil and Constitutional Rights (November 19, 1981), as reported in Leadership Conference on Civil Rights, *Without Justice* (February 1982), p. 8.

12. *The New York Times* (February 1, 1984).

13. Ibid.

14. *Bob Jones University* v. *United States,* 461 U.S. 574 (1983).

15. Reynolds's remark is quoted in *Hearings Before the U.S. Senate Judiciary Committee on the Nomination of William Bradford Reynolds to Be Attorney General,* 99th Cong., 1st sess., p. 961 (1985).

16. *Riddick* v. *School Board of Norfolk,* 784 F. 2d 521 (4th Cir. 1986). The Supreme Court refused to review the case, thereby deferring the issue for the future. Other upcoming issues include whether a school desegregation order may be based on housing discrimination, and when suburban school districts may be included in a desegregation order.

17. *Regents of University of California* v. *Bakke,* 438 U.S. 265, 407 (1978) (Blackmun, J., concurring).

18. *Regents of University of California* v. *Bakke,* 438 U.S. 265 (1978).

19. *United Steel Workers* v. *Weber,* 443 U.S. 193 (1979).

20. Reynolds was quoted in *The Wall Street Journal* (December 8, 1981).

21. *Firefighters* v. *Stotts,* 467 U.S. 561 (1984). The activities of Linda Chavez described in the footnote are reported in *Nat. J.* 81 (January 14, 1984).

22. 467 U.S. 578–80.

23. *Congressional Quarterly Almanac 1985,* p. 221.

24. *Wygant* v. *Jackson Board of Education,* 476 U.S. 267 (1986); *Local No. 28, Sheet Metal Workers' International Association* v. *EEOC,* 106 S. Ct. 3019 (1986); *Local No. 93, International Association of Firefighters* v. *City of Cleveland,* 106 S. Ct. 3063 (1986).

25. *Johnson* v. *Transportation Agency of Santa Clara County,* 107 S. Ct. 1442 (1987).

26. Recent polls supporting affirmative action are reported in *The New York Times* (March 15, 1987).

27. The story of the 1982 extension of the Voting Rights Act is told in Pertschuk, *Giant Killers* (New York: Norton, 1986), chap. 6.

28. *Thornburg* v. *Gingles,* 106 S. Ct. 2752 (1986).

29. See *Hearings,* n. 15, pp. 268, 376, 449.

30. *Bowen* v. *American Hospital Association,* 106 S. Ct. 2101 (1986).

31. *The Wall Street Journal* (June 27, 1983), p. 6.

32. *School Board of Nassau County, Florida* v. *Arline,* 107 S. Ct. 1123 (1987).

33. See *Hearings,* n. 15, pp. 469–81 (handicap case discussion).

34. Senator DeConcini's statement is from his press release, June 19, 1985.

35. Mitchell, Address to the Georgia Bar Association (June 6, 1969).

36. The landmark cases are *Brown Shoe Co.* v. *United States,* 370 U.S. 294 (1962), and *United States* v. *Philadelphia National Bank,* 374 U.S. 321 (1963).

37. *Continental TV, Inc.* v. *GTE Sylvania, Inc.,* 433 U.S. 36 (1977).

38. "The Speech" is in "A Time for Choosing" and was delivered October 27, 1964.

39. *The Wall Street Journal* (March 4, 1982).

40. *The Wall Street Journal* (January 4, 1988).

41. Brett, "Monsanto: Great Expectations Unfulfilled," 30 *Antitrust Bull.* 39, 55–56 (1985).

42. Feulner, "Foreword," *Mandate for Leadership II: Continuing the Conservative Revolution* (Washington, D.C.: Heritage Foundation, 1984).

43. Ibid., pp. 408, 410.

44. The air bag case is *Motor Vehicle Manufacturers' Association* v. *State Farm Mutual Insurance Company,* 463 U.S. 29 (1983). *The Wall Street Journal* report was on June 27, 1983.

45. The disgusted comment is by Bandow, "A Do-It-Yourself Agenda for President Reagan," 8 *Cato Policy Report,* no. 6, p. 1 (November–December 1986).

46. *The Wall Street Journal* (June 27, 1983), p. 6.

47. The Mississippi case is *Brown* v. *Mississippi,* 297 U.S. 278 (1936).

48. *Mapp* v. *Ohio,* 367 U.S. 643 (1961).

49. *Gideon* v. *Wainwright,* 372 U.S. 335 (1963).

50. *Escobedo* v. *Illinois,* 378 U.S. 478 (1964); *Massiah* v. *United States,* 377 U.S. 201 (1964).

51. *Murphy* v. *Waterfront Commission,* 378 U.S. 52 (1964).

52. *Miranda* v. *Arizona,* 384 U.S. 436 (1966).

53. *United States* v. *Wade,* 388 U.S. 218 (1967).

54. *Berger* v. *New York,* 388 U.S. 41 (1967); *Katz* v. *United States,* 389 U.S. 347 (1967).

55. *Fay* v. *Noia,* 372 U.S. 391 (1963); *Townsend* v. *Sain,* 372 U.S. 293 (1963).

56. The Washington lawyer is quoted in Jackson, *Judges* (New York: Atheneum, 1974), p. 270.

57. The Burger Court's decisions on criminal procedure are comprehensively analyzed in Kamisar, "The 'Police Practice' Phases of the Criminal Process and Three Phases of the Burger Court" in Schwartz (ed.), *The Burger Years* (New York: Viking/Elisabeth Sifton, 1987), p. 143.

58. Meese's comments on criminal law are collected in *Nat. J.* 2646 (November 23, 1985).

59. Meese was quoted in *The New York Times* (November 19, 1986); see also Caplan, *The Tenth Justice* (New York: Alfred A. Knopf, 1987), p. 120.

60. The Yelverton and Giuliani comments are in Solomon, "Meese Sets Ambitious Agenda That Challenges Fundamental Legal Beliefs," *Nat. J.* 2640–42 (November 23, 1985). The Frey comment is in Kamisar, "The Case of Meese vs. Miranda," *Los Angeles Times* (February 11, 1987).

Index